Chaos or Control

T0385322

Chaos or Control

Change and Authority in the Church and Society

Timothy Bradshaw

Paternoster:
thinking faith

MILTON KEYNES • COLORADO SPRINGS • HYDERABAD

First published 2009 by Authentic Media
9 Holdom Avenue, Bletchley, Milton Keynes, Bucks, MK1 QR, UK
1820 Jet Stream Drive, Colorado Springs, CO 80921, USA
OM Authentic Media, Medchal Road, Jeedimetla Village,
Secunderabad 500 055, A.P., India
www.loveauthentic.com

Authentic Media is a division of Biblica UK, previously IBS-STL
UK. Biblica UK is limited by guarantee, with its registered office at
Kingstown Broadway, Carlisle, Cumbria, CA3 0HA. Registered in
England and Wales No. 1216232. Registered charity in England and
Wales No. 270162 and Scotland No. SCO40064

British Library Cataloguing in Publication Data

A catalogue record for this book is available from the
British Library

ISBN: 978-1-84227-643-3

Cover Design by David McNeill
Print Management by Adare
Printed and bound in Great Britain by J.F. Print

Contents

Introduction

This book is written in response to, and in the midst of, the fever gripping the mainline churches in the West. It is an attempt to take bearings at a time of extraordinarily fast change in social values and institutions, changes which are affecting churches and the general public, who are both beginning to feel nervous and confused at the dizzying pace of change in Western morality and at the declining influence of Christianity. It would be good if the attention of the 'think tankers' could be attracted, as well as that of theologians, church leaders and people, and those interested in the questions raised by changing social mores in Western society: How should the church cope with powerful pressures for liberalizing change? Does it have sufficient resources in Scripture, tradition and living guidance of the Spirit to discern the right way in doctrine and practice? I am also increasingly convinced that the crisis in the church is a microcosm of the crisis of values in Western society generally, and that an examination of the church as a patient needing healing will therefore also provide an insight into the plight of secular society and its spiritual problems. Ultimately the sacred and secular affect each other deeply. At present the latter tends to think the former is irrelevant, although its recent encounters with Islam have begun to chip away at this attitude of amused contempt.

Western society is in the process of undergoing profound change in moral ethos and structure of relationships. This is well documented in terms of the concept of 'postmodernity' and economic analysis as the 'commodification' of more and more areas of life. This has been summed up as the triumph of the consumer principle over aspects of life way beyond the formal marketing of manufactured goods. The autonomous self has the right to choose, and fetters on such choice are the equivalent of contracts 'in restraint of trade'. The various waves of the feminist movement also figure in this vortex of impulses. The result is that traditional social morality is being revised, constraints on choice removed, forms of life hitherto frowned upon as wrong are being endorsed and given legal status and protection.

This whole process affects the churches, and indeed is affected by changes in the churches themselves. The traditional mores were closely bound up with Christianity, particularly through the established churches and their role as upholders of accepted ethical norms. These connections are now purely formal and symbolic, scarcely defended as significant for social policy at all. In England and Scotland, the established churches no longer seek to play the role of the ethical resource centres for the nation, but step back and act as one among many religious groupings. The relativistic libertarianism of the day is well advanced within churches themselves, resulting often in severe conflict, and the crisis of authority emerges. This has meant that churches are divided in themselves, and so cannot speak powerfully to the social situation on issues such as euthanasia, abortion, biology and identity, homosexuality, consumerism, the third world. The crisis of moral values in society and the crisis of authority in the churches are deeply linked.

Many inside and outside the churches fear a moral and spiritual vacuum or chaos: 'everyone does what is right in his own eyes', the final sentence of the book of Judges. Are there no authorities or norms any longer? In the Anglican Communion this crisis was focused in the 1998 Lambeth Conference at which the liberal and conservative theological forces engaged, argued over Scripture and tradition, over the leading of the Spirit, over claims to legitimate changes to the moral tradition, over local contextual conditions. This process was quite correct as a Christian discussion of an ethical problem raised by a member of the Communion, the American Episcopal Church. The assembled bishops voted by a large majority on the issue of human sexuality to maintain the traditional lines, an authoritative consensus about the interpretation of Scripture, although constitutionally not a 'binding' decision. The American bishops, however, ignored the consensus, ignored all pleas against precipitate action that would create a crisis, and consecrated a bishop who was divorced from his wife and a self-declared practitioner of gay sex with a male partner. This immediately raised the issue of the nature of authority in the Communion, which had been a sort of family in kind, but now was clearly far more divided. One learned commentator suggested that this raised the issue of the need for a magisterium along Roman Catholic lines. American Episcopalians decided formally that they had no core ethical doctrine by which they were bound, nor did they feel bound by the global vote since they are an 'autonomous' church who attend the Lambeth Conferences as merely consultative occasions.

This illustrates the nature of the crisis: the libertarian conscience stresses freedom for the individual and denies the authority of history or social context as a shaping or conditioning reality to be obeyed or respected in the interests of the wider good. This is at the root of this book's concerns, the 'chaos' factor that springs out when form is opened up completely. But, on the other hand, it is not difficult to see that complete chaos or freedom does not seem to be goal of postmodern, feminized and consumerist society. Rather people are feeling a new set of norms, a set of norms which is gradually making itself felt on the churches. These norms are very roughly described by people as 'political correctness', an assertion of a range of rights ascribed to different groups in society. A problem with this new moral authority system for the church is that some of its norms conflict with those of the gospel values as understood through most of the church's history. Another question arising for the church is how far it can agree with the new order, how it must beg to differ even with legislation enacted by the government. This reflects disagreements among Christians within and between churches, and raises important questions for ecumenism; but will the future shake-out result in a conservative–liberal bifurcation overriding denominational allegiances?

We need to try to describe and explore this great challenge to society and church, asking how Christianity can meet the swirling pressures for change, how in practice is the church dealing with these pressures, how authority should be viewed in the light of the gospel. At one end of the spectrum of answers is the well meaning pluralistic new style liberalism of revisionist theologians and bishops, at the other claims of fundamentalism and authoritarian church structures, notably Roman Catholic but also a sector of evangelicalism. But surely there is a middle way, ensuring a gospel-based core of faith and practice, with room for development and also for legitimate disagreement? This book will argue that Scripture – the voices of the prophets and apostles – gives an orientation which is clear enough as a base for the churches, together with core practices of Christian life and worship flowing from the apostolic life.

Christians need to tackle the pressing question of how the church can face cultural pressures – and influence them and learn from them – while maintaining a definitely Christian orientation. This issue presses desperately on the Christian church. But equally the Western experiment of a wholly secular civilization is in trouble; we need to think very hard about whether by exiling God we have in fact cut off the moral oxygen necessary for a living body politic. This book will suggest that the fruits of Western liberal democracy, and a humane free-market economic order, are dependent upon the gospel tree from which they grew. Remove that tree and the fruit may well wither. In other words, the health of the church is vital to that of society and state. The influence of the Gospel of Jesus indirectly shaped society, culture and politics over the centuries,

enabling a unique synthesis of individual creative freedom with a
Christlike form, one that accepts the other person as God's creation.
The scandalous doctrine of the cross of Christ, breaking down barriers
between hostile tribes, lies behind the core praxis of liberal democracy.
The danger of society and state deliberately rejecting this ethos is of losing
this synthesis and seeing individualist freedom grow wildly, resulting in
the state needing crack down and control society harshly, suppressing
humane freedoms. I try in this book to bring a theological angle onto
this problem for western society, suggesting that the Christian tree has
produced the social capital of the British nation state, and cutting it
down very deliberately by secularists is a costly act of vandalism, with
little popular support in fact.

Part I

Crisis of Authority in Church and Society

1

Deconstruction of
Christian Social Values

This book argues that the crisis afflicting the church in sexual ethics is deeply entwined with the crisis of values gripping Western society generally. This particular church crisis has a significance wider than the seventy million Anglicans worldwide. It reflects divisions running through Western culture generally, and arguably the cultural shifts have affected church opinion and practice radically. No longer has Christianity the same place in society as a formative factor for social and personal ethics. Western culture now feels a crisis of moral authority: where do its values come from in the brave new world of secularism? Obviously the decline of Christianity as the core driver of ethics and practice has affected society generally. The West is in effect conducting an experiment in seeking to manage society without a religious core, making up its values and priorities as it goes along. The problem for Western states may even be put specifically in terms of the problem of Christianity: it now is regarded as a deep embarrassment, a problem rather than the source of social virtue underpinning so many institutions and practices – such as schools, hospitals, universities, charities, social services, and altruism – as the driver of vocation to help others. For some reason, states are keen to divorce such values and practices from Christianity and churches. Curiously, it may be that the problem of the secular West is that of Christianity, and the problem for Christianity is the effects of the dizzying pace of change in human behaviour as the old moral constraints are jettisoned.

Nietzsche's prophecy – The death of God

Is the West confirming the prophecy of Nietzsche's madman that Christianity is dying and that death means the unravelling of the deep grammar of social and moral practices that were basic to the development of western civilization?

> 'Have you ever heard of the madman who on a bright morning lighted a lantern and ran to the market place calling out unceasingly: "I seek God! I seek God!" As there were many people standing about who did not believe in God, he caused a great deal of amusement. Why! Is he lost? Said one. Has he strayed away like a child? Said another. Or does he keep himself hidden? Is he afraid of us? Has he taken a sea voyage? Has he emigrated? – the people cried out laughingly, all in a hubbub. The insane jumped into their midst and transfixed them with his glances. "Where is God gone?" he called out to them. "I mean to tell you! We have killed him – you and I! We are all his murderers! [...]There never was a greater event, and on account of it, all who are born after us belong to a higher history than any history hitherto!' Here the madman was silent and looked again at his hearers; they also were silent and looked at him in surprise. At last he threw his lantern on the ground, so that it broke in pieces and was extinguished. "I come too early," he then said, "I am not yet at the right time." This prodigious event is still on its way, and is travelling – it has not yet reached men's ears. Lightning and thunder need time, the light of the stars needs time, deeds need time, even after they are done, to be seen and heard. This deed is as yet farther from them than the farthest star – *and yet they have done it!*" It is further stated that the madman made his way into different churches on the same day, and there intoned the *Requiem aeternam Deo*. When led out, and called to account, he always gave the reply: "What are these churches now, if they are not the tombs and monuments of God?"[1]

Today's twenty-first-century British culture has apparently turned in the direction signalled by Nietzsche. God has been banished from the public forum and market square, in Europe and America although in different ways. European and North American culture arising from and shaped by the social ethic rooted in the Judeo-Christian religious tradition has become increasingly secular, although precisely how that is defined is quite contested. North American society was founded on the principle of the separation of church from state, although the founding fathers had no idea that their society would be anything other than essentially Christian in character and certainly did not regard themselves as 'secular' in the sense of atheistic or anti-religious. They did regard themselves as supporting a nation state free of clerical rule, but understood themselves as Christian laypeople participating in a democratic process. Of course

---

[1]Friedrich Nietzsche, Complete Works, ed. Oscar Levy, vol. 10, *The Joyful Wisdom*, Edinburgh: 1910, p. 167.

slavery was a deep contradiction on this constitutional ideal, but a stain the Americans themselves eradicated as a result of Christian humanist logic. Today the USA legally is increasingly secular as regards public displays of Christian symbolism, often because of other religions objecting to this on the grounds of the constitutional separation of church and state – the last thing the founding fathers imagined would have been Muslims objecting to Christmas trees in public squares. The American experience of secularism is deepening as Christianity is increasingly pushed out of view and considered a matter of taste, no more significant that any other religion and indeed more suspect than most, despite the very large percentage of church attendance in the USA. The nation is apparently quite strongly Christian, the state is not and cannot be by the American Constitution, a document which, for Oliver O'Donovan, marked the end of 'Christendom' with its deliberate pushing away of institutional religious bodies from formal links with the state.[2] As the USA becomes more pluralist, less Christian and more atheist, the state is faced with difficulty as to any single coherent body of values to assume as shared by the nation, or perhaps nations in its borders. Examples such as the ongoing debates about the legitimacy of abortion and homosexuality show the tensions at work in that Western society.

It is interesting to compare how state and nation cohere in non-Western civilizations. In Islamic 'secular' states, such as Turkey and Egypt, the clerics' influence is kept out of the formal structure of government but their message is assumed as the moral norm for the nation. In Turkey, for example, a Christian missionary organization could not build a church, despite the description of 'secular' given to the state. The Turkish constitution set up by Attaturk after the First World War deliberately excluded Islamic religious rule and asserted 'secularism' over against clericalism. The Turkish army was given a role to maintain this system, since the Turkish nation was and is deliberately totally Muslim and pious Muslims wish to live under Islamic government. This system is being tested severely now as an Islamic party in government presses for change, paradoxically in the name of 'liberalism', working for an Islamic government which itself would not be liberal.

There is little doubt that the *state* in Western European culture has very deliberately rejected Christianity as the driver for public policy, although some European states retain established churches, state-funded church schools, and historic customs derived from centuries-long Christian social practices. The *nations* of the West are not the same as their *states* and there is often a far greater level of support for Christianity as a cultural good and identity than is evident from the attitudes of secular governments or mass media. The census in the UK,[3] for example, in 2001, showed that over seventy percent of the population identified themselves

---

[2]Oliver O'Donovan, *The Desire of the Nations,* Cambridge 1996 p. 244.
[3]www.statistics.gov.uk/CCI/nugget.asp?ID=954&Pos=3&ColRank=2&Rank=1000

as Christian culturally, although a far lower percentage actually attended churches regularly. Nation and state diverge radically on their attitude towards Christianity. Nietzsche was right to connect European morality with faith in God and a massive change in that morality once that faith was evacuated. The state, if not yet the nation, seems to be confirming Nietzsche's prophecy. Christianity has been largely uprooted from Western European states in terms of identity or social policy influence. The public seem to accept that Christian principles cannot now be used to decide public policy, or even such matters as medical ethics; the state, notably in its educational professoriats, has had remarkable success in this shift.

What criteria can be used for the purpose of creating values is not clear, but in the UK Christianity is, the state insists, a matter of private taste, albeit one with a strong sentimental tug. The European Union decided that the identity of Europe should not be deemed Christian in any sense,[4] not even historically, a most peculiar decision in terms of the facts of cultural history and political history in Europe. Nietzsche foresaw that the decline of faith entailed the unravelling of the whole moral structure of Western society, which does seem now to be happening, and since the Church exists in society, the changes are having an effect on Christianity. An important point to note is that Christianity is pushed away from being a matter of public truth, it is not considered objectively true even among very many Christians who 'do not want to impose their views on others', thus implicitly conceding that their faith is not based on facts relevant to society.

Privatization of Christianity

Grace Davie is a sociologist of religion who does not agree that modern society is incompatible with Christianity[5] and points out that the West is unique in seeking to conduct society on a secular basis, and that this must be regarded as an experiment with an uncertain outcome. There is no doubt that Christianity has been banished from the public forum and that the great cathedrals and churches of Europe might well be dubbed 'tombs' of God, museums pointing us back to an earlier age of widespread faith, faith rooted in the person of Christ, a revelation which has shaped the deep grammar of Western civilization over the centuries through its impact on individual lives. Of course as the state continues to silence Christianity as relevant to public policy, it will help erode the faith as important to the nation. Religion is a problem for the modern Western

---

[4]A decision taken in 2006 in the draft European Constitution. See : http://www.articlearchives. com/society-social-assistance-lifestyle/religion-spirituality/1480221-1.html accessed 9.5.2009.
[5]Grace Davie *Sociology of Religion*, London, Sage: 2007.

state: the vast inheritance of Christianity is embarrassing for state policy proposing multi-culturalism and diversity of cultures. Western cultures particularly have embraced the notion that the state has to be neutral and to be neutral might entail pressing down on Christian values and traditions to create a more level playing field for all other faiths. There is a powerful sense in which 'multi-culturalism' has become the established ideology or faith of Western states.

Grace Davie has produced a striking thesis about religion in Britain, 'believing without belonging'.[6] Her argument is that the Christian faith is not to be measured merely by church attendance. Even if we say that a large element of the 2001 Census figure contains a purely sentimental claim to be 'Christian' culturally, the figure will include many who believe, but do not belong to institutional churches. They believe but do not belong. For them faith is individual, possibly quite eclectic in holding some Christian views and practices, but not others. The distinction between Christianity and Church may prove a significant one. Certainly as regards pressure felt by the state for implementing Christian principles, the phenomenon of believing without belonging considerably weakens any organized impact. The phrase 'privatized' religion is very much connected with this refusal to belong or to participate in institutional church life. Christianity is leaving the public forum, and a dualism is quite common in Christian attitudes in the work place: faith is a personal private matter, not to be aired in public. It can thereby become a well kept secret, an individualistic version of faith detached from the realities of society and issues of public debate

Nietzsche's madman declared that the 'death of God' was a reality but one that would take a long time to take effect on culture, since the Christian moral synthesis held together European morality, and in this he seems to have proved right. Only now, at the start of the third millennium, are we experiencing the full impact of secularization in our 'postmodern' era with its celebration of unrestrained diversity and relativism. The privatizing of faith is surely part of this weakening of Christian impact, a stage in its being kept in its own area, a private hobby for some and not the majority, a matter of taste, not a matter of real importance.

Western states assume they can keep the moral fruit of Christianity, while cutting them free from the Christian root. Theologian Hendrikus Berkhof used the analogy of wanting the fruit, while cutting down the tree responsible for growing it.[7] The moral imperative of caring for the sick of all tribes and clans, not just for one's own family and kind, is attractive and to be kept. Accepting the rule of law and democratic decisions likewise arose from Christian ideals and practices especially of the Free Church tradition. Not forcing one's views on another is similarly

---

[6]*Religion in Britain since 1945: Believing Without Belonging*, Oxford: 1994.
[7]Hendrikus Berkhof, *Christian Faith*, Grand Rapids: 1979, p. 515.

an ideal arising ultimately from the Christian heritage. Such ideals are desired by Western states, but not the Christian religion that gave them birth. Nietzsche predicted that this core morality would unwind with the 'death of God', and certainly the state is finding it hard to maintain altruism without its Christian base – why should anyone care for the sick for anything else than a good pay packet? The notion of Christian vocation to do such a thing has faded fast, and indeed been pushed out by educators who regard such vocational motivation as destructive of self-esteem – a Nietzschean criticism. The hangover of Christian morality itself dissipates, the fading smile on the face of the Cheshire cat. The authority of the Church declined, leaving the authority of its attractive moral system, but that now is apparently dissolving quickly for several reasons.

As Nietzsche announced, the death of God means the undoing of the morality rooted in the Christian revelation, notions such as altruism may be considered natural to the human condition for the liberal mind, but that liberal mind is the product of a long process of cultural development stemming from the Christian revelation. It may well be, as Nietzsche thought, that the natural state of man is not altruistic but seeking after power and domination in Darwinian fashion. Christianity, for Nietzsche, was a debilitating creed, producing an attitude of servitude in people and this he equated with the altruism propagated by the churches to disempower the naturally strong and bold. This is, he argues, the fundamental doctrine of the cross, a doctrine of resentment by the weak against the strong, notwithstanding that it has generated much Western social service. Nietzsche showed that Kant's morality was based on the assumption of a certain sense of moral duty, but that this sense was in fact culturally relative, a kind of residue of the Christian cultural mores. This, said Nietzsche, was an imprisoning mores and predicted its gradual demise in favour of a totally individualistic will to power and desire.

In many ways Nietzsche's caricature of Christianity has reflected the progress of the public moral imagination of the West, or at least the imagination of its planners, rulers and opinion formers, who believed that religion was a superstitious, authoritarian brake on progress and should be put out of the public forum altogether. The old moral synthesis was eroded by a complex of factors. Intellectually Nietzsche's rejection of Kantian morality again seemed to vindicate itself. Nietzsche not only predicted the death of God and its deep consequences; he also rejected any overarching moral system since that fettered the freedom and creativity of the human being and his will to power. The Christian moral ethos, widely accepted in society since mid-Victorian times as a positive social force for good in all sorts of ways, was successfully depicted as an unnecessary clog on joyful freedom, on the welfare of women, on social progress globally. In this too, Nietzsche seems to be charting how things are going as the authority of Christianity and churches wears off in the public mind, and especially in the corridors of power, the state.[8]

Kantian morality – detaching from revealed religion

The philosopher who unwittingly paved the way for attempting to keep the fruit of Christian morality, while removing the tree of faith in the transcendent God of Jesus Christ, was Kant. Kant had argued on the basis of a human sense of moral duty that we need to postulate God, freedom, and immortality to make sense of this moral experience. God then became defined by our moral sense. Nietzsche points out that this moral sense of duty is the product of a longstanding Protestant culture in which Kant grew up, and that once God falls out of the picture, this moral sense will erode with it. Kant's move was not intended to promote the self as value-free in its autonomy, but his assumption that a morality imbues the human self naturally and universally has proved to be very questionable indeed. Kant's legacy is depicted by critics to be the exaltation of the self as its own moral legislator, freed from 'heteronomous' law impinging from outside the self and dictating to it.[9] While it was far from Kant's intention, the liberated self of today owes something to his turn to the self as sourcing rationality and morality. It was left to Nietzsche to take this further and strip out any inherent moral sense, leaving the individual will as the core of who we are. We can choose to be what we want and we should choose radically and adventurously. The traditional structures and patterns of life are just that, products of a tradition often imposing taboo and restricting what we desire, according to Nietzsche, now a dominant intellectual influence.[10]

The authority of the once accepted moral law, a kind of secularized version of Christian morality, is wearing thin and being displaced by the authority of the self and its desires, no longer to be held back by the fuddy duddy, hide-bound reactionary morality of Christianity. This tendency is strongly reflected in contemporary movements in Western literature, for example Philip Pullman's *Dark Materials* trilogy, written for children. The movement of sexual liberation of the 1960s has made pornography mainstream and acceptable on film and TV without the old limitation that it might 'deprave or corrupt', since depravity and corruption are now meaningless terms. Actual sexual intercourse between actors can now be performed in films given a general cinema certificate,[11]

---

[8]See e.g. Jeremy Paxman, *The Victorians*, London: BBC Books 2009.
[9]See e.g. Colin Gunton *Enlightenment and Alienation*, Basingstoke: Marshall, Morgan & Scott, 1995.
[10]Alasdair MacIntyre, *After Virtue*, London: Duckworth 1985.
[11]For example the film *Nine Songs*, 2004 directed by Michael Winterbottom.

and sexual violence, supposedly off limits, hardly attracts the attention of the British censor today, as demonstrated by the British Board of Film Censors giving a 15 certificate to the French film 5x2, released in the UK with subtitles in 2005, a film beginning with a graphic depiction of the anal rape of a woman.

Whether individual freedom and will can ever be as 'free' as Nietzsche assumes to be possible is an interesting question. Just as smoking cigarettes, drinking alcohol and taking drugs are addictions controlling the lives of many who are supposedly 'free' and making their own lives entirely of their own desire, so ordinary people push their shopping trolleys around aisles of products at supermarkets in the grip of a consumerism fuelled and reinforced by the advertising industry. How free is the individual to break away from this contextual grip, any more than from that of Christianity or morality, and is there not always going to be a prevailing influence conditioning the individual? When we consider 'authority' in Western culture, we speak of individual freedom and choice, but at the same time we cannot help noticing the grip of our economic and hedonistic context, pulling the individual to exercise 'free choice' along certain paths.

Marxist criticism of Christianity

Karl Marx, another German critical thinker who wrote before Nietzsche, famously criticized the whole economic basis of capitalist society and the ideology that helped keep it standing, notably Christianity. His theoretical criticism of Christianity and Western capitalism remains important, despite the failure of communist regimes, as his condemnation lies near the root of much UK educational syllabus construction, and indeed of what is loosely termed 'political correctness.' The economic order was found to be unjust and destructive. Capitalism meant that workers were kept from the proper rewards for their labour and kept from owning the means of production. This deep pathology led to inhumane behaviour and all the social ills so easily seen in industrial towns of the West. Wholescale revolution of the economic order itself is therefore required to heal the plight of humanity and set relationships aright in the long term, to end 'self-alienation'. Not a few commentators have pointed out that Marx's atheistic reading of history borrows from and reflects some major biblical themes regarding social justice and the path of history,[12] but Marx is very definitely hostile to religion. He takes up Feuerbach's criticism of religion according to which God is a projection

---

[12]See, for example, 'Augustine' in Bertrand Russell, *History of Western Philosophy*, London: Allen & Unwin, 1946, p. 383.

of the human spirit reflecting cultural and psychological realities alone. Marx wrote an early essay on religion in 1844,[13] in which he says that man makes religion, that religion is a reflection of human consciousness and therefore of a perverted consciousness born of a perverted society. Religion plays a baneful role in society in distracting the attention of the poor and oppressed from the cause of their misery. 'Religious distress is at the same time the expression of real distress and the protest against real distress. Religion is the sigh of the oppressed creature, the heart of a heartless world, just as it is the spirit of an unspiritual situation. It is the opium of the people'.[14] Religion therefore needs to be prised away so that mankind can see clearly and take the necessary action against unjust economic forces. Religion is a false authority, for Marx, needing to be displaced by the truth of the Marxist view of history and class struggle.

According to Marx, religion in its institutional form, the medieval church, oppressed people externally, and Luther 'freed mankind from external religiosity, but only by making religiosity the inner man. He freed the body from its chains, but only by putting the heart in chains.'[15] Marx was one of the first analysts to identify the phenomenon of the 'inner chains' of a ruling ideology operating at a subliminal level in the human heart, a social authority and control. The problem now for Marx was the removal of these inner chains of religiosity, chains which prevented proper material action to set people free from their oppression. Religion and ideology possess the people's minds as strongly as any physical drug, it is a product of the economic perversion and alienation. Here we might note a degree of similarity with Nietzsche's criticism of Christianity as an ideology which weakens humanity and renders the potentially strong and resourceful person a self-loathing and useless being. Marx and Nietzsche both find this religion unhealthy and a perversion of being. Ideology for Marx goes wider than merely religion, as the whole theory of capitalism depends on working people being controlled by the acceptance of the market and hopes for economic improvement.

Since the collapse of the Soviet Union, and the satellite communist states Marxism as a workable political system has ceased to be an option. Even the People's Republic of China is blending capitalism with state communism and allowing private enterprise within state control. Marxism as an authoritative system, as a cause to be fought for by active revolution, has faded. But as a means of analysing economic systems and histories it has gained a new life and mutated into a new critical ideal in the West. In particular the Marxist criticism of Western colonialism, interpreted as simply a cynical exercise in economic exploitation and

---

[13]'Critique of Hegel's Philosophy of Right', in Karl Marx, *Early Writings*, Harmondsworth: 1975, p. 243 f.
[14]Ibid., p. 244.
[15]Ibid., p. 251.

oppression, has taken root through Western education.[16] The very worst of motives were attributed to British colonial rule and only evil results. 'Post-colonial guilt' has become the lens through which western history of the last few centuries is viewed. The older view, that colonialism was a venture in civilizing less fortunate regions of the world, is written off as bogus self-justification.[17] Moreover, Christianity and Christian missions are interpreted along with this colonial crime syndicate as an ideologically motivated force and pretext. Racism and a superior attitude to other civilizations are woven into this critical bundle of negativity towards Christianity and its legacy. Marx identified religion as a controlling and pernicious ideology, a virus of the mind; now his own negative reading of Western capitalist societies has mutated into just such an authoritative mental orientation, a keenly anti-Christian 'dog whistle' message.

Add to this the claims that homosexuality was oppressed by Christianity, and that women too were oppressed by this patriarchal religion, and the neo-Marxist portrait is almost complete. Christianity is paraded in shame at the bar of history, and found guilty, a cultural equivalent of the yellow star the Jewish people of Europe were made to stitch onto their clothes. This negative assumption, an irrationally harsh self-criticism of Western cultural history, now dominates much of the Western educational world and the media – in Europe Marxist theory has found a new life as kind of virus in the cultural bloodstream. Europe, certainly Britain, has become allergic to its own history and identity. The very loose term now given to this mindset or world view is 'political correctness', and close to its core lies a thoroughgoing rejection of Christianity as racist, sexist, homophobic and illiberal in all sorts of ways. There can be no question that this reading of Christian history is very authoritative indeed in the West. It is a core assumption and is of course therefore bound to be dripping into the culture of church life in many ways. This overthrows the previous view that Christianity has been the root all manner of virtue and good, of great reforms in society, of education, medicine and nursing, science and literature, of democracy itself.

This has almost become the mental norm within which thinking takes place, defining what is reasonable to think. Here we are reminded of the analysis of how society would fare in the power of mass media and state control in the novels of George Orwell, particularly *1984* and *Animal Farm*. There he speculates on 'thought crime' and 'crime stop', on 'new speak' and of historical records being weeded of offensive material. Authority in modern society – as Orwell predicted on the basis of Marxist societies and the power of mass media – works through the subliminal and presuppositional, and at this level of social conditioning Christian

---

[16]See, for example, Karl Marx, 'The British Rule in India', in Karl Marx and Frederick Engels, *Selected Works*, vol. 1, London: Lawrence & Wishart Ltd, 1950, pp. 312–318.
[17]See for example, The BBC TV programme and book: Jeremy Paxman, *The Victorians* London, BBC Books 2009.

presuppositions have been displaced by a mutated version of the Marxist criticism of Western Christian history and practice. Christianity, especially Christian history, is suddenly bad news, a matter of apology.

So while Marxism proper seems to have been defeated, it has evolved into another form and survived in the liberal capitalist West as a negative ideology among secularists, notably in the professions. This is part of the reason why virtually any other ideology or religion has more authority in the West than Christianity, since political correctness attaches its criticism solely to that religion, alone guilty of the unforgivable sins attributed to it. The doctrine that deep sections of British society and institutional life are 'institutionally racist', a doctrine pronounced by an elderly Scottish judge and named after him as the MacPherson doctrine, has roots in this Marxist ideology and adds to the fashionable idea that Christianity is hostile to ethnic minorities and so suffers from a deficit in moral authority, indeed the history of the West is deemed evil and Western cultures need to do a very long penance indeed. Rational argument for this absolutist reading is lacking, but it has taken deep root. Robert Skidelsky pointed to the irrational nature of the MacPherson doctrine in his analysis of the report: 'The definition of racism, which Chapter 6 reaches, after a long and meandering discussion, is that it is anything perceived to be racist. The perpetrators of racist activity may not know they are racist at all. All they have to do to be so called is to treat people in a way which is interpreted as being racist. Racism, in short, is insensitivity to the feelings of members of ethnic minorities. It is a cultural failure. The Metropolitan Police Service caused offence to the black community and therefore was 'institutionally racist'. The Report only just falls short of dubbing the Commissioner of the Metropolitan Police an unwitting racist for denying that his force was institutionally racist. 'We assert again that there must be an unequivocal acceptance that the problem actually exists as a prerequisite to addressing it successfully', it sternly proclaims. The notion that the perception of a fact makes it a fact is a legal and philosophical monstrosity.'[18]

Post-colonial multiculturalism

This Marxist type of critique probably underlies further charges laid against Western culture, especially Anglo-Saxon culture, by historians such as Edward Said in his book *Orientalism*. There he attacked the attitudes of the Christian Western imperialists towards Islam as inferior, a bizarre object of interest to be studied and patronized. Islam should have been taken more seriously, not turned into a detached exotic and reactionary phenomenon with little to commend it. The West had failed

---

[18]David Green (ed) *Institutional Racism and the Police: fact or fiction?* London, 2000 p 3.

to understand Islamic civilization because it was unable to empathize with and respect it. Western cultural study and practice was again found guilty and in need of apology and repentance, in need of accepting the equality of Islamic culture with its own Western civilization. Again, the West is put in the stocks for some healthy self-abasement. Islam should be encouraged in its self-esteem, Christianity encouraged to see itself as bad news.

In turn secularists in positions of influence used this idea to push back Christian presence from the public forum, on the grounds that other faiths might take offence at it. This was and is a spurious claim, but somehow it took root. The practice of multiculturalism became in effect another Orwellian phenomenon, that 'some are more equal than others', Christian culture being set at a discount while other faiths were celebrated. This again has had the effect of giving Christianity a negative image. Notwithstanding the historical constitutional place of the established church, the blasphemy laws and apparent privileges of Christianity, culturally it has suffered what amounts to steady discrimination at many levels of national life, now being accepted as normal and fair. An increasingly negative view of Christian history now tinges cultural interpretation and presentation. This has reversed, not to say banished, the authority of the historic Christian ethos in Britain, Europe and even the USA. The strong multicultural doctrine now ingrained in British social policy has reinforced relativism as the core value of cultural cohesion: the formal claim is that all cultural values are equally good. This means that global ethics are now in question: each culture has its own set of values, and none are better than others – such is the crude fundamentalism of multiculturalism, and again this strikes hard at the notion that values rooted in Christianity are normative for Britain and the West.

In practice this cultural relativism is effecting a drastic weakening of Christian social authority. In the USA there is a fast-growing number of examples of the rejection of Christian practices in favour of purely secular and functional practice. An article entitled 'Christian Conscience on the Critical List' by John Flynn reported a conference held by the Pontifical Academy for Life.[19] This conference concluded that the right of doctors, pharmacists and hospitals not to provide treatments that violate their moral principles is increasingly under threat. The rights of conscience for doctors and pharmacists not to administer treatments or drugs to effect abortions is being challenged on the grounds that such refusal denies human rights to patients demanding such procedures. The human rights of conscience of the Christian professionals is being made secondary.

A similar, controversial instance of the the authority of the Christian voice being suppressed in public debate in Britain occurred when the Roman Catholic Adoption Agency was told that it had to comply

---

[19]See www.zenit.org, a Roman Catholic news service, 4 March 07.

with new 'Sexual Orientation Rules', compelling the agency to accept homosexuals applying to adopt children, despite the conscientious objection of the agency to homosexuality and homosexual adoption. The rights of gays to adopt trumped the right of Roman Catholics to hold their traditional ethical view.[20] The state has declared this view now to be unacceptable and virtually illegal, offensive to gays and so almost criminal. Christian ethics have become a kind of secular heresy, their authority has become a taboo in British law, if not in mainstream British opinion. Marx's hope to uproot the Christian religion from a favoured position in public perception has come to pass, or is doing so quickly. This perception surely has much to do with the declining confidence in historic British identity as having any value or merit. The rejection of Christianity from a perceived good to a perceived wrong interweaves with a collapsing cultural self-confidence in Britain about its identity, history and purpose.

What's left?

It must be noted however that the Marxist theory of history itself owes a considerable debt to the Judeo-Christian tradition. Both teach that history has a purpose and a goal, an eschatology leading to a state of harmony and peace, when war will be no more. Marxist thinking burns with a longing for social justice and with Old Testament prophets condemns the piling up of material goods at the expense of the poor: 'You who trample upon the needy, and bring the poor of the land to an end.'[21] A real irony is that the neo-Marxian criticism of cruelties involved in colonialism and capitalist excesses coincides precisely with Christian criticisms of such wrongs. Wilberforce campaigned to abolish the slave trade, for example, and so changed an economic order. The British Navy in the nineteenth century stopped the massive Arab slave trade. Shaftesbury campaigned for safe factory working conditions. The error of the fundamentalist neo-Marxian view, or its offspring 'political correctness', is the complete failure to accord Christians their major role in such reform towards social justice, democracy, care and openness to truth. In fact we might argue that political correctness, like Marxism, has a root in the Christian imperative to love your neighbour as yourself, but its negativity towards the tree that grew it gives it a bitterness of taste, turning it into an irrational anti-Western ideology rather than an engine of fairness for all rather than some.

The authority of the politically correct neo-Marxian analysis comes from a dominant reading of history, albeit a very biased one, that is taking root

---

[20]See the debate in the House of Lords in *Hansard*, 21 March 2007.
[21]Amos 8:4.

as a myth in the educational and media establishment. Another aspect of authority emerges as interpretation of history, interpretation testifying to virtue or vice, and the Marxian reading of Christian history emphasizes only vice and oppression. The Nietzschean attack on Christianity claims the authority of the unrestrained desire of the individual; the Marxian attack claims the authority of the record of history and its moral meaning. This radical critique is the core of Western 'political correctness', the rejection of so much traditional Christian history and morality.

Left-wing writers are beginning to notice the surrender of the left to multiculturalist relativism: the authority of the claim of absolute equality of all human beings has been heavily qualified by the acceptance of the 'left' of different rights for different cultural groupings. Nick Cohen's *What's Left?*[22] accuses the 'left' of betraying its core principles of upholding equality and freedom by siding with the Islamic extremists who perpetrated terror attacks on the capitalist West, thus exchanging the left wing core principles for a commonly held hatred of the USA and supporting all manner of illiberal religious practices formerly totally unacceptable to the left. Such ultra-right wing religious ideologies and movements have gained the support of the left. Christopher Hitchens, also from the left, agrees with Cohen:

> This betrayal (because there is no other word for it) has been made possible in part by a degraded version of multi-culturalism. The hard left has junked its historic secularism, to say nothing of its principles of equality for females and homosexuals, to make common cause with Muslim outfits some of which are associated in other countries with the extreme right. It has done this by the use of nonsense terms such as 'Islamophobia', which are designed to give the no-less nonsensical impression that Islam is some kind of persecuted ethnicity.'[23]

Cohen and Hitchens, two powerful voices from the left, are deeply perplexed that a 'degraded version of multi-culturalism' has undermined the global socialist ideal by recognition of the legitimacy of a religio-cultural group on the grounds of its claims to being badly treated by the colonial West. Another very well reasoned exposure of this degeneration of the left into bias and false ideology is *The Fall-Out* by Andrew Anthony.[24] A Marxist reading of cultural history has led to recognition of movements opposed to Marxist and humanitarian ideals. Not only has Christianity suffered disorientation from the advent of multiculturalism, so have socialism and feminism – the Western sisterhood has been totally silent on the fate of young Muslim girls removed from school

---

[22]Nick Cohen, *What's Left? How the Liberals Lost Their Way*
[23]Christopher Hitchens, 'A Man with a Score to Settle', Sunday Times, 21 January 2007
[24]Andrew Anthony, The Fall-Out, London: Jonathan Cape, 2007.

and sent into forced marriages, for example, rendering feminist values entirely 'culturally relative' to the West, not for women universally. This powerfully illustrates what appalls Hitchens, Cohen and Anthony about the psychological impact of multi culturalism on Western values and assumptions. They are no longer absolute in the face of claims by assertive non Christian religious 'communities', or their self appointed leadership. The irony of this is that it is secular politicians and bureaucrats who are implementing religious social morality, deeply affecting the fate of Asian women in the UK. Bss Warsi pointed to the growing acceptance of polygamy in the UK, for example.[25]

We now turn to examine the new version of liberalism arising from this paradigm shift of values in the UK, following the ejection of Christian social mores.

---

[25]See Hansard http://www.publications.parliament.uk/pa/ld200809/ldhansrd/text/90428-0001. htm.

2

Secularist Liberalism

Liberal democratic capitalism, until the uncertainties of the 2008 'credit crunch' anyway, is deemed to have overcome the Marxist political and economic system, and indeed theory. The West seemed to have produced a good balance between freedom and form, the individual and society, which the Socialist model could not replicate, crushing as it did the innovative capacity of the individual in the name of the state. Such has been the success of the liberal democratic ideal that Francis Fukuyama wrote a book entitled *The End of History,* in which he assumed that the liberal democratic capitalist ideal of political and economic being has conquered the world finally and for good.[1] This thesis may have seemed plausible until the Islamic extremist assault on this materialist secular capitalist vision with Al Qaeda's successful suicide attack on the 'Twin Towers' of Manhattan, September 11 2001, symbols of American capitalist success. This attack was in effect a religio-cultural protest against materialism as an idolatry, an attack in the name of Islam, however much many other Muslims denied the validity of this justification of mass murder. It was certainly a statement of one authority system against another, in the eyes of the Islamist bombers. Liberal democracy was not universally admired after all, as the Rushdie affair had shown earlier across the globe. Liberalism has not only been rejected by militant Islam,

---

[1]Francis Fukuyama, *The End of History and the Last Man*, London: Penguin, 1992.

but has itself started to mutate under pressure of powerful religiously based alternative values.

From Christian to secular liberalism

Liberal democracy arose from Western Protestantism and its doctrine of human worth and social morality, which accords equal value to all persons, whatever their condition. It has mutated from a movement rooted in the Protestant tradition of truth, transparency and individual virtue, particularly the Nonconformist ecclesiology stressing the importance of all members in church governance, undeniably creating pressure for the franchise for ordinary people. The very name of liberalism indicates the imperative to promote 'freedom'. This means freedom of thought and expression: liberalism has opposed authoritarianism politically and intellectually, and according to it questioning of authority is an ideal and suppression of free thinking is to be deplored. Liberalism also advocates equal treatment and fairness for all, and attacks privilege. It is not however Marxist in its analysis of the human condition, since it assumes that if individuals are set free then they will prosper and fulfil their potential. This is an optimistic view of human nature, with a moralistic assumption that those who work hard will succeed, deservedly. Marxist socialism insists that the whole capitalist order needs to be broken down, where liberalism traditionally taught that 'free trade', following the law of the free market and removing state interference, will best help the individual and so indirectly the prosperity of nation and state. Traditional liberalism regarded the state with suspicion, as an agency likely to use its power against freedom in many ways.

Liberalism in Britain grew from a Christian base, notably William Gladstone's political implementation of this ideology[2], and the mass support he garnered from Christian voters, especially the Nonconformists, although he was a high-church Anglican. In Europe otherwise liberalism tended to be facing authority structures backed by both state and church, and so was essentially 'secular'. The Roman Catholic Church in particular opposed liberalism in its various aspects into the twentieth century,[3] and liberal uprisings against authoritarian regimes in the nineteenth century were often opposed by the state backed by that church, while in Britain it had almost no power to affect state policy. In the twentieth century the Roman Catholic Church backed the right wing regimes against movements

---

[2]See eg David Bebbington, *William Ewart Gladstone : faith and politics in Victorian Britain*, Grand Rapids, Mich : Eerdmans.

[3]The 1864 '/Anti-modernist Decrees' and 1870 decree of infallibility were particularly strong examples of the Vatican's highly defensive attitude in reaction to liberal change; see eg Stanley G. Evans *The Social Hope of the Christian Church*, London: Hodder 1965 ch 8.

of liberalism and socialism, notably in Spain. British democracy, trade unionism and socialism have their roots not in secular Marxism as much as Methodism and Christian social ethical imperatives. British political evolution, rather than revolution, has progressed from a Christian base and framework of value; never having had a popular 'revolution', there has never been a moment in British political and constitutional history where Christianity has been attacked and pushed away in the name of secular government. Education developed in and from church schools and universities. Hospital care, particularly the nursing tradition inculcated by Nightingale and other Christian women such as Agnes Jones and Mary Seacole, undoubtedly arose from the Christian moral ethic. Truth and right were not relative but global absolutes, and so to be asserted globally.

Gladstone's liberalism sought to promote individual opportunity and fairness. Free trade, of course, to Gladstone and British liberalism, existed within a Christian moral framework, thus it could not countenance the trade of prostitution for example, nor slavery, which offended morality – which was unquestionably assumed to be Christian morality. While the free church liberal voters in Britain were generally not happy with the establishment of the Anglican Church, for Gladstone this establishment was very important for the heart of the national moral good, enshrining Christian faith as the driver of social morals. This assumption of the authority of Christianity as the source of social morality prevailed in mainstream British politics until after 1945. But such was the confidence in the scope of this moral tradition and faith through the nation as somehow given and rooted, that the role of the church in promulgating this ethic was regarded as secondary or less than important. This in fact is a kind of Kantian assumption, that all people feel the universal sense of moral duty, and that God, freedom and immortality are rational postulates arising from this given moral sense. We can now see this moral base was the fruit of a very long cultural tradition, rooted in Christianity.

Church adoption of the secular assumption

This can be exemplified by the 1944 Education Act, implemented by the Conservative politician R. A. Butler. At that stage in history, most schools in England were Church of England schools, many were state schools which taught religious education along Christian lines, some were Roman Catholic, and a few belonged to other denominations. But the church schools needed a vast injection of funds to maintain their standards and upkeep. The state had to reach an accommodation with the churches. Butler, himself an Anglican, devised a settlement whereby some church schools were 'aided', some 'controlled', giving up church control with more state funding than the aided schools. This was devised to get most Anglican schools into virtual state control, under the two different categories of 'aided' and 'controlled' schools. Rome was happy with the deal as they got funding and kept control. Anglicans handed most of their schools over to state control, as Butler had assumed they would. He, and the Anglican Archbishop William Temple, assumed that this change of management would make no change on the moral influence of schooling on children, although some more conservative churchmen disagreed. But some twenty years later Butler expressed profound dismay at the poor quality of religious education and its effect on children, so bad was the situation as to imperil the Christian nature of the nation, he said.[4]

The assumption that that fruit would remain when the tree was removed proved mistaken, clearly the continuing influence of traditional church teaching was a significant loss. Hastings' historical judgement is that these educational choices deeply strengthened the rapid advance of secularizing the middle classes in the 1960s, a judgement that seems hard to gainsay. Liberal attitudes had assumed the Christian moral ethos was present, as if a law of nature, but Nietzsche was right in his criticism of Kant: the Protestant moral sense of duty quickly unwound as faith in God and church influence declined. The authority of moral sense quickly detached from the traditional liberal ethos, leaving freedom as its main focus of virtue and criterion of worth. The key question became 'why should this activity not be permitted, if desired?', a question no longer answerable by 'because Christianity rejects it'.

The sudden death of Christian Britain in the 1960s

Callum Brown, in his book the *Death of Christian Britain,*[5] argued that the death of Christian Britain indeed set in late, roughly around 1958, and deepened during the 1960s to the present collapse of major influence or authority in the state and even the nation, although a nostalgic loyalty lingers on. Brown discusses the concept of secularization as one of deep paradox, even irony. This notion, in Britain, was conceived in the minds of worried clerics in the nineteenth century; as they perceived urbanization and lower church attendance and commitment, it was a church anxiety. But the figures do not reveal a steady decline of church attachment, and strikingly the highest level of church growth occurred from 1945 to 1958, a spurt particularly affecting women and their attitudes. The sharp decline set in from the 1960s. 'Secularization' as a steady process from the Enlightenment or French Revolution of 1789, is a 'myth', and

---

[4]Adrian Hastings, *A History of English Christianity*, 1920–1990, London: SCM Press, 1991, p. 421.
[5]Callum G. Brown, *The Death of Christian Britain*, London & New York: Routledge, 2001.

one derived from over-anxious church fears. Brown does not discuss Butler's 1944 Education Act, nor Hastings' historical judgement that it was a factor in the secularizing of middle classes, but the two scholarly interpretations fit together well. The detaching from the church of the middle class who were schooled in the 1950s and teenagers in the 1960s matches Brown's description of deeply changing attitudes and moving away from the authority of Christian ideals.

Why this analysis is particularly significant for Christianity and the difficulties of the Anglican Communion regarding the Christian understanding of sexual behaviour is that changing attitudes to sex were central to the abandonment of the Christian ideal and of the churches. In particular, says Brown, the changing attitudes of women seem crucial – who were quickly adopting 'liberated' sexual behaviour patterns and rejecting the social constraints that had surrounded and stifled sex before marriage and single motherhood. The Christian ideal of marriage as the context for sex and child rearing, with the woman as the key person in enforcing this ideal, and 'gossip' as the big shaming and restraining factor, suddenly broke up. The Church of Scotland, reporting on this phenomenon, picked out 'the promiscuous girl'[6] as the key problem causing the spread of secular attitudes, driving a wedge into social loyalty to Christian commitment. This was a sudden and violent change – secularization came as a storm not as a long process. When the piety of women eroded their sexual behaviour and ideals changed, there was no natural moral sense, as the liberal Anglican R. A. Butler also discovered, and the 'Christian character of the nation', which he assumed to be a fixture, began to disappear before his eyes.

The 'death of Christian Britain' came violently in the 1960s, rather than as a long, slow, inevitable process. A vibrant Christian culture, notably among women, had existed through the nineteenth century up to 1958, according to Brown. The caring professions had had deep roots in this vibrant Christian culture, notably nursing. Nightingale had reformed and founded this profession, moving it from a degraded kind of institution represented by the gin-sodden predatory Sary Gamp in Dickens' *Martin Chuzzlewit*, to the deeply committed, scientifically informed and altruistic profession represented by the school of nursing developed at St Thomas' Hospital in London and generalized into becoming a world-renowned system. This profession was based on the motivation of the Christian gospel of Christ-like care for all, rich and poor, not just for family, clan, or tribe. The ethic running through this profession remained very strong until well into the 1960s, and nursing magazines reveal that the grass roots profession resisted the secular nursing theory coming in from the USA very strongly.[7]

---

[6]Ibid., p. 180.
[7]A. E. Bradshaw, *The Nurse Apprentice*, Aldershot: Ashgate, 2001.

Not only was the Christian ethic of valuing the individual person still very definite even in the mid 1960s, but ward prayers were still being said on wards then, led by nursing sisters themselves. The uprooting of the Christian base for nursing in Britain involved a fierce battle, but 'they', the bureaucrats who knew best, ultimately had their way. Soon altruism, vital to the caring professions, was in search of a rationale, and then was rejected as exploitative of professionals. Caring now has to be rooted in contract rather than covenant – contract and cash: 'paid to care' rather than called to care is the new order of the day. The 1960s saw not just a gentle fading out of Christianity by default, but a fierce battle in some contexts, in which the state failed to support the Christian ethos. The influence of the neo-Marxist polemic on Christianity seems evident in this deconstruction of the nursing tradition on the grounds that the idea of vocation to care was exploitative and manipulative, and that the motive of altruism was unprofessional.[8]

Feminism

The feminist movement, ironically given the immense power vested in the hands of the women who ran hospitals and wards, also helped kill off the Nightingale tradition. The feminist movement of the 1960s asserted empowerment over altruism and rejected the notion of a woman's vocation to care as a piece of ideology designed to keep women down as passive servants. Callum Brown demonstrated the sudden end to this female Christian culture as sexual liberation and self-fulfilment replaced the moral framework which supported the agenda of church and family as the ideal way of a woman's life. New possibilities opened up to women and these suddenly became popular and acceptable. This weakened the authority of the Christian ideal and churches massively and led to the 'death of Christian Britain', culturally and hence politically. The role of women in society always was utterly crucial, and their work of raising children, sustaining marriages, and handing on the Christian religious and moral tradition, was immeasurably important, through the nineteenth and twentieth centuries and before.

This contribution was however never properly marked nor appreciated nor rewarded. The term 'housewife' became one of disdain, in comparison with virtually any other female performer of a job or task. The churches themselves did not accord sufficient status to women, who were the core of their membership. Florence Nightingale found this when she offered her services to the Church of England, only to find that there was no niche in the structures of the church for them. She found the 'secular'

---

[8]See A.E Bradshaw, *The Project 2000 Nurse*, London Whurr 2001.

world the place where she could put into practice her vocation to serve the sick, initially through the Army in Scutari, later through hospital nursing in London. Society and church simply failed to acknowledge the contribution of women. The feminist movement was therefore correct to protest at the failure to accord sufficient status and reward to women, notably those raising children in stable marriages and handing on the virtues to their children for the good of social peace and well being. Women were not even given the vote until the suffragette protests and campaigns at the start of the twentieth Century. This failure to value the place of women for the deep grammar of society and culture resulted in the legitimate feminist protest.

British culture has now inverted this expectation and virtually compelled women into the work place. But his has removed women from their key community building and sustaining role. The chief executive of the Joseph Rowntree Foundation is quoted as saying: 'Every community regeneration project I've ever seen has been driven ultimately by women residents from the bottom.'[9]

It is an irony that feminism succeeded in overthrowing the value of the mere 'housewife' even more than society had done pre-feminism. Radical feminism attacked the very legitimacy of marriage, women focusing on raising their children, homemaking, and of course passing on the Christian way of life. The Marxist doctrine of 'ideology' was used here to say that women were victims of a false world view imposed on them to keep them under control for the good of men, who basically manipulated women. Since the original attack on the role of women as wives and mothers, a role deemed to be damaging and repressive, later waves of feminist or 'womanist' thought sought to make this role a legitimate one for those women who desire it, which can be their free choice – indeed religious motivation for such a choice may even be permissible. One might go a step further and suggest that the original feminist attack on marriage, and relating to men in committed relationships as wives and mothers, was itself a form of bondage and thought control.

Sexual liberation

Feminism was certainly a major edge in the secularist attack on the traditional Christian pattern of marriage as the building block of society.

---

[9]Madeleine Bunting 'Again social evils haunt Britain.' http://www.guardian.co.uk/commentisfree/2009/jun/14/society-community-uk-morality.

Marriage is now merely one choice among many as an arrangement for child rearing and form of relationship. But feminism was but one line of attack on the institution of marriage and family. As Pannenberg says in his discussion of secularization, 'The opposition of individual freedom to all institutional rules and claims on the individual can also be directed against the institution of the family: in the case of children against the authority of parents and in the case of parents against the ties and limitations of individual freedom which are bound up with marriage and family.'[10] Once marriage has been placed in the new secular context, it becomes an institution resting merely on human choice, not divine pattern and purpose, and so the secular context changes it into a lifestyle option. This is one important example of how the secularization of liberalism fundamentally alters the deep grammar of social institutions. In the first place 'freedom' is used as a wedge to open up the Christian forms of life, but then the state begins to impose its own ideology. The state in fact begins to displace the family, parents, and local bodies in framing morality and even issuing contraception, at school, to girls below the age of consent.[11]

Religiously grounded or validated social institutions bear an authority and purpose which secularism cannot maintain, since all becomes a matter of choice and taste rather than a divinely given patterning of relationships for the good of society and humanity. What some have chosen, others can reject, unless of course the kind of secular society is a Marxist or fascist dictatorship denying freedom and imposing patterns of life, which then command no more authority than mere arbitrary force. Liberal secularism regards such religious claims as repressive and preventing the individual from attaining freedom and self-fulfilment, and psychology after Freud has driven this message home with the utmost power. Restraints on sexual activity lead to neuroses and deviance, far from being deviant, as Christianity teaches, unrestrained free sexual activity is absolutely healthy, as long as it is consensual and not visiting violence on others.

The homosexual movement followed in the wake of feminism in the mid 1960s, succeeding in removing homosexuality from the list of psychological disorders, and then succeeding in changing laws banning homosexual practices, later removing educational safeguards against them, and finally getting legal recognition for homosexuals and homosexual partnerships with virtually all the rights attaching to marriage. Whereas homosexuals had been oppressed legally, now the boot is very much on the other foot and homosexual rights are as powerful as any other. This has been an amazingly fast and successful campaign against the

[10]W. Pannenberg, *Christianity in a Secularized World*, London: SCM Press, 1988, p. 37.
[11]See Sunday Times July 20 2008 'Schools encouraging under age sex.'

traditional Christian and 'common sense' view of society, which was to tolerate but discourage homosexuality.

Callum Brown's analysis of the process of the death of the traditional Christian moral ethos – that the 1960s were the critical pivotal years of change when the social control mechanism of the church fell away, making single parent motherhood, for example, accepted and no longer stigmatized and repressed by the disapproving surrounding culture[12] – is strongly exemplified with the progress of homosexuality. Peter Berger's 'plausibility structures' describe a similar phenomenon.[13] The change in English sexual mores might be illustrated by the case of Cynthia Payne who was convicted in 1978 of running a brothel, but in 1987 a jury acquitted her of all such charges for running precisely the same 'parties' in her home. The 1967 change in the law over homosexuality[14] likewise gives a benchmark of such change and move away from church teaching on the basis of the freedom of the individual to decriminalize homosexuality with the only proviso being mutual consent and the parties being over 21. Professor H. L. A. Hart and Lord Devlin[15] debated the relationship of morality to law and there can be no doubt that Hart's secular pragmatism reflected the future, as against Devlin's more traditional Christian view that law needed a basis in morality if a unified society would accept a common law. What might be said now is that the change embodied a new morality, not a departure from morality, the new morality being rooted in the freedom of the autonomous self, constrained only by the need not to harm others. The wider notion of social harm and shaping patterns of behaviour is not part of this picture. The 1960's ushered in the era of contempt for inherited 'taboos' not based on physical functional necessities. There can be no doubt that the advance of secularism went hand in hand with the removal of traditional moral patterns of life. Individual freedom removed traditional form, notably that of marriage and child raising. Family Court judge Mr Justice Coleridge spoke of an epidemic of family breakdown which is overwhelming the courts, calling for a national commission to address this breakdown and its tragic effects on children. 'What I hope in all humility I am drawing attention to is the endless game of "musical relationships" or "pass the partner"'. While individual pleasure is important, the social effect of hedonistic individualism is catastrophic.[16]

The 1967 Act made 21 the age of consent, higher than the age for heterosexual consent, and this bar was lowered as the gay campaign

[12]Callum Brown, *The Death of Christian Britain*, London: Routledge, 2000.
[13]Peter L. Berger, *A Rumour of Angels*, Harmondsworth: Penguin, 1969.
[14]1967 Sexual Offences Act.
[15]P. Devlin, *The Enforcement of Morals*, Oxford: Oxford University Press, 1965; H. L. A. Hart, *Law, Liberty and Morality*, Oxford: Oxford University Press, 1963.
[16]http://www.telegraph.co.uk/family/5561776/Family-breakdown-is-now-a-national-tragedy.html.

waxed stronger and stronger in the next decades, until in Britain the Civil Partnerships Act was passed in 2006, interestingly with some Anglican Bishops voting for it in the House of Lords.[17] The unquestioned assumption driving this legislation and all other changes to the law, notably the repeal of 'Section 28', an educational measure banning the promotion of homosexuality in school sex education lessons, was that some human beings are homosexual as a matter of their very being, with no regard to theories of social construction as a major factor in this phenomenon. The sweeping success of the homosexual campaign has been based on a view of human nature, even natural law, validating the claims of the homosexual lobby and negating the claims and pastoral policies of Christianity, which regards homosexuality as a problem to be negotiated morally rather than a biological given fact of nature.

It is interesting to note that this particular change was not based on democratic majority vote in society, rather it was a change led by the imperative of freedom of the individual. If the authority of the Christian faith and churches had been pushed to one side, it was not by the voice of the people, but rather by an authoritative doctrine and influential new intellectual establishment. It is important to note that Christian thinkers approved the 1967 Act on the grounds that morals cannot and should not be enforced, that they need to be rooted in personal conviction, and that the state should not be in the business of dictating the sexual habits of its citizens. The Church of England certainly, if not all British churches, adopted a dualistic attitude in its moral advice to society: inside the church we believe this to be right, but outside the church we believe church teaching does not apply. The question of truth applying globally has clearly been answered in a relative manner, according to context.[18]

The modern liberal state withdrew from supporting Christian moral norms in sexual morality during the 1960s in terms of the criminal law, and has lent its power to enforcing very different moral norms as regards all kinds of sexual relationships and child rearing, lent its power in fact to suppressing the traditional Christian view, to the level of criminalizing it. The church increasingly adopted the view that the individual should be free to choose, and that the church had no business interfering or pontificating, certainly outside the church but incipiently inside as well. The authority of freedom and abolition of constraints on how we behave has become paramount, 'judgementalism' was to be avoided – what could be the basis of any judgement on the behaviour of others?

In Britain homosexual partnerships are now on a par with marriage in terms of legal and financial rights and privileges, and so increasingly are partnerships between men and women not sealed by marriage. Marriage is seen as just one option among many, not as the 'building block of

---

[17]Civil Parrtneships Act 2006. See Hansard for the voting of the bishops and speeches.
[18]Oliver O'Donovan, *Resurrection and Moral Order*, Leicester: IVP, 1986, p. 20.

society' or the best way to raise children, in the eyes of the legislators. Laws relating to the age of consent, to taxation, to inheritance, to adoption of children, are all now thoroughly detached from Christian influence. Freedom to do as the individual pleases sexually has attained maximal authority, but Christian freedom to argue for this freedom to be shaped and guided is now on the edge of being banned.

Tolerance of homosexual acts in private was not enough for the homosexual movement, nor its normalization by psychiatry. The task of getting Western culture to regard gays as a people group, an oppressed community, began – fuelled by the 1969 Stonewall Riots in Greenwich Village, USA – the precursor to the 'Gay Pride' marches of 'out and proud' homosexuals wanting public recognition of an identity. The homosexual movement has also campaigned successfully in getting an offence onto the statute book in Britain making stirring hatred against persons on the grounds of sexual orientation, equivalent to the same offence as stirring up hatred on racial grounds.[19]

In a decade then, the whole cultural context for the traditional Christian view of sexual morality has been fundamentally changed. Christians now find themselves in the position of homosexuals before the 1976 Criminal Justice Act, told that they are more or less tolerated, but only in private. The welter of gay rights legislation has been followed up by efforts to suppress Christian Union meetings, for example, in University premises, by a prosecution of a bishop for refusing to employ an actively homosexual youth worker and seek to have the bishop given 'equal opportunities training'.[20] The gay rights campaign now seems to wish to destroy the traditional Christian view altogether: not to 'live and let live' in a pluralism.

The traditional Christian is now countercultural and only just tolerated by the law of the land. Our British context is suddenly very frosty indeed towards Christianity unless that Christianity bows the knee to the revolutionary guard and undergoes re-education. The gay campaign clearly will not cease its war until the church, notably the established

---

[19]For this Act see http://www.opsi.gov.uk/acts/acts2008/pdf/ukpga_20080004_en.pdf, schedule 16. Thanks to a last-minute intervention by Lord Waddington, a freedom of expression clause was appended:
'29JA Protection of freedom of expression (sexual orientation)'. In this Part, for the avoidance of doubt, the discussion or criticism of sexual conduct or practices or the urging of persons to refrain from or modify such conduct or practices shall not be taken of itself to be threatening or intended to stir up hatred. Had this not been inserted, the Christian view on homosexuality would have become criminal if published.
[20]See   www.telegraph.co.uk/news/uknews/1577982/Bishop-fined-in-gay-discrimination-case.html.

church, complies with its moral code. There are to be no 'grey areas', no areas where we can agree to differ on this issue.

Crisis of Authority in the Anglican Church

The crisis of values afflicting western society and church can be usefully illustrated by the strife in the Anglican Church. The crisis tearing the Anglican Churches over sexuality is threatening to split the communion in a profound fashion, and opens up the question of authority in the church and indeed the question of how the church is defined.

Attempts have been made at resolving the disagreement about homosexuality by appealing to the merits of accepting a range of different opinions reflecting diverse cultural contexts, not subject to over-arching metanarrative. Liberals want each member church to be free to decide its ethics and doctrine autonomously. The Communion has not before needed any 'teeth' to enforce any practice or teaching, like the Eastern Orthodox it has relied on an acceptance of tradition by all on the analogy of a mutually trusting family, but now this consensus is breaking up and there are no 'systems' in place to adjudicate between the traditionalists and revisionists, or indeed to define terms of membership of the Communion. In particular the Archbishop of Canterbury is a figure of moral authority, but not of jurisdiction over other churches in the Communion.

The disruption of the Chuch – Consecrated diversity

How the church should minister to people who see themselves as homosexuals, therefore, is proving a church-dividing question. The fierce disagreement was triggered by the consecration by the American branch of the Anglican Communion, ECUSA,[21] of Gene Robinson as bishop of New Hampshire on 2 November 2003. Living an openly homosexual lifestyle, he had previously been married for some time and had fathered two children with his wife. It was not however his divorced status that caused the furore but rather his validation of a homosexual lifestyle incorporating gay sex as a pattern declared to everyone. The consecration was carried out in the face of great opposition by the archbishops of the Anglican Communion, and against the resolutions of the Lambeth Conferences, global meetings held every ten years. Prima facie, this consecration conflicts with a clear line of biblical teaching and ecumenical church tradition. ECUSA behaved as if a totally autonomous body without any obligations to the church's tradition or to sister Anglican churches in the communion, let alone to other denominations. The fact that ECUSA's

---

[21]This acronym stands for 'Episcopal Church of the United States of America', it was subsequently been changed to TEC, 'The Episcopal Church', in 2006.

Presiding Bishop, Frank Griswold, was made to step down from the Anglican Roman Catholic International Commission, ARCIC, signalled severe Roman Catholic disapproval and damage to ecumenical relations between Rome and Canterbury flowing from ECUSA's unilateral action.

Notwithstanding the crisis it has provoked, ECUSA, renamed as TEC, has maintained its stance resolutely since, and the fever within the worldwide Anglican Communion has grown increasingly intense, to the point of the deepest possible fracturing of relations between provinces and within provinces themselves. O'Donovan accurately observes that Anglican liberalism used to be a kind of fudging middle position to reconcile the tensions of Evangelical and Catholic poles of identity, but the New Hampshire crisis has finalized a deep reconfiguration of the spectrum: 'The historically centripetal middle had become a new centrifugal pole.'[22]

Conservatives in TEC, bishops, clergy and people, have appealed outside their Province to Canterbury, with the resulting commission producing the *Windsor Report*,[23] recommending the formation of an Anglican 'covenant' to which all member churches would be committed. This proposal is currently under intense debate within the Anglican Communion. TEC and other Provinces favouring the acceptance of homosexuality as normal and not an aberration stresses their autonomy as independent episcopally governed churches, subject to no higher authority and legally permitted to order their own affairs under their own arrangements. The intense disagreement over human sexual behaviour has shown how decentralized the Anglican Communion is and how it has relied on a shared conservative family consensus as its bonding agent, a personal kind of practice of fellowship surely close to that of the early church. It is a tragedy that this has now been broken.

Conservative parishes in TEC have appealed to friendly bishops outside the USA who support their traditional stance on homosexuality, with the result that some congregations have put themselves under the authority of African bishops, seeking to maintain their Anglican identity while detaching from their revisionist TEC bishops. This wholly unprecedented move shows how deep the divisions go and what a threat to the unity of Anglicanism this crisis has become. The crisis raises the question of authority in the starkest way – where is the truth to be found, and why are the sources of authority now so ineffective as guiding norms for the Anglican Communion? Is the Anglican Communion now being faced with a fork in the road, the left hand road being that of a 'free for all' liberalism, the right hand road being a heavily controlled authoritarianism? In fact the fork is more complex than this, since TEC

[22]Oliver O'Donovan, *Sermons on Subjects of the Day*, 1. p. 3, online at www.fulcrum-anglican. org.uk/page.cfm?ID=130.
[23]*The Windsor Report*, London: Anglican Communion Office, 2004.

acts against its own conservative dissidents in an authoritarian way, not brooking opposition to its decision to accept and encourage homosexual practice, hence the conservative flight to alternative bishops from Africa. TEC has decided to remain episcopally governed, and the bishops are enforcing their revised ethical policy on their conservative dissenters rather than upholding their freedom. The polarity of freedom and control is working itself out in complex fashion in the Anglican Communion, as in Western society generally: liberalism can be deeply authoritarian.

The premonitions of Crockford's Preface

The current crisis has been a long time coming, but it has not come out of the blue; storm clouds had been gathering and some acute conservative theologians forecast the weather pattern of the impending hurricane. The ordination of women in Anglican churches was the issue exercising the minds of the bishops of the Communion prior to the Lambeth Conference of 1988 and the Preface to the very Anglican *Crockford's Clerical Directory* of 1987/88 was written, as by custom, anonymously and this one addressed the state of the Anglican Communion with some robust criticisms. In fact this led to the tragedy of the author of the preface, a distinguished Anglican scholar and churchman, Dr Gareth Bennett, committing suicide having lost his anonymity and being hounded by the press. His declared aim was to offer a 'trenchant' analysis of what seemed a very worrying state of affairs, sharply focused by the fact that some provinces of the Communion had ordained women to the presbyterate, and ECUSA threatened to consecrate a woman bishop without consulting with the Communion. The Lambeth Conferences were not used to such unilateral and radical behaviour, behaviour which broke the unwritten understanding of mutuality and consultation. ECUSA was presenting the Communion with deep problems and recklessly causing crisis, in effect conducting a kind of revolution and still expecting to be accepted as a legitimate member of the Communion. Bennett's anonymous article conducted an analysis of the shape of the Anglican polity in relation to ECUSA's behaviour.

Anglicanism, for Bennett, had always been slow in producing a coherent doctrine of the church, its Reformation had focused on freeing the English church from the rule of Rome, and only later was a wider ecclesiology forged. This emerged through the writings of Jewell and Hooker, seeking to steer away from mere Erastianism or state control, from Popery and from Protestant sectarianism. The Church of England found authority 'in scripture as this was interpreted in the life and practice of the undivided Church of the first four centuries of the Christian era', said Bennett, adding 'Such a conservative ecclesiology, with its great stress on the institution of episcopacy and the independence of the local church, came to be recognized by other Christian denominations as a distinctive Anglican position.[24]

This basic stance led to the flowering of Anglican patristic scholarship and is the ecclesiological position taken as the basis for Anglican ecumenical discussions. But Bennett immediately asks whether this apparently clear position was ever fully accepted throughout the Church of England by its various constituent parties. Indeed the church has existed with these parties isolated from each other, especially in terms of an ecclesiology. According to this final *Crockford's Preface*, four factors worked to maintain the unity of the Church of England. The establishment was one vital aspect. *The Book of Common Prayer*, 1662, was another, with its literary power and spiritual depth, providing a much loved theological language throughout the church. The common ministry and ordination was the third unitive factor identified, and – perhaps now surprisingly to contemporary readers – the fourth was stated as the 'the conservative theological tradition of the English universities with their strong links to the Church of England.[25] Anglican scholars and churchmen, even well into the twentieth century, tended to a conservatism in theology, and tended to approach theology through history. This package was essentially a practical one rather than a carefully worked out system or doctrine of the church.

Anglicanism spread around the world by the missionary movement and as Anglicans accompanied the British Empire, and left its distinctive churches around the globe, all under the authority of the mother church until the formation of the Protestant Episcopal Church in the United States in 1784. For the first time a new national Anglican church, self-governing, was set up. This move was copied by the other Anglican churches world wide until by the 1930s an Anglican Communion had come into existence. But what, apart from their common historical heritage, held these churches together? Bennett raised this incisive question for discussion – and his question still seeks a definitive answer today, twenty years later, as the 2008 Lambeth Conference has shown. What did hold together this collection of autonomous churches, all free to change their doctrine and practice and indeed ecumenical relations? *The Windsor Report* with its proposed Anglican Covenant is the possible final answer to the pointed question raised by Bennett in Crockford and by TEC now as it seeks to exercise its autonomy in the strongest possible way, untrammelled by any sense of control from

---

[24]'Preface' in *Crockfords Clerical Directory*, London: Church House Publishing, 1987/8, pp. 59–60.
[25]Ibid., p. 60.

the wider Anglican family – while still claiming the Anglican label for itself.

Bennett sets out how the Anglican Communion has tried to define its stance on authority in its member Provinces or regional churches. In particular lists of fundamentals were drafted to define what member churches must hold in order to remain in communion with the others. The Chicago–Lambeth Quadrilateral of 1886 and 1888 described a four-fold Anglican commitment: the use of the canonical Scriptures, the historic Catholic creeds, the historic episcopate locally adapted, and the sacraments of Baptism and the Eucharist. This remains a significant marker for the Anglican churches, but as Bennett points out they are understood in various ways and interpreted differently. He pointed to Stephen Sykes' book *The Integrity of Anglicanism* (1978) which spoke of 'dispersed authority' in the Communion, and found its common identity in its liturgical tradition of worship rooted in the *Book of Common Prayer*, echoing the old phrase *lex orandi lex credendi*, 'the law of praying is the law of believing.' Worship is where the essence of the Anglican tradition is to be located. Sykes thought of the various consultative bodies, such as the Lambeth Conference and Anglican Consultative Council, as functioning to gather together the strands of authority to discover a common mind. Bennett points out that the shared liturgical tradition diversified as the *Book of Common Prayer* was superseded by all manner of modern regional prayer books, and in England it has fallen largely out of use in parish worship.

What Sykes' book did show was the refusal by the Communion at the time to accord any institution in the global communion a central authority. The national churches are constitutionally autonomous in their exercise of the Lambeth Quadrilateral and shared ways of being Anglican. The 1978 Lambeth Conference did not succeed in developing any common authority structure, preferring to celebrate diversity and the right of each province to act according to its own canons over the presenting issue of division at that time, the ordination of women. Lambeth 1978 urged mutual respect for the sincerity of rival practices. Bennett's verdict on this conference was that 'They had consecrated the notion of an ever-increasing Anglican diversity and the obligation to 'accept', at least in the sense of cooperating with, anything decided by a particular province.' Bennett asks whether this approach condemns the Anglican Communion to diversity without determinable parameters, the conference 'had never faced the possibility that a notion of authority so obscure in conception and so imprecise in its exercise might in fact be no authority at all.[26] Bennett judged the Anglican Communion to be a 'loose association of independent national churches with some weak consultative bodies,[27] diagnosing very precisely and

---

[26]Ibid., p. 61.
[27]Ibid.

acutely the nature of the Anglican Communion structure and its centrifugal tendency.

The 1988 Lambeth Conference in fact was faced with ECUSA unilaterally appointing a woman bishop, Barbara Harris, without any reference whatsoever to the wider Communion, acting as a totally free agent in relation to its sister Anglican churches, and causing a crisis in the family. It was not disciplined in any way, and its strategy of doing as it liked and then presenting a *fait accompli* to the Lambeth Conference worked well. This was to be the same policy as was used in the consecration of Gene Robinson subsequently, as time was to show.

The Lambeth Conference of 1998 had very heavily reaffirmed the conservative moral tradition on homosexuality with a seven to one vote, despite great efforts by ECUSA and its dominating influence on the organizing secretariat. ECUSA was acting not only against historic and ecumenical consensus, but against the strongly declared present mind of the Anglican Communion. It was taking advantage of the lack of a worked out set of rules to cope with the crisis it was causing, arguing that it was a wholly autonomous local church which was acting under its own rules. Gary Bennett's analysis proved correct, the Communion proved a loose association relying on a sense of mutual fellowship and consultation, a sense simply ignored by ECUSA. In fact Lambeth 1998 passed a resolution accepting *The Virginia Report*, a report examining the very problem of the need for the Communion to develop more definite central controls to offset the autonomy of each province. There is no doubt that the Communion again revealed a common mind for stronger instruments of unity and definition over against the present state of unrestricted diversity.

The Lambeth Conference of 2008 deliberately refrained from discussion of the divisive issues. The Archbishop of Canterbury did not invite Gene Robinson to the Conference, however, indicating that the Communion had not accepted as a *fait accompli* the consecration of someone who announced their primary identity to be homosexual – the fact of his being divorced was not considered problematic since the Anglican Communion has made no issue out of clerical divorce, even serial divorces by bishops, despite New Testament teaching against this. A large body of 250 traditionalist bishops decided not to attend the conference and to attend a different assembly in Jerusalem instead, thus highlighting the fracture in the Communion. The current situation is that the Communion is working on a 'covenant' as a common basis for all members, but TEC is opposed to any binding element as a threat to their self-governance and autonomy. Bennett's verdict about the dangers of unlimited diversity have surely been vindicated.

Chaos or control?

This illustrates the nature of the crisis: the libertarian conscience stresses freedom for the individual and denies the authority of history or social context as a shaping or conditioning reality to be obeyed or respected in the interests of the wider good. This is at the root of this book's concerns, the 'chaos' factor. But on the other hand it is not difficult to see that complete chaos or freedom does not seem to be goal of postmodern, feminized and consumerist society. Is Western Society as it faces its crisis along with much of Western Christianity, stuck between chaos and unlimited autonomous freedom, or a centralized control system overriding open and reasoned discussion? Or is there a form of freedom lived out by the church which confers freedom rightly shaped? This question is directly linked to the crisis of values also facing our society in the West. We now turn to examine a crucial dimension to this crisis, that of relativism, a form of consecrating diversity.

3

Cultural Relativism

From equality to privilege

The steady rejection of Christian ethics as an authority for policy by the British state paradoxically comes at a time when Britain is redefining its identity as 'multicultural', that is welcoming other religious cultures into the nation, as institutions, and into policy-making committees and seeking to accept their practices sometimes even despite these offending the existing legal norms. This has affected secular liberalism in its attitude to religion. Religion, provided it is not Christianity, is suddenly welcomed by the secular liberal state in Britain, if not in some other European states which have embraced secularism in a more intellectually worked out fashion, such as France. Multiculturalism in Britain probably originated in typically pragmatic fashion, with roots in a Christian ethic of welcoming strangers, but it deepened into an ideology, one used perhaps cynically by secularists to help suppress traditional Christian customs, practices and assumptions with the spurious argument that such practices in the public forum are 'offensive' to other faiths. This is generally not true, but has been used in bureaucracies at all levels to marginalize Christianity, notwithstanding the nation's cultural identification with the faith.

In secularist Britain today minority groups are increasingly given identities different from the historic majority culture. Rather than stress the one national 'community' with a shared set of values, UK policy is to underplay commonality and stress divergent 'communities'. In taking this view, the state totally ignores individuals who prefer not to be labelled by their religion or continent of ethnic origin, but came here or stay here because they want to own a mainline British identity and value system: such people are in effect handed over to their minority 'communities' and their self appointed leaderships. Part of the motivation for this multicultural policy is to make new immigrant communities feel welcome and their traditions valued, hence for example the efforts by local authorities to translate notices into the languages of immigrants, rather than expect them to learn English as the common unifying language. The segregationalist approach to multi culturalism, or pluralism, reverses the integrationist vision of uniting people into a common national identity and history, from which liberal democratic values developed. The change to a version of apartheid began with the government's Swann Report of 1985. This advocated thorough going 'pluralism', influenced by the thinking of the Indian sociologist Bhikhu Parekh, now Lord Parekh, also influential in the ideology behind the MacPherson Report and its concept of 'institutional racism' in mainline British institutions. This was taken further with the 'Parekh Report' 2000, published by the campaign group, The Runnymede Trust. This advocated a kind of Indian model of society and state as 'a community of communities', going beyond 'the racism and culture-blind strategies of social inclusion'. In other words this report proposed communalism, different cultures being identified as having their own special identity and custom, jostling alongside others. This is a wholly new configuration of the nation state known for almost two millennia and an apparent return to tribalism on the territory of the British isles. It is significant that at the time of writing the new BBC head of 'Religion and Ethics' is a trustee of the Runnymede Trust, a campaigner for communalistic multi culturalism, and a Muslim.[1] Pressure for this kind of vision for the future of the UK is significant, but it enjoys little public support, especially after the '7/7' London bombings in 2005 by British Islamist fanatics. The strong pluralist model is however strong in educational departments, although as Julios says, 'Despite such educational efforts to foster a multicultural ethos within the British educational establishment, a combination of socio-economic and political developments abroad and at home saw steady decline in support for the country's official multi cultural model.'[2]

The paradox is that the very secular state is keen to grant major exemptions from important legal provisions, whereas for Christianity the approach is quite the reverse, as the gay adoption controversy cited above shows. For example, halal slaughter has been allowed for Muslims, avoiding animal cruelty laws covering slaughter of animals. Millions of animals are now slaughtered under 'halal' custom, unstunned and bled

---

[1] see eg *Daily Telegraph* 12th May 2009.
[2] Christina Julios *Contemporary British Identity*, Aldershot, Ashgate 2008 p. 115.

to death, with a ritual prayer intoned, with their throats cut – a practice illegal under normal UK law and Western cruelty rules generally. Politicians are implementing a form of community apartheid with the multicultural imperative.[3] At the same time the historic Christian culture has been repressed on the spurious grounds that symbols of Christian culture are oppressive to minority faiths, for example nativity plays in schools at Christmas, Christmas trees in public places, and Christian symbols on postage stamps. The central faith tradition is not regarded as equal, in practice, in the multicultural salad bowl. It must be said that minority faiths rarely desire suppression of Christianity in the UK.

All this is very postmodern in that it accepts the validity of widely divergent value systems, even where these conflict.[4] The 'modern' liberal ethos depended on a unity of truth and value. The 'diversity' agenda has come to replace the common agenda in important aspects of life. Another way of putting this is the growth of 'relativism' and celebration of competing or jostling, if not at times jarring, practices and moral assumptions. NHS Health care policy shows this.[5] The fact that this system seems incoherent and contradictory, if not unstable, is itself a demonstration of the break-up of the old notion of truth as overarching and normative for all. Diversity is authoritative, but some minority exemptions from normal law can spread into the non minority community and gain a normativity. Thus the halal exemption from normal law for Muslims is becoming applied to non Muslims so as to be 'inclusive' of the minority custom. Schools have fed halal meat to non Muslim children on the grounds of convenience An exemption to normal animal welfare is therefore eroding that law itself.[6]

Tolerance of intolerance

The very notion of tolerance, the notion that led to much of the multicultural agenda against that of integration, has itself been put into the centrifuge of relativism. This is because some faiths and practices that are not tolerant have been tolerated in the name of the diversity agenda. Pluralism has deepened from a welcoming of different groups of people into a classificatory system into classifying people groupings for

---

[3]See privileged legal arrangements in the 2003. Employment Equality (Religion or Belief) Regulations 2003 http://www.hmso.gov.uk/si/si2003/20031660.htm as interpreted by the Muslim Council of Britain: http://www.mcb.org.uk/faith/index.php.
[4]See the harrowing testimony given to the House of Commons Select Committee report http://www.parliament.the-stationery-office.com/pa/cm200708/cmselect/cmhaff/263/8021905.htm.
[5]http://www.dh.gov.uk/prod_consum_dh/groups/dh_digitalassets/documents/digitalasset/dh_093132.pdf.
[6]http://www.timesonline.co.uk/tol/comment/faith/article3160175.ece.

the purposes of attributing rights, different kinds of education, language provision, diet and cruelty laws. It seems that for some tax purposes polygamy is being recognized as a cultural practice for some groups, whereas it is a crime for others.

The power of this Western 'multicultural' mindset or worldview is hard to pin down, but just as socialism used to be a powerful idea in Europe, held by leading thinkers, educators, politicians and religious leaders, so with this new ideology of today. It is an 'idea' with a life and practice and the idea has permeated all public institutions in the name of the 'inclusivity agenda'. This contains deep tensions and contradictions – for example, Islam is to be included and so is homosexuality, yet Islam rejects homosexuality very firmly indeed. A major point about our new cultural ideology is that it is not based on rationality or the law of non-contradiction, it is based on the concept of diversity, and the notion that all views and lifestyles must be accepted as valid. The multicultural agenda is designed to favour minority communities, and so Christianity is automatically a victim of this policy since it is taken to be the existing mainstream. Condor points out that the UK government's praise of multi culturalism has become a national self glorification, and assumes that this is what all cultures should wish for as the superior social ideology. Ironically this is now a form of jingoism for Britain. Other nations or cultures which disagree with this programme are by implication less enlightened and less fortunate.[6]

The world now does seem to be facing a dialectic of East and West, with the East migrating into the West and bringing its religious ideology with it, finding a friendly welcome from a liberalism now lacking in confidence about the legitimacy of its own civilization and culture. Even the core principle of freedom of speech seems to be less than absolute now, as Western critics of Islam are threatened with assassination and the intellectual elite does little to protest. A major paradox of multiculturalism is that liberal freedom of thought and expression was a basis for accepting minority faiths and ideologies, but that this very freedom of thought and expression is itself no longer regarded as universally binding; rather it should defer to cultures which suppress it.

Cartoons of Mohammed, for example, were provocatively printed in a Danish newspaper in order to secure the principle of free speech,[7] but this tactic backfired as Mullahs toured the Middle East whipping up hostility towards Denmark and Western commentators did not defend the cartoonists but rather deemed them offensive and rejected the very idea of their being printed. The West had not supported the cartoonists.

[6]Susan Condor 'Representing, resisting and reproducing ethnic nationalism: Official UK Labour Party representations of "multi cultural Britain"', in http://eprints.lancs.ac.uk/11178/.
[7]The Danish newspaper *Jyllands-Posten* on 30 September 2005.

The UK was notable for not reprinting the cartoons at all, and so going furthest in not upholding freedom of speech to satirize and offend. The threat of violence, coupled with, or masked by, a claim to respect religious sensitivities compelled UK self-censorship. Even historic plays have been censored by theatres to avoid 'possible' offence to Muslims, as when the Christopher Marlowe's play 'Tamburlaine the Great', when performed at a leading 'liberal' London theatre, was shorn of a key passage in which the tyrant burns the Qur'an, an important part of the story of his arrogance and pride.[8] Likewise in Western universities critical textual study of the Qur'an is in effect banned, in stark contrast to all study of the Old and New Testaments where open scholarly criticism of all kinds is mandatory.[9] Multi culturalism in the UK has taught the state that liberal values, including freedom to criticise religion, are not universally held and other cultures reject them in favour of theocratic values.

A supreme instance of the clash of civilizations over freedom of speech came in the Netherlands with a short video entitled 'Submission', made by a radical film maker Theo Vangogh. It was scripted by a woman from a Muslim background, who sought to criticize Islamic attitudes to women,[10] in effect making a feminist protest against patriarchy – a cause of immense popularity in the West, the very basis of the feminist movement. She was elected to the Dutch Parliament. But public sympathy for her gradually drained away and she was stripped of her Dutch citizenship after her asylum papers were queried. Western liberalism ultimately did not regard her freedom of speech as absolute, did not uphold her right to reject her own religion and its attitude to women. The Western media's attitude to her was to put her in the dock and ask why she had presumed to cause such trouble, the implication being that the rights of Muslim women should not be made a topic of discussion given the consequences of such a criticism. The Western assumptions made normally about the rights and indeed duty of women to reject male headship and control, the theme of her film, suddenly were quite unimportant: the really pressing issue was the 'offence' caused to Islamic culture. Europe ejected her for her criticism of patriarchal religious authoritarianism, precisely what Western feminists have been targeting as evil for decades, and she was forced into exile in the USA.

This was another Munich moment by the 'liberal' democracies and by the sisterhood of feminism, to use a telling phrase of Alexander Solzhenitsyn. In his 1970 speech, 'One Word of Truth', on receiving his Nobel Prize,

---

[8]Daly Alberge, 'Marlowe's Koran-burning hero is censored to avoid Muslim anger', *The Times*, 24 November 2005. In fact there was no actual anger, merely fear of it.
[9]See, for example, Melanie Phillips, *Londonistan*, Londno: Gibson Square, 2006, pp. 161–2.
[10]Theo Vangogh, *Submission*, Part 1, 2004, available as a Google video.

The spirit of Munich is in no sense a thing of the past, for that was no flash in the pan. I would go so far as to say that the spirit of Munich is the dominant one in the twentieth century. The civilised world quailed at the onslaught of snarling barbarism, suddenly revitalised; the civilised world found nothing with which to oppose it, save concessions and smiles. The spirit of Munich is an illness of the will-power of the well-to-do, it is the usual state of those who have surrendered to the lust for comfort at any price, have surrendered to materialism as the main aim of life on earth. Such people – and how many there are in the world today – choose passivity and retreat just so that normality can last a bit longer and the onset of brutishness be put off for another day; as for tomorrow, you never know, it may turn out all right...[11]

Lisa Jardine's BBC article on this expressed concern for Western liberalism, depicting Hirsi Ali as 'the canary in the mineshaft', a forerunner of someone whose freedom of opinion was suffocated.[12] The Netherlands in particular was the cradle of religious toleration and freedom of speech and thought: it was, thought Jardine, a bad sign indeed that Hirsi Ali was sent away by that nation simply because she criticized her own faith, Islam. Truth and freedom of thought had been made culture relative, contrary to the basic Western liberal ethos. Violent threat, and fear of it, has a greater authority than the principle of free speech, the liberal tradition has mutated drastically. John Locke's famous 'Letter on Toleration', a classic text on freedom of speech, repudiates the notion that intolerance should be tolerated, since it would repress tolerance.

Jardine's justifiable worry about the future of liberalism is a 'modern' rather than 'postmodern' one, she believes the right to freedom of speech and opinion is absolute, and that fierce debate is the way to resolve differences. Instead she fears we are moving into an era of pragmatic expediency suppressing opinion when it is awkward for a religious grouping, even when violence is rewarded by this suppression. Freedom of speech, including the freedom to offend and ridicule, has long been a Western principle, indeed sharp criticism has led to important reforms, as well as being vital in the scientific enterprise where free minds are utterly central. Defending public morals used to be one ground of censorship, but the case of *Lady Chatterley's Lover* in 1960 broke the mould by showing the book was of literary merit, in accordance with the 1959 Obscene Publications Act. Western societies today know very few limits on pornography and freedom of speech, but minority faiths seem to be given a status exempting them from criticism, and especially satire, since this would be 'offensive', or even 'might be perceived as offensive', another kind of evolving thought crime quite new in Western culture. Christian customs of a public nature have been removed by secularists,

---

[11]Alexander Solzhenitsyn, *One Word of Truth – The Nobel Speech on Literature 1970*, London: Bodley Head, 1972, p. 20.
[12]Lisa Jardine, 'Liberalism under pressure', available online at http://news.bbc.co.uk/1/hi/magazine/5042418.stm, accessed 15.05.2009.

not by minority faith adherents, on the grounds that Christian practices 'might be perceived as offensive' to minority faiths, an extraordinarily wide criterion with which to strike at historic Christian practices in the public square.

The Home Office decision to avoid making a specific criminal offence of 'honour killings' of women was another instance of the British state choosing to be accommodating and not risk 'causing offence',[13] the group right overriding the rights of individual women at risk of violent reprisal. This policy in effect concedes to conservative clericalism, the voice taken to represent the group. What seems to be happening is that the state is assuming a secular pluralist managerial role, distributing rights and exemptions not according to any moral merit or value but solely to pacify communal demands and so keep the peace in the short term, whether or not such distribution is fair or consistent. As Bobbitt[14] points out, a nation state depends on its having a minimum core of commonality and loyalty binding the nation together; if this dissolves then the practice of a democratically run nation state becomes less feasible and a 'state nation' is likely to emerge to control, rather than to reflect, the groupings clustering together on the territory that once hosted a unified nation.

Christmas and Easter were removed from a Yorkshire college calendar, which cited policy documents from Ofsted, the state regulatory body, for the excision. 'Winter Lights' festivals are occluding 'Christmas Lights' in many Local Authorities, the impetus coming from secularist bureaucrats rather than other faiths.[15] A new form of authoritative 'best practice' seems to be developing, amounting to a theoretical privileging of 'other faiths' – an approach assuming that the one 'non-other faith', that is Christianity, giving the definition 'other faith' meaning, is discounted and not privileged in the same way whatsoever. In contemporary Britain the old style liberal value of free speech has been rolled back by hard line Islam in an unholy alliance with the new style 'liberal' elite, as Kenan Malik put it:

> What we are talking about here is not a system of formal censorship, under which the state bans works deemed offensive. Rather, what has developed is a culture of self-censorship in which the giving of offence has come to be seen

---

[13]See www.parliament.uk/homeaffairscom/ June 2008 for the Home Affairs Select Committee evidence on this growing problem of forced marriage in the UK. See also http://news.bbc. co.uk/1/hi/uk/5054286.stm.
[14]Phillip Bobbitt, *The Shield of Achilles*, London: Anchor, 2002, p. 146 ff.
[15]See http://www.yorkshirepost.co.uk/news/MP-slams-college-for-dropping.4489167.jp and for an example of the Winter Lights controversies see http://www.oxfordmail.co.uk/ news/3810153.Council_set_to_axe_Christmas/. Absurd examples include a sudden ban on hot cross buns, traditionally served at Easter in Poole hospital, lest they be found offensive http://www.dailymail.co.uk/news/article-447750/Hospital-banned-hot-cross-buns-avoid-offending-non-Christians.html. Halal food however has now become an absolute right throughout the hospital system.

as morally unacceptable. In the 20 years since the publication of The Satanic Verses the fatwa has effectively become internalised.[16]

Freedom to attack or ridicule Christianity has become absolute in the UK,[17] the ancient blasphemy laws – being an ancient form totally devoid of substance – have fallen into the cobwebs.[18] These laws should be abolished as they give other faiths the wrong impression that Christianity is protected from attack and ridicule, whereas the reverse is true. Academically Christianity has been engaging with criticism – hostile and friendly – since the Enlightenment, and it is taken for granted that no questions are 'off limits' to the text of Scripture. The strange new phenomenon is that other world religions which have not engaged with nor integrated free critical thought are treated with wholly uncritical 'respect' by academics, and secular politicians national and local. The authority of Western critical and moral reason is set aside in favour of cultural relativity. This is taking place institutionally as well as theoretically.[19]

The diversity agenda has been one important reason why Christianity has been pushed out of the public forum by the media and political classes and into the dimension of the private hobby, regarded as having no relevance to public policy making, and Christians themselves have not resisted this 'privatization' of faith. This process has been pushed as the concepts of 'diversity', 'inclusiveness' and multiculturalism have become normative in Western thought and practice in a way negative towards the 'non-other faith', Christianity. It is the secularists who have brought the situation about whereby the 'non-other faith' is accorded far less deference and authority in the West than are 'other faiths', on political grounds of fear of violent reprisal and more commonly of a deep imperative to affirm the cultures of racial and ethnic minorities. On the one hand the civic doctrine now is that 'all religions are the same', on the other hand as Orwell put it 'some are more equal than others.'[20]

[16]Kenan Malik, 'Walking on Eggshells', *The Guardian*, 1 October 2008.
[17]Mark Thompson, Director General of the publicly funded BBC, the most powerful opinion forming media in the UK, has announced that Islam should be treated more kindly than Christianity since the former is new to the UK, the latter not. BBC news, 15 October 2008. This is certainly BBC policy.
[18]BBC's decision to screen *Jerry Springer – the Opera* in 2005, depicting Jesus in a nappy, despite protests from Christians on a large scale, revealed the death of the blasphemy laws as enforceable against Christianity.
[19]Non Muslim councillors of Tower Hamlets London Borough were told to obey the Muslim fasting rules at all meetings held over the Ramadan season. http://www.telegraph.co.uk/news/2638808/Councillors-told-not-to-eat-during-Ramadan-meetings.html. Accessed 16.05.2009.
[20]See the formal protest from the Church of England about government marginalization of the church, 8.6.2008 http://news.bbc.co.uk/1/hi/uk/7442285.stm.

This gradual Christian cultural experience of oppression is an important phenomenon to analyse theologically. Christ crucified is at the heart of the Gospel, a great placard of divine humility and humiliation, a gross offence – 'a stumbling block to the Jews and foolishness to the Greeks' (1 Cor. 1:23) – right from the very start of the life of the earliest church. We have evidence of a cartoon poking fun at the faith with the graffiti found in Rome picturing a man on a cross with the head of a donkey being worshipped, with the Greek inscription 'Alexamenos worships his god'. Christianity is a faith – as Nietzsche so disliked – which absorbed hatred by love and not by 'taking offence'; it overcame tribal vendetta and resentment. That was the victory of Christ in terms of human power: that could be said to be the core of Western civilization as it evolved.

But Christianity is also about the truth: 'by open statement of the truth' says St Paul, 'we commend ourselves to every man's conscience in the sight of God' (2 Cor. 4:2). To be free to speak and say what we think, to criticize, to debate honestly – that too is a Gospel imperative. Jesus went to his death telling the truth, not fudging it, not keeping quiet or covering up what he really thought. A white lie might have got him to safety. But the truth was all important. This too is a characteristic of Western civilization, the freedom to ask questions by science as Darwin did, the freedom to question the texts of Scripture and trust their truth will fight their own battles without the need for violent protection, manipulation or coercive strategies. The clear approval by Western society of religious censorship on behalf of hard line Islam is not a good sign culturally nor theologically. It is worth noting some illiberal effects of segregationalist multi culturalism, rather than than the softer form of encouraging mutual harmony and integration. Communal segregation is an Indian model and has been pressed by Lord Parekh, from India. This praises the idea of communalism, over against the Western assumption of the individual subject to the law of the nation state, without reference to tribal allegiance and custom. Further, we can remember that the first state to ban Salman Rushdie's Satanic Verses was India. It thereby chose to suppress individual freedom of thought in the interests of appeasing a large cultural minority, and to encourage the idea that violence pays off in shutting up cultural criticism and satire. The West has for several centuries stood for the very reverse, for freedom of thought and speech, for facing down blackmail, coercion and threat. Now however the UK is travelling down the Indian route, and cultural relativism has begun to suffocate liberal values, and freedoms basic to the thriving to Western culture. Kenan Malik's recent book *From Fatwa to Jihad*,[21] argues that multiculturalism has led to a culture of grievance which renders secular and progressive arguments less sayable. As Galileo by the Medieval Papacy, so Darwin would have now been silenced by 'offended' mobs

---

[21]London: Atlantic, 2009.

whipped up by clerics, not having read the 'offending' texts. We now turn to consider the way the state manages the segregation and tribalism it is encouraging and the lack of common virtue as an ideal in British culture and society.

After inter racial riots in the North of England, 2001, the UK government began to worry about social 'cohesion', and commissioned a Home Office Report chaired by Ted Cantle. This diagnosed the problem of virtual apartheid communities, but its cure was only to focus on respect for different communities, not to seek to foster real integration. The London bombings of 2005 underlined the problems of failing to foster ownership of a national community by 'other' faith groups. How should society be managed in this new, more tribal, context? As we will now see, 'the manager', detached from any core moral value other than a commitment to relativism, is a key figure in current UK society. How is state management to control rampant individualism as upheld by western secularism, and reactionary communalistic demands for special privilege, now that the Christian balance has been repressed?

4

The Emotivist Culture

'the therapist, the manager and the aesthete'

In the well respected judgement of Alastair MacIntyre, Western society has now jettisoned 'virtue' as its core imperative and is driven by emotivism, the feelings rather than concerns of justice and reasonableness. He famously points to the triad of 'the manager, the therapist and the aesthete' as the key figures in current secular Western culture, now that 'virtue' has ceased to be the goal of what society is for and how it conducts itself.[1] And it is worth adding Bobbitt's view of the way the Western state is evolving from the nation state to 'the market state', from the state existing for a common group called the nation, it is now being dominated by the forces of the market, and becoming more like a supermarket to be used for its services than anything more noble. Bobbitt sees the nation state as in real peril because of the loss of common bonds of value.[2]

The 'intimate' society suffocating reason

To illustrate this we can consider the 'celebrity culture' and the authority of 'celebrities' who have no virtues but generally are physically good looking and in the entertainment or sporting industries. In the realm of politics anyone seeking high office needs to be youthful and attractive:

[1]A. MacIntyre, *After Virtue*, London: Duckworth: 1992, pp. 72–74.
[2]'As a result, it is increasingly difficult in multicultural, multiethnic states to get consensus on public order problems and the maintenance of rule-based action, which are core tasks of the State' (Bobbitt, *The Shield of Achilles*, London: Anchor, 2002, p. 225).

to be wise and experienced but older than middle aged is to be virtually unelectable. Politicians now need to be aesthetically pleasing, even if morally bankrupt and intellectually barren. The turn towards subjective feeling as the main criterion of life, rather than reason and morality, can only deepen the fissured nature of society as a common rational purpose and vision becomes more and more difficult to maintain and appeal to.

Western moral relativism, 'after virtue', operates on an emotivist level rather than a rational one and this may explain the illogicalities and inconsistencies common in society. The practice of relativism means that an individual can assert his own moral view on a subject, while also asserting the reverse view as equally valid to someone else: the truth is relative to the individual and how she feels at the time. An interesting example of this occurred after a party of British sailors had been captured by Iranians off the coast of Iran,[3] then released amid a welter of propaganda. On their return the sailors were at first told they could sell their stories to the press.

Public outcry at this mawkish celebration of the emotions by people who had been assumed to be robust military service personnel forced the Ministry of Defence to change its mind and ban the selling of these stories, restating the longstanding traditional policy and imposing a restraint on the sailors who had not rushed into print already. But until that restraint, giving the sailors guidelines, they had been free to sell. The sailor cited felt to do so was wrong, but that it was not wrong for others to do so, as long as they sincerely felt they should do so. The test was one of sincerity of emotion. This typifies Western social moral judgement today, a move from moral principle to emotion. With the rejection of Christian ethics as a source of morality and the collapse of Marxist states with their suppression of individual freedom, such decisions, to sell or not to sell, have no wider context to shape them, and no higher principles to which appeal can be made. The Ministry of Defence's role in this is important, since that body emerges as the one defining the terms for the sailors, firstly permitting sale of their stories, thus opening up a pathway previously closed and so granting it respectability. The sailors were suddenly placed in a new context. Then, because of the disgust of the British public expressed vehemently at the prospect of service personnel being encouraged to sell experiences of war, the Ministry went back and replaced its ban. The sailors then had the old traditional context replaced. It must have been very confusing and disorientating for them. The sailors, the Navy, the Ministry of Defence, were 'all at sea', without a moral compass. The ultimate criterion seems to have been

---

[3] See *The Times*, 26 March 2007, for a report of the capture.

public feeling, when the government discerned public disgust it changed policy: emotion makes a fickle guide.

Emotivism is displacing objectivism in the law enforcement of the UK. Rather than enforcing the law of the land, enacted by Parliament, there is a growing tendency for senior police officers to emote and speak of the feelings of victims and of 'what communities want' the police to do.[4] This relativizes law enforcement from one community to another, and fragments the common law of the nation in principle.

Richard Sennett argues that contemporary Western society has ended 'public culture' in the sense of political common purpose and endeavour argued out and debated reasonably and morally, and has grown into 'the intimate society', wherein

> the reigning belief today is that closeness between persons is moral good. The reigning aspiration today is to develop individual personality through experiences of closeness and warmth with others. The reigning myth today is that the evils of society can all be understood as evils of impersonality, alienation and coldness. The sum of these three is an ideology of intimacy: social relationships of all kinds are real, believable and authentic the closer they approach the inner psychological concerns of each person. This ideology transmutes political categories into psychological categories. This ideology of intimacy defines the humanitarian spirit of a society without gods: warmth is our god.[5]

The social withdrawal coincides with the cult of the emoting individual, and the erosion the proper difference between public role and private, leading to the loss of any sense that we have a role in public life – what we do is watch celebrity emotive political leaders passively, we do not engage in political action or reasoned debate. A successful politician now is one whose personality and narrative warms the hearts of the voters, rather than one who presents a rational and moral agenda for society.[6]

Alasdair MacIntyre argues in his *After Virtue* that Nietzsche is the core philosopher for today, making the individual will utterly central, letting will replace reason as the one imperative to decide how we behave and order society. The media tells the British morning by morning of the spread of gun and knife crime among teenagers in inner cities,[7] of drug taking, of school children needing to be given special rewards simply for behaving normally and not being disruptive. 'Respect' is gained through power, wealth and, failing these, violence. The 'noble savage', Rousseau's

---

[4]The longstanding promise of the British police constable is to implement the law 'without fear or favour', arguably eroded by the new emotivist policing policies.
[5]Richard Sennett, *The Fall of Public Man*, Cambridge: Cambridge University Press, 1977, p. 259.
[6]Thomas Mann's novel *Mario and the Magician* London: M. Secker, 1930 [Penguin Books 1975] articulates this political phenomenon for Weimar Germany.
[7]See eg http://www.guardian.co.uk/uk/2009/mar/12/knife-crime-prison-sentences.

doctrine of the human being, unencumbered with cultural constraints of loyalty and duty, seems to be today's iconic personage. The youth of Britain, very rich and very poor brought together by the same moral vacuum and coarseness, are to be kept under control only by external surveillance cameras and 'anti-social behaviour disorders'. The one restraining moral imperative they are given is to respect the values of others, with the proviso that their own cultural heritage of Christianity is deeply tainted and best avoided.

As Pannenberg notes, self-fulfilment and self-actualization comprise the core message for individuals in Western society, any objective moral norms 'are largely regarded as values imposed by human beings which are communicated to individuals through socialization and are internalized by them. So moral norms of any kind appear as an alien determination of the individual in contrast to his or her claim to self-fulfilment.'[8] In other words, what were called 'morals' appear to be invented by the controllers of society to spoil fun, and are based solely in the desire of the management to keep order. The expectation that all children would have a basically informed conscience to which teachers could make appeal has gone. It is no surprise that discipline in large state schools is reportedly increasingly difficult to maintain,[9] that moral authority is simply eroding – as Nietzsche predicted. The autonomous self is no longer being ordered by a moralized autonomy but by heteronomous surveillance, threats, and bribes to gain even normal behaviour.

Secularism has apparently managed its negative task well, evacuating Christian morality, but in terms of a positive task it has left a vacuum or the naked individual will and desire, unshaped and unordered, a law unto itself. Authority in society has been moved into the self, the sense of freedom and need for fulfilment, the refusal of fetters of reactionary 'morality'. At the same time the authority of government, now loosed from a positive narrative of the nation's history and detached from a common moral tradition, declines. Likewise the authority of the law fades in terms of anything beyond the fear of getting caught; and cynicism grows as to whether the authority of law rests on 'what is right'. It was interesting to note the initial defence of MPs and Peers revealed to have claimed unreasonably large expenses in the political scandal of May 2009. This was to appeal to 'the rules': claiming to have remained inside the letter of the law, while maximising every possible avenue of claiming. The public did not accept this, thinking that holders of public office should act with virtue, with moral rectitude, not simply keeping technically inside a set of rules. Here we note that rules themselves do not create virtue and that rules need virtuous adherents to use the rules aright. This point

---

[8]Wolfhart Pannenberg, op cit., pp. 16–17.
[9]See eg http://www.guardian.co.uk/education/2009/apr/05/schools-behaviour-teachers-parents accessed 16.05.2009.

also applies in discussing some of the social services scandals, notably the horrific treatment and death of Baby P, whose broken back was not detected by a GP, and whose social workers all claimed to have fulfilled 'the rules' technically – and yet without wisdom, care and virtue needed for real welfare of the vulnerable.[10]

C. S. Lewis, in his *The Abolition of Man*,[11] lamented this development in the wake of secularism. He pointed to the Greek view that mankind embodied reason, will, and morality, the last symbolically located in the chest. Lewis argued that modern man had no 'chest' any longer, no moral orientation to direct the will. Reason alone was supposed to do this, leading to a very functionalist understanding of how humans act. Now, however, we could argue that reason has also been displaced, that pure will and desire alone dictate how we live, the authority of morality and reason have faded. The intimate society, as Sennett warned, is dangerous because if detaches people from important engagement with how society is run, from important disagreements and hard debates. The result is a sort 'soft despotism' and passivity, breeding deep frustration and reaction by those not benefiting from the system. In particular young males find 'respect' and identity in gangs where society accords them no role and no pathway to success. The loyalty of the gang, with its honour codes and vendettas, is a distortion of common moral duty to all people.

The authority of expressed feelings and the right to have these 'respected' and not ignored or given offence has become a major factor in British culture and law, behind this, which conflicts with the Western tradition of free critical thought and speech. This emotive authority threatens to criminalise some reasoned debate over human sexuality. The role of the therapist, and equivalent masseurs of the feelings and psychologies, reflects the turn to the self characteristic of Western society and the focus on deep human feeling needing to be expressed and to be recognized as the root of self understanding. The therapist leads us to healing of our fractured and unhappy feelings about ourselves in relation to others, in a totally amoral, non judgemental way. 'After virtue' we are victims of our unshaped desires and feelings, and so political management turns to the 'spin doctor', basically the advertising industry, to try to control and herd public feeling. The rise of the internet and its vast range of alternative messages, makes this control of feeling very difficult and strengthens the cult of pure individualism. But some individual opinions are being repressed by state management.

---

[10] See on the MPs' expenses scandal http://news.bbc.co.uk/1/hi/uk_politics/8039273.stm and on 'Baby P' see http://www.timesonline.co.uk/tol/news/uk/article6235066.ece.
[11] C.S Lewis *The Abolition of Man*, London, 1946.

Managerialism

As they look on at the unravelling of social order as morality fades Western politicians and bureaucrats face the problem of the breakdown of a common cultural moral vision, and the inner restraint the Christian tradition taught and inculcated. This break-up of the common tradition has meant breakdown of respect for a common law and pattern of good behaviour, even for the state and its apparatus. The legitimacy of democratically elected governments reduces as fewer and fewer voters bother to vote, from apathy or cynicism at the politicians offering their services to the public, or conviction that the major political parties are not concerned with the real issues and problems of the ordinary electorate. The problem has worsened as politicians themselves are now accused of individualist greed, lack of personal morality and detachment from the overall common good. The British scandal of MPs abuse of expenses and allowances has caused this further unwinding of social cohesive values. Politicians and bureaucrats now see their task as managing society so as to keep the peace. This is in fact the explicit rationale for the European Union, a collocation of nations pooling state sovereignty in order somehow to prevent war by unifying national economies and law. It is essentially a bureaucratic, managerial ideal, liberal and secular, with no other underlying value system apart from practical efficiency and the well being of its own organization.

This is precisely today's management ideology, a vision of effectiveness and efficiency: for manufacturing and marketing, for example, for achieving the goals of the company and expanding it. This too is what today's Western politics is about: the effective and efficient government of a nation, rather than any idealism of a socialist nature or a traditionalist nature. The nation today is not much different to a large company such as McDonalds – it tries to sell fast food, adjusting to new dietary fads, reinventing itself from time to time, keeping pay levels acceptable, and maintaining itself as its primary goal. Management has become a matter for 'experts' trained for the task of keeping such an organization going, whether the state civil service, local government, schools or businesses. MacIntyre[12] points to the archetypal theorist of bureaucracy, Max Weber, as a key thinker representing this vital aspect of life in Western democracies, that is to say managed bureaucratically by expert managers, whose aim is to manage. Rational bureaucracy is the way modern society must run itself, and bureaucratic rationality is the rationality of matching means to ends economically and efficiently, for Weber. MacIntyre points out that this enterprise is a closed circle, the 'ends' for which the manager or bureaucrat works are set by the business enterprise, set by 'rationality', and reason cannot arbitrate on the values represented by those ends.

---

[12]MacIntyre, After Virtue, p. 25 ff. See eg http://www.timesonline.co.uk/tol/news/politics/article6534773.ece.

Bureaucratic authority concerns effectiveness, and its rationality can only speak of that criterion.

The state has increasingly displaced the traditional forms of community and seeks to manage local concerns directly, 'micromanage' being a term that has come to be used. The family – the key social unit – has taken on many forms, notably the fatherless family, and the state acts as the breadwinner for this popular form of family, with 'anti-social behaviour disorders' as a form of authority over teenagers running out of control. Society is becoming very individualized, a phenomenon already identified by nineteenth-century sociologists, who pointed to the demise of traditional *'Gemeinschaft'* or community in which individuals gained identity and value,[13] and the alternative forms of voluntary association. But today those voluntary clubs, societies and professional bodies are now being superseded by state-sponsored agencies and regulatory bodies. Minority faith cultures are strongly encouraged and affirmed and indeed financed, but otherwise local culture dwindles – and this has hit the poorest white population very hard. The American study *Bowling Alone*[14] argued that local leagues are disappearing and individuals are no longer 'belonging' to such clubs, preferring isolated sporting activity. This has a very negative impact on social trust: we live as insulated beings, having little to do with our neighbours.[15] This is in direct contrast to ethnic minority communities with clan and tribal systems, arranged marriages, and enduring ties back 'home'.[16] This is old-style *Gemeinschaft* with all its strengths and weaknesses, notably in terms of women's rights and freedoms.

A manager cannot, on the Weberian terms of contemporary society, discriminate between different values or ends on rational grounds; his rationality relates to efficiency. And for Weber and modern managers 'the choice of one particular evaluative stance or commitment can be no more rational than that of any other. All faiths and all evaluations are equally non-rational; all are subjective directions given to sentiment and feeling.'[17] This leads MacIntyre to make the link between such modern managerialism and Nietzschean emotivism, since value becomes a matter of choice, not of reason, reason only applies to the effectiveness of what is being managed. Management, 'after virtue', becomes value free in an objective or global sense, it serves its own project. 'Bureaucratic

---

[13]Tönnies' distinction of *Gemeinschaft* and *Geselschaft* indicates a given community as opposed to a chosen group (see, for example, Nisbet, *The Sociological Tradition*, London: Heinemann, 1970, pp. 47ff.).
[14]Robert D. Putnam *Bowling Alone: The Collapse and Revival of American Community.* New York: Simon & Schuster, 2000. Putnam shows how Americans have become increasingly disconnected from family, friends, neighbors, and democratic structures.
[15]See www.statistics.gov.uk/socialtrends38 such statistics reveal the same applies to the UK
[16]See eg The Parekh Report 2000 op cit.
[17]MacIntyre, *After Virtue*, p. 26.

authority is nothing other than successful power', a very Nietzschean idea. In today's society success by the manager or chief executive means jobs and prosperity for those below her; she will jet across oceans, pay bribes (or commissions) to secure large contracts and keep the company going, her success brings a 'trickle down' benefit to those beneath, she becomes the Übermensch, the Overman. This message of success at all costs is undeniably prevalent in all Western nations, and it increasingly applies to state governments in the scramble to maintain employment and sell, for example, jet fighter aircraft to other states – almost whatever the nature of those states and the uses of those aircraft. Of course the ownership of the companies is in the hands of shareholders, who will want to make a profit, and will therefore put into post managers who will achieve that goal of the company or government department.

MacIntyre's analysis of how emotivism and managerialism combine helps explain the rapid progress in the business, administrative and governmental dimensions of secularism and 'political correctness', with its alternative sets of quasi-moral, emotivist, imperatives. 'Values' once running through old fashioned companies are now completely changed, replaced by the virtues of 'efficiency' and 'best practice' to keep the project running smoothly, exemplified by the embracing of 'gay rights', maternity leave, and prayer rooms for minority faith groups, and so forth. Managerialism is affecting the professions very deeply: whereas hospitals in Britain used to be controlled and run by the medical professionals, doctors and nursing matrons, now the specialist administrative management class has grown enormously and controls the professions. The authority of the expert and his wisdom has been supplanted by that of the managerial enterprise. In the instance of the hospital and its management, this change has broken the community of professional caring undertaken as a ward team with its own structure: now individuals are managed as individuals with no place in the old holistic pattern. Education of children, and in research universities, is likewise now a matter not of inculcating wisdom, reason, moral sense, but of managing skills and downloading state ideology into the mind.

Managers will no doubt devise all manner of ways of motivating their subordinates to get them to work together most efficiently, to control behaviour and avoid conflict, to evoke 'commitment' to the cause of the company, that cause which is the justification of managerial authority, an authority exercised in the name of efficiency. For Weber bureaucratization is performed by functionaries allocated tasks and proceeds by way of calculable rules. The more bureaucracy is perfected, the more it is 'dehumanized', so as to remove unquantifiable elements of human emotion such as love and hate. The detached expert is needed to replace the old 'master' of the family firm who may be tempted to be influenced by gratitude or non-calculable feeling. At this point we can move to the experience of the employees and ask how it feels from their side of the fence, as the recipients of policy made by these experts in management. There is no doubt that the managerial culture has also embedded itself into the churches: 'human resources' departments surprisingly now appear in Anglican bureaucratic machinery, hardly a description with any theological merit whatsoever.

Economic changes have had drastic effects on working people in the West, and the plight of young males especially and their self-understanding as family wage earners. Heavy industry has virtually vanished from Britain, ending 'blue collar jobs' with good pay and Trade Union protection. Factories are closed and moved to other parts of the world where labour costs are far cheaper. This drastic change has had a deep impact on male employment patterns and on how men feel about themselves in society. It may also have affected education, since the demand for technologically skilled workers with good mathematical skills has fallen. Richard Sennett has pointed to the message to working people that they must be 'flexible', they must expect now to have to move jobs, to retrain and go into other jobs, to have a skill mix to enable them to be moved on to new tasks in new businesses. In his book *The Culture of the New Capitalism*,[18] he surveys major differences between earlier forms of industrial capitalism and the more global, more febrile, ever more mutable version of capitalism that is taking its place. He shows how these changes affect everyday life – how the work ethic is changing; how new beliefs about merit and talent displace old values of craftsmanship and achievement, giving workers pride in what they did and so a positive understanding of themselves in the world of work, in society and at home.

In contemporary Western society, what Sennett calls 'the spectre of uselessness' haunts professionals as well as manual workers as they increasingly become units processing information like superior accessories to computers and telephone lines. In recent years, reformers of both private and public institutions have preached that flexible, global corporations provide a model of freedom for individuals, unlike the experience of fixed and static bureaucracies. The old idea of a job for life with the same firm has gone for ever, it seems.

Sennett argues that, in banishing 'old ills' of inflexibility, the new-economy model has instead created new social and emotional traumas. The individual employee is taught that the job is far from secure, that a move is always close.[19] Only a certain kind of human being can prosper in unstable, fragmentary institutions: the culture of the new capitalism demands an ideal self, oriented to the short-term, focused on potential ability rather than accomplishment, willing to discount or abandon past

---

[18]Richard Sennett, *The Culture of the New Capitalism*, New Haven, CT and London: Yale University Press, 2006.
[19]Richard Sennett, *The Corrosion of Character*, New York and London: W. W. Norton, 1998.

experience in the interest of moving to ever new functions, at the behest of management. Sennett deplores the modern American and British workplaces as 'high risk, low loyalty' contexts for individuals who are schooled into the merits of flexibility and change, yet find the system for most disappoints and makes them feel failures. This wholly negative sense of worthlessness was brilliantly portrayed by Arthur Miller in his figure of Willy Loman, the ageing and now unwanted salesman, in *Death of a Salesman*. Loman, who has served his company most of his life, is dismissed despite his protestations of loyalty and former successes, mistakenly fearing that his wife and family will no longer respect him and that he will lose respect in his community. Willy, desperately trying to get his retired boss's son, Howard, to retain him, even at a low salary, protests:

> 'I'm talking about your father! There were promises made across this desk! You mustn't tell me you've got people to see – I put thirty years into this firm, Howard, and now I can't pay my insurance! You can't eat the orange and throw the peel away – a man is not a piece of fruit!'[20]

The difference between Miller's salesman and today's equivalent is that Willy would not have been given the expectation that loyalty to the firm would be counted as a virtue; he would be told to be flexible, to move on, to get some training for a new job, his earlier success being irrelevant. Even if one can and does become a successful Weberian 'expert' in the bureaucracy or firm, one has no security, no esteem, no value, one is very dispensable indeed – and this today is deemed a virtue. 'It could be said', according to Sennett,

> that capitalism was ever thus. But not in the same way. The indifference of the old class-bound capitalism was starkly material; the indifference which radiates out of flexible capitalism is more personal because the system itself is less starkly etched, less legible in form… The old habit of Marxism was to treat confusion as a kind of false consciousness: in our circumstances it is an accurate reflection of reality.[21]

We are confused about who we are in society, whether we are needed or just a set of reconfigurable functions, superior computer chips. The contemporary practice of 'reengineering institutions in which people are treated as disposable' brutally diminishes the sense of mattering as a person, being necessary to others, as Sennett puts it.[22] He thinks this has corroded character in contemporary Western humanity.

---

[20]Arthur Miller, *Death of a Salesman*, Act Two, Harmondsworth: Penguin Books, 1949/1961, p. 64.
[21]Sennett, *The Corrosion of Character*, p. 146.
[22]Ibid.

Western capitalism as a system now encourages individualism, looking over one's shoulder to 'watch one's back' for the redundancy notice; we distrust our bosses who we think do not have our best interests at heart but rather regard us as units of labour. Economic globalization has been a very important driver to this process, as multi-national companies buy up smaller firms and detach any sense of local loyalty from working ethos. The internet likewise has refocused individual interest from lasting real relationships, even with such realities as local shops, libraries and services, onto internet purchasing through computer screens and 'virtual reality' perspectives. The liberal secularized individual is, to use Marxist analysis, alienated from many realities, replaced by virtual life on the screen. He is not pitted against others, rather he is a matter of indifference, far worse in Sennett's view, corroded in character and meaning, passive and functionary. In literary terms, we are in Huxley's *Brave New World*, in which people are bred for particular purposes in genetic factories, never actually give birth physically, are kept contented materially, and supplied with 'soma', a recreation drug to cope with depression. Western liberal secular society is very much 'managed', and aware of being managed, but to what end? The manager, the therapist and the pleasure providing aesthete combine: we need to feel good about ourselves in this colder and very individualistic world in which we are all dispensable and expected to 'be let go', and be offered counselling, computer games and downloads of music into our ear pieces by way of distraction.

'The ontology of human beings ('human nature') is thus seen to be, in some sense, out of joint with the cultural and social requirements of a modern civilization, indeed our human nature has to be suppressed by the sociological requirements of an industrial civilization.'[23] This is Weber's pessimistic view of how the demands of bureaucracy will impact on personal life, in Bryan Turner's summary. It is interesting to compare this with Francis Fukuyama's view that liberal secular capitalism brought us to the final 'end of history', a consumer society in which material needs are apparently met, but to no greater purpose: 'is this the promised end?'[24] If a system of life has no higher purpose, it will engender cynicism rather than respect and enthusiasm, especially when the promised success for flexibility and preparedness to change leads only to 'failure'. One may ask whether this high risk, low loyalty regime demands something akin to Nietzsche's 'slave mentality' of employees, that they give themselves totally to be functionaries of the system, prepared for instant undeserved dismissal and lack of appreciation – as a virtue, as if absorbing the pain

[23]Bryan S. Turner, Preface, *From Max Weber, Essays in Sociology*, eds. H. H. Gerth and C. Wright Mills, London: Routledge, 1991, p. xxviii.
[24]*King Lear*, V.iii.264.

of the negative somehow for the good of the system, in a sort of self negation.

Both Marx and Nietzsche would say that this acceptance of flexibility to serve whatever cause the bureaucracy or company is promoting is the result of being manipulated by whatever emotivist managerial means is to hand. MacIntyre argues that such manipulation is deeply characteristic of Western society, and hence the best manager now is the best actor, as is clearly the case in the world of political management and 'spin'. The public and employees are best managed in terms of emotivist rhetoric and gestures, words are used as means to manipulate, rather than as conveyors of truth and argument, emotivist tools of management. And the one goal of Western secular capitalisms seems to be encouraging consumption at all costs, the Argos Catalogue being the Bible, the authoritative text. The authority of the manager is powerful, we believe in management, that more administrators can and will bring improvement, and we are willing to submit its decisions about redundancies and flexibility, the slave mentality towards our superiors who know best. The answer to the problems of the UK's failing institutions seems to be to appoint more managers to devise more paper procedures and regulations. But 'boxes' can be ticked on paper, totally divorced from good action, notably in caring professions. Compassionate care was assumed as a basic virtue for the caring professions, but is no longer regarded as such, leading to public disquiet.[25]

Self-dramatization and identity advertising

The therapist is the third character presented by MacIntyre as iconic of our contemporary emotivist society, alongside the manager and the aesthete, therapy being typically needed by the wealthy in the form of their expensive personal psychologists and the poor in terms of social workers, over eating, alcohol and drug taking, anaesthetics for deep unhappiness. Since the 1980s when MacIntyre wrote his book the therapy model has grown in importance immensely. Rates of depression and medication are soaring, and the management of feelings is of utmost importance in Western society. The police in Britain make a point of 'feeling the pain' of victims of crime, of showing they are not racist, homophobic nor Islamophobic; they have been trained in empathy rather than law enforcement, or so it seems to the public.

Narcissism in the modern Western context, accompanied by the absence of regard by anyone else or any institutional affirmation, has become a

---

[25]See eg Health Care Commission. Investigation into Mid Staffordshire NHS Foundation Trust. London: *Commission for Healthcare Audit and Inspection*, 2009:12.

common youth phenomenon. We dig into ourselves for an identity, not finding one in a given community nurturing us from birth. The appalling campus killings by 'loners' resentful of their failure to attract attention and commendation, exemplifies such agonized self-obsession and desire to gain attention at any cost, by bitterly resentful sociopaths. This is the ultimate act of self-dramatization on the national and international stage. Peter and Brigitte Berger's *The Homeless Mind*[26] argues along Weber's line that the contemporary bureaucratic situation gives the individual a position of equal anonymity, without meaning. When an individual's private life is barren and without meaning, reaction can be irrational and violent.

Berger points to the flight into irrational counter worlds as one reaction, and the world of the internet is the perfect 'virtual' world for such escape. There individuals can develop new identities, multiple identities, and chat 'online' to other such persons, possibly also indulging in fantasy identities. A kind of Gnostic escape into wholly new and far more exciting realms is easy to achieve through the computer screen. The narcissistic self can develop and mutate into other forms of itself, 'relating' to other virtual characters in ways never to be dared in real-life encounters.[27] This might be therapeutic for the participants, and yet a move away from genuine flesh and blood relating to others. It is certainly a matter of the feelings being deployed in cyberspace rather than a rational activity. In terms of the Christian doctrine of creation and incarnation this smacks of escape from reality and into a realm of stories and myths, of projected artificial stimulus, a world similar to that of the pagan gods and goddesses and semi-transcendent values.

The extraordinary phenomenon of public self-exposure of problems on 'reality' TV programmes reveals a desperate need to be looked at and noted by society, on the part of people who feel 'nobody' otherwise. Becoming famous for five minutes, even for revealing gross personal problems formerly kept private, is a regular television format. This turns the private into the public and 'shocks' the gawping viewer, or rather no longer shocks at all. The 'celebrity' figure is someone who evokes response, even one of disgust, and if ordinary people can experience being taken notice of by a wide public audience, that is therapy, gaining recognition however absurd that may appear, the key gain is being acknowledged by wider society. That society is indeed 'emotivist', and many are happy to watch TV programmes spotlighting chaotic relationships by way of a grotesque populist theatre of private lives being made public. Gawping at public executions and at the disturbed antics of those in 'Bedlam' might be said to be precursors of such TV shows. The need to get oneself

---

[26]P. and B. Berger, *The Homeless Mind: Modernization and Consciousness*, New York: Vintage, 1973.
[27]See, for example, Sherry Turkle, *Life on the Screen*, London: Simon & Schuster, 1997.

advertised, put into the public forum, 'publicized', can also readily be met by internet websites and 'chatrooms' of all kinds.

We can dramatize ourselves and find recognition, find escape from the anonymity and failure of ordinary life in many ways, through the contemporary forms of the media and virtual reality. Indeed the need to be seen and noted as a figure in society shows itself in the many people who decide to speak loudly into their mobile phones as they walk down the street, sit in a train carriage or on a bus, animatedly sharing the most mundane details of their private life, in the public forum, declining the older practice of maintaining a discreet and quiet mode of conversation. It is ironic that such speakers do not seek to talk 'to' their neighbours on the train, bus or fellow walkers in the street, they project their voices into phones ignoring the personhood of the surrounding unfortunates suffering the barrage of loud words as pure nuisance.

Bobbitt convincingly claims that techniques of mass media also threaten the claim of the State to ensure the conditions of freedom.

> This is most easily seen in the immense power of the modern electronic media and the press. More than any other development it is the increased influence of the news media that has delegitimated the State, largely through its ability to disrupt the history of the state, that process of self portrayal that unites strategy and law and forms the basis for legitimacy ....the ideology of media journalism is the ideology of consumerism, presentism, competition, hyberbole – as well as scepticism, envy and contempt (the reactions it rains on government officials).[28]

Bobbitt captures the fragmentation and fractiousness caused by the mass media, now of course available 'on line' from all over the world, including Arab language services from the Middle East cultures and states. Bobbitt must be correct in concluding: 'No State that bases its legitimacy on claims of continuity with tradition, that requires self-sacrifice, that depends on a consensus of respect, can prosper for very long in such an environment.'[29] Bobbitt points to the mass media as disrupting the national narrative and tradition, fragmenting the common loyalty to one national cause as worthwhile. But in the UK the government educational system seems more than willing to denigrate the common national narrative, often in line with the Marxist critique outlined above.[29] The historic national culture and history is very deliberately being delegitimated by the nation's educators, it is little surprise that any social ethical core is fast fragmenting and moral authority being relativized.

Dramatization and publicization of the self in contemporary Western culture connects strongly with the great stress now placed on 'identity' for the individual, very much the autonomous individual and the

---

[28]Bobbitt, *The Shield of Achilles*, op cit., p. 226.
[29]Ibid.

narcissistic self, no longer gaining a life role from job or family structure, a role conferring an objective identity for the local community. In Western civilization individuals no longer have an identity objectively, but they choose one and seek to fashion themselves accordingly. Fashion and identity in fact are closely interwoven, and can be thrown away and reinvented in today's throwaway culture. Insecurity in the dizzying pace of change has made concern for 'my identity' vital and to get notice of that identity out into the public forum, since that is who I am. Globalization is a key factor in this process, with powerful global forces controlling all manner of agencies affecting life contexts and removing any sense of local rooting. Even phone calls trying to sell double glazing or mobile phones now emanate from a different continent thousands of miles away. Bauman says:

> The fast globalization of the power network seems to conspire and collaborate with a privatized life politics; they stimulate, sustain and reinforce each other. If globalization saps the capacity of established political institutions to act effectively, the massive retreat from the 'body politic' to the narrow concerns of life politics prevents the crystallization of alternative modes of collective action on a par with the globality of the network of dependencies. Everything seems to be in place to make both the globalization of life conditions and the … atomization and privatization of life struggles self propelling and self perpetuating. It is against this background that the logic and the endemic illogicality of contemporary "identity concerns" and the actions they trigger needs to be scrutinized and understood.[30]

Life feels precarious and shifting even as its aims and the very contexts of existence, and the increasing sense that the individual, even if banding together with others, can have no impact politically or economically on what is happening, has led to individualization of interests and inner meanings. Compulsive shopping, 'retail therapy' to use an ironic popular term, becomes a pastime along with exercising at gyms, jogging, pilates, harmless activities to occupy people and transport them to another world than the worrying one of daily life. 'Shopping expeditions,' explains Bauman, 'fill the void left by the travels no longer undertaken by the imagination to an alternative, more secure, humane and just society.'[31] Moreover rearranging one's identity becomes another activity undertaken in the context of our acute insecurity. And this is very much an individualized response to the context, 'just as community collapses, identity is invented'[32] The era of identity building divides and separates

---

[30]Online samples of the curriculum http://curriculum.qca.org.uk/uploads/QCA-07-3329-pCitizenship3_tcm8-396.pdf, http://curriculum.qca.org.uk/uploads/QCA-07-3335-p_History3_tcm8-189.pdf illustrate the massive emphasis on the merits of cultural diversity, for example.
[31]Z. Bauman, *The Individualized Society*, Cambridge: Polity Press, 2001, pp. 149–150.
[32]Ibid., p. 151.

us, yet the 'precariousness of the solitary identity-building prompts the identity builders to seek pegs on which they can hang their individually experienced fears and anxieties' and find communities of interest to counter loneliness and anxiety.

This fragmentation of the nation into sub-group cultures, each with its own equally valid and true sets of morals, ideas, customs for living, is the overwhelming impression of today's Western society, and this is seen as a good thing. Reason, intellectual and moral, has a low place beneath cultural values which can offer their own form of 'reasoning' on moral questions: why is polygamy any worse than monogamy, for example? There is no answer to that question, once a core basis of moral discussion has been broken up. The situation is to be 'managed', feelings soothed by the cultural therapists, attention diverted by the hedonistic 'arts' on screen. The managers, the state bureaucracy, have no common moral base shared with society or rising from it, they administer rights to competing groups on a purely pragmatic basis. Soaring rates of sexually transmitted diseases and multiple abortions among young people reveal the collapse of a shared morality alongside a technological managerial approach by educators and health services.[33] A kind of animalisation of teenagers, managed by the state agencies, is underway, following the 'death of Christian Britain.' The Church of England, moreover, seems to have accepted that it no longer has a responsibility to the nation to commend a 'form' of sexual mores.

The secularised nation state is becoming amoral in terms of a form of 'the good life', and entirely clinical and functional as regards state policy. The pattern of society emerging seems to be that non minority faith citizens are ruled by secularist mores, its historic Christian forms being deliberately uprooted by all possible means, as regards public policy; the role of the family in shaping children's moral behaviour is being sharply overriden by educationalist policy. The state faces a managerial nightmare: individual freedom is now absolute, and bureaucratic control is the only way of preventing chaos. At the same time a new tribalism and fragmentation, is arising from the severe multi cultural policies, devoid of a common authority, individual freedom without moral form beyond utilitarian management, taking us on the road to ever deepening tribalization and fragmentation. The intellectual dimension to this fragmentation of morality and reason is 'postmodernism' to which we need to attend in order to help map the western individualist rejection of trust in authority.

---

[33]see eg http://www.timesonline.co.uk/tol/life_and_style/health/article6318571.ece.

5

Postmodern Fragmentation
The Current Intellectual State

Deconstructing rational foundations

European cultural fragmentation finds expression intellectually in 'postmodernism', that broad term seeking to describe the drive to cut loose from a single global rationality and morality of the kind characteristic of Christianity and the Enlightenment. The movement undoubtedly finds its roots in the work of Nietzsche and his deep attack on Christianity and the rationalist tradition. The crisis in the church has to be interpreted in the context of this radical intellectual and moral tendency of consecrating diversity.

The intellectual movements associated with postmodernism are themselves diffuse, and most easily understood in the light of what has happened in Western culture rather than an abstract philosophy. As we have rehearsed above, Western culture is now dominated by the 'diversity agenda' against the unity agenda, where the stress was on one unified system of rationality, of morals, of liberal democratic norms. 'Deconstruction' is a word closely associated with this culturally self-critical diversity agenda, the rush away from shared norms towards the virtue of multiplicity even to the point of contradiction. Indeed the notion of contradiction implies an overarching logical coherence, which 'postmoderns' barely acknowledge in their rejection of rationality.

Postmodernism of the academic kind revels in 'deconstructing' what is universal and overarching – or foundational, to change the metaphor. For

Derrida, philosophers have made the mistake of looking for, or assuming, that essential truth consists in the essence of things. Such essential truth is deemed to be oppressive of the individual and of diversity, in the language of Derrida 'logocentric'. His diagnosis is that the power of the word, the Logos, dictates to us and suppresses us, we need to break up the unitary power of the word over against us by getting inside it and breaking it up to reveal its real diversity and irrational aspects. Derrida is well known for his treatment of text and denial that an author's intention decides its meaning. Rather the text is pregnant with all manner of unintended meanings, as if an insect had laid eggs in a body which later hatch out against the will of the host. Derrida worms his way into the text to unpick it and show the many threads of possible meaning, deconstructing any one final controlling meaning. In fact all of life is this kind of text, a kind of alphabet soup of meanings, according to our radical postmodern philosophers. Philosophers should look at language itself, but not regarding individual words as having a meaning given by a 'rational' or 'causal' link with the objects, ideas or actions they allegedly designate. Words are not markers referring to more real entities. Language rather contains only differences and meaning is created by the distinction between the sounds, for example 'pin' and 'pen', meaning being 'deferred' as the ongoing process of 'difference' proceeds. These distinctions form part of a system. The philosopher should see how language works by the differences contained, and by the chain of expectations which the writer or speaker sets up, and which require the listener to defer the moment when he or she decides what a sentence may or may not mean. Deferral and difference are meanings simultaneously conjured up by the word 'differance'. This is a philosophy of unsettlement and provocation, a gadfly biting the complacent and disturbing the current orthodoxies. Authority becomes a very dubious word and concept in this light – texts previously considered authoritative will lack meaning and intention, and institutions previously trusted as virtuous authorities find themselves reinterpreted as subtle controlling agencies exercising power without justification – even hospitals can come under this condemnation in the light of Foucault's analysis.

An interesting development regarding politicians' strategy for retaining public esteem is to move attention from the past to the future and new promises, 'drawing a line on the past' and 'moving on', a very 'postmodern' view of truth. The postmodern 'feel for' truth is a coherence view rather than a correspondence view, not seeking to find a confirming reference to the truth claim but moving on for new experiences from the old ones which may have proved disappointing. This coherence view chimes in with the picture of life as intratextual, of being within a text of interlocking signs and meanings, the signs pointing to other signs rather than a reality or authority outside the 'text'. We are not responsible to any authority outside the text of social signs, and these themselves will shift and change, so life is a matter of negotiating the slalom of pointers and these will shape our orientation to life. This is the 'cultural-linguistic' view of culture and of society.[1]

This philosophy, or anti-philosophy, meshes with much experience of contemporary Western life as it flits like a bat at dusk going from insect to insect in jerky flight: a philosophical version of 'surfing the net', one prompt leading to the next without any necessarily logical or rational connection. This philosophy reminds us of dreams or narratives which later, under analysis, disclose layers of meaning not initially apparent. Or 'deconstruction' seems akin to the joke: a narrative is suddenly put into a very different unexpected light, a word given radically new meaning, and the juxtaposition is 'funny' by its very absurdity. This rereading of texts and narratives can make them invert their apparent meanings and their intended meanings, the authors' intention being virtually irrelevant to the ongoing soup of meanings possible to new readers. Life and thought is on the surface, indeed there is no depth beneath the surface and the shifting movement of meanings is the essence of things, or to change the metaphor, there is no 'overarching' meaning or reference point, or again there is no lighthouse rising above the surface of the sea to give the drifting ship bearings.

Derrida is rejecting dualisms of being and becoming, of value and fact, of changeless and changing, so ingrained in the Western cultural psyche, in favour of a sort of ironic monism of language received and broken up, constantly interrogated with deep suspicion and contemporary cynicism. Derrida echoes Diogenes the cynic, barking at the world from his barrel, taking nothing whatsoever on trust and suspecting the motives of everyone. We seem to be living and thinking, even these acts can hardly be separated as we sail through the one great Sargasso sea of language and text, surfing the great internet which is reality, moved from one website to the next, finding one interpretation after another. The notion of an authoritative voice in the midst of this cacophony becomes impossible and not desirable. The process of experiencing the texted signs, of questioning them 'playfully', perhaps strengthening the analogy of the joke, opening up apparently established meanings to new suggestions. Just as Derrida rejects the idea that a text should be understood by its author's intention, holding instead that it has a life of its own and is part of a world of texts, so he rejects the idea that there could be an authoritative God 'over' the world. To use Lindbeck's categories, postmodernism envisages our life in the cultural linguistic field, but experiencing meaning also as in the 'experiential-expressivist' mode rather than the 'cognitive propositional' mode of reason and

---

[1]G. Lindbeck, in *The Nature of Doctrine* (London: SPCK, 1984), posits this as a way of defining the role of Christian doctrine which does not refer beyond its own linguistic web of meaning.

logic, the overarching Logos no longer in place. Lindbeck's attempt at a 'post liberal' account of Christian doctrine as a language game with no reference beyond itself, chimes in very well with the state of Western culture and its fragmented, flitting, shifting kaleidoscope of meanings, without an overarching norm to refer to as authoritative.

Diversification of the self

Postmodern deconstruction runs deeper into the human self, removing even the 'authority' of myself as a rational or moral entity, an enduring 'identity' or same entity now as last year or into the future. Just as the cognitive propositional model has been rejected by postmodernism, or post-liberalism, so has the picture of a human being as a reasoning individual, the Kantian self of the Enlightenment. The postmodern claim is that the self is in fact de-centred, is not really a single centre but multiplex, more a collection of drives and will. The world of the internet again may offer the easiest way to illustrate how this can be taken seriously rather than being a perverse and difficult claim by some abstruse philosophers who love to fly in the face of common sense experience. Sherry Turkle's book *Life on the Screen* is subtitled 'identity in the age of the internet'[2] and explores the interactive effect on the self-understanding of the internet user and game player. She explains MUDs, 'multi user domains', which are 'virtual reality' games participated in by users at their computer screens linking up to a particular virtual world. The Star Trek game is an example in which thousands of players spend up to eighty hours a week playing exploration and war games.

> Through typed descriptions and typed commands, they create characters who have casual and romantic sexual encounters, hold jobs and collect paychecks, attend rituals and celebrations, fall in love and get married. To the participants, such goings on can be gripping: "This is more real than my real life", says a character who turns out to be a man playing a woman who is pretending to be a man. In this game the self is constructed and the rules of social interaction are built, not received.[3]

It is apparently not uncommon for dedicated MUD players to be in several of such virtual worlds at the same time, their computer screens boxed into quarters, with each showing a different game world and different character of theirs taking part and relating to other virtual characters. The MUD players can be at work on their computer, leaving the MUDs running in the background but sending messages from time

---

[2]Sherry Turkle, *Life on the Screen*, Phoenix and London: Simon & Schuster, 1995.
[3]Ibid., p. 10.

to time, virtual reality interweaving with real-time activity. Turkle quotes Doug, an American student who plays four characters in three MUDs, a seductive woman, a macho cowboy, a rabbit, and a furry animal in a MUD that makes him feel like a sexual tourist. 'I split my mind', says Doug, 'and I just turn on one part of my mind and then another when I go from window to window'. Turkle says that for many computer users these windows have become 'a powerful metaphor for thinking about the self as a multiple distributed system. The self is no longer simply playing different roles in different settings at different times, something that a person experiences when, for example, she wakes up as a lover, makes breakfast as a mother, and drives to work as a lawyer. The life practice of windows is that of a decentred self that exists in many worlds and plays many roles at the same time.'[4] In contrast to roles taken by actors in the theatre, MUDs offer parallel identities and lives and leads participants to treat on and off screen lives with surprising equality. 'Why' asks one of Turkle's interviewees, 'grant such superior status to the self that has a body when the selves that don't have bodies are able to have different kinds of experiences?' Such experiences are 'real' for the players, as they interact in different genders and forms.

Turkle relates this to the French movement of postmodernism which she learned in the 1960s and 1970s, the view that 'the self is constituted by and through language, that sexual congress is the exchange of signifiers, and that each of us is a multiplicity of parts, fragments, and desiring connections.'[5] But this view seemed to her at the time very abstract and out of touch with real experience since that demanded the autonomous ego as a responsible, intentional unitary agent. The centred self did not seem to be an illusion, but the bedrock of reality, despite claims of psychologists and postmodern philosophers otherwise. Since becoming a computer expert and game player with lives 'on screen', however, she now finds the French postmodernists more convincing. 'In my computer-mediated worlds, the self is multiple, fluid, and constituted in interaction with machine connections; it is made and transformed by language; sexual congress is an exchange of signifiers; and understanding follows from navigation and tinkering rather than analysis…and I meet characters who put me in a new relationship with my own identity.'[6] Language, as text, makes and transforms by way of the continual stream of messages and instructions typed and sent to control and interact with characters on screen. That computers, machines, have been important catalysts in carrying forward and incarnating postmodernist experiences of the self is a deep irony not lost on Turkle. In the various MUD lives she experiences being 'decentred', 'fluid', 'nonlinear' and 'opaque' in post

---

[4]Ibid., p. 14.
[5]Ibid.
[6]Ibid., p. 15.

modern mode, in contrast to the modernist view of reality and truth as 'linear', 'logical', 'hierarchical' and 'having depths to be plumbed' and understood.

Her book also shows how Derrida's 'textuality' and rejection of text as owned only by the author can be readily explained through computer usage. A student of hers came to understand Derrida's viewpoint through the computer software of 'hypertext', a way of creating links between texts, songs, photographs and videos, as well as travelling along links made by others. The student understood what Derrida was saying about writing being constructed by audience as well as author and the significance of what is absent from the text. The texts linked together by the student's hypertext 'get their meaning in relation to each other...The links have a reason but there is no final truth behind them.'[7] This view of things chimes in with contemporary Western culture and its understanding of reason, meaning and authority, and may help explain why apparently flat contradictions do not matter much to the contemporary psyche: freedom of thought is one thing, Qur'anic fundamentalism another, but they should be allowed to jostle together, not be brought into conflict and adjudicated under the aegis of an overarching logic or arbiter of a final truth; consistency does not matter, indeed it would require a unified field of knowing which postmodern culture somehow finds difficult. *Wikipedia* illustrates the point being made here: the text on screen can be added to and tinkered with ad infinitum, there is no regulator to check whether its 'references' are 'correct'.

On the other hand, the liberal or 'modern' theory of knowledge assumes that what is on the surface of things refers back to some deeper latent reality, or again that the 'signifier' refers to a more real 'signified' reality. The postmodern world seems to be 'all at sea', concerned about processes, happy to be led along by open possibilities almost because they are there, no longer with fixed meanings since they will mean something else in a different virtual world. Not only are meanings fragmentary and diverse but so apparently are we as individuals, and the personal computer has been very much part of an acceptance of this self understanding and of its attendant problem – identity crisis. Turkle cites Frederick Jameson as saying that in the postmodern world 'the subject is not alienated but fragmented.' The alienated lost soul or self is the figure from the Enlightenment and Romantic movement, a figure even found in Marx's diagnosis of the human problem resulting from economic conditions. In the postmodern era, however, Jameson suggests, since the self is decentred and multiple the concept of alienation breaks down and what is left is an anxiety of identity.[8]

---

[7]Ibid., p. 18.
[8]Turkle p 49.

Computer experience gives people a way of thinking about identity crisis. Turkle thinks that 'life on the screen' is a way of participating in this multiple way of being but also of making it an object to our consciousness and self-understanding. Cycling through the worlds of the windows on screen we more clearly see who we are and how we are and ponder our disjointed, fragmented identity as we take part in ongoing serial and parallel relationships, learning about ourselves through our reactions to these varied experiences and pushing boundaries we had assumed were defining us. The self is multiplied and diversified into the pin cushion of feelings and experiences suggested by David Hume in his criticism of reason and causation, or indeed suggested by the Buddhist vision of the human being as a series of temporarily experiencing systems, not ultimately held together in a permanent self or soul, but to be reassigned and absorbed elsewhere in due course.

Turkle's book returns over again to sexual experiment and experience 'on screen', the participation in virtual reality eroticism with others whose identity is not truly known and indeed whose gender is not necessarily known.[9] We can apparently decentre ourselves sexually, becoming gendered differently and learning different responses to those previously thought to be ours. Turkle adduces examples of people being much more assertive on screen and learning to be so at home, or learning to live split lives to ensure they did not threaten their home relationships.[10] Some claim to gain a deeper self understanding by this game playing technique of living in different worlds of semi-reality, as if the process enables them to 'get above' themselves and gain a position of self-observation not possible before. This process of 'tinkering' and experimenting and surfing the net itself prompts such new insight rather than the cognitive analytical way of thinking, although clearly the participant is analysing what is happening rather than simply being drawn into a subjective emotional engagement. Experimentation is fine, there are no limits, freedom is supreme and form temporary and there to be liquefied.

It seems clear that morality is bracketed out of such activities, they are somehow deemed value free since they are games in the imaginations – and yet other players are drawn in too. Turkle describes the process as raising teasing and interesting questions. Describing participation in one

---

[9]'should it make a difference if unbeknownst to the husband his cyberspace mistress turns out to be a nineteen-year-old male college freshman? What if 'she' is an infirm eighty-year-old man in a nursing home? And even more disturbing, what if she is a twelve-year-old girl? Or a twelve-year-old boy?' (ibid., p. 225).
[10]'Some people have sex as nonhuman characters, for example as animals on FurryMUDs. Some enjoy sex with one partner. Some use virtual reality as a place to experiment with group situations. In real life such situations (where possible) can create enormous practical and emotional confusion. ...Different people and different couples deal with them in very different ways' (ibid., p. 224).

erotic MUD she says: 'TinySex poses the question of what is at the heart of sex and fidelity. Is it the physical action? Is it the feeling of emotional intimacy with someone other than one's primary partner? Is infidelity in the head or in the body? Is it in the desire or in the action? What constitutes the violation of trust? And to what extent and in what ways should it matter who the virtual sexual partner is in the real world? The fact that the physical body has been factored out of the situation makes these issues both subtler and harder to resolve than before.'[11] Turkle's research put her in touch with Rudy, whose girlfriend – he discovered to his deep perplexity – adopted a male persona in a chatroom to engage erotically with women. Rudy's response was to declare himself deeply unsettled at her need or desire to do this and that although he believed that humans are all bisexual it upset him that she might be 'a dyke'. He criticized the online chatrooms for making it too easy to explore such things, far harder than going out in the real world and engaging in them which would be 'making a statement'. Her playing this game was not real and yet it was real and it led her along into uncharted emotional territory, possibly having an impact on her relationship with Rudy. 'The status of these fantasies-in-action in cyberspace is unclear. Although they involve other people and are no longer pure fantasy, they are not "in the world". Their boundary status offers new possibilities. TinySex and virtual gender-bending are part of the larger story of people using virtual spaces to construct identity.'[12]

The cyberspace experience of disembodied eroticism, or a newly constructed medium for interactive erotic engagement, takes the diversification of sex further outwards, and perhaps illustrates anew Foucault's view that sex is a dominating 'reality' somehow betwixt and between the physical and the mental, to be deployed in all manner of ways and especially seductive when considered to be offending the social norms, and somehow dangerous. This cyber sexuality can be regarded as an extension of the modern libertarianism, the difference being that it invites a self understanding as multiple and parallel, a phenomenon that will tend to deconstruct or relativize morality as known in the Christian and enlightenment traditions – indeed a pluralizing of 'self', or human being, entails a radical challenge to any notion of morality, rather moralities seem more relevant and chosen matters of taste. The postmodern call to reinvent ourselves as we choose, and often, has clearly affected the churches and the deep disagreements over sexual morality. Individual freedom wishes to abolish inherited moral forms of life, and label them 'taboos' in need of deconstruction.

---

[11]Ibid., p. 225.
[12]Ibid., p. 226.

Foucault: The social construction of sexual identity

This phenomenon, while no doubt driven by the totally successful gay rights movement, would be given a wider and longer background by the French philosopher Foucault, who describes Western civilization as producing a 'scientia sexualis', ways of 'telling the truth about sex geared to a form of knowledge-power', which is the confession.[13] By this Foucault means that Western civilization has in all sorts of ways maintained the urge and practice to express inner feelings to gain a sense of redemption, and that this has found institutional forms since the medieval church's penitential and inquisitorial systems developed. It has now spread into many forms of relationship, children and parents, teachers and pupils, patients and psychiatrists, indeed MacIntyre's iconic therapist figure is a recipient of just such inner secret truths brought out from the private realm.

Here the point may be raised as to whether homosexual 'coming out' is not some form of just such an urge to confess and so to gain liberation, acceptance, release, justification. Confession, says Foucault, became one of the West's most highly valued techniques for producing truth, whether confessing voluntarily in public or under coercion to an interrogator. Truth emerges from confession in Western cultural understanding, according to Foucault, and this does seem to fit the phenomenon of homosexual testimony or confession about desires and practices – although precise details of the latter are not nearly so well aired in public for general information. 'The obligation to confess', now normal in medical, educational, parental, therapeutic contexts for example, 'is now relayed through so many different points, is so deeply ingrained in us, that we no longer perceive it as the effect of a power that constrains us; on the contrary, it seems to us that truth, lodged in our most secret nature, "demands" only to surface; that if it fails to do so, this is because a constraint holds it in place, the violence of a power weighs it down, and it can finally be articulated only at the price of a kind of liberation. Confession frees, but power reduces one to silence',[14] this is the 'ruse' of confession which deceives us to think that we want to confess rather than being ordered to do so by a power. Foucault here seems close to Nietzsche's 'slave mentality' view of Christianity: Christians claim to desire to be slave-like in their self-abnegation and humility, in their desire to repent and confess sin, as a virtue. In fact, says Nietzsche, they are deceiving themselves since they cannot attain what they truly desire and see others having, so they make a virtue of the state of self-negation to the public as a sort of message.

---

[13]Michel Foucault, *The History of Sexuality*, vol. 1, trans. Robert Hurley, London: Penguin, 1978, pp. 62–4.
[14]Ibid., p. 60.

Confession is a ritual in which the speaker is the subject and object of the truth brought forth from the inner depths, and it happens in the context of 'power' relations, says Foucault, since it takes place with another, or virtual other, an authority who judges, consoles, forgives and reconciles. The expression alone of the confession 'produces intrinsic modification of the person who articulates it; it exonerates, redeems and purifies him; it unburdens him of his wrongs, liberates him and promises him salvation.'[15] This resonates with the agonizing joy of 'coming out' by homosexuals, whose articulation of their perceived inner selves, like the pain of giving birth, creates a new person, a rebirth into the community 'as' a homosexual. The state sponsorship of this process gives this confession an authority which can confer liberation and status, which can even turn a friendship into a new single being out of two, a 'civil partnership'. The state has become part of the movement for sexualizing society, 'a process that spreads sex over the surface of things and bodies, arouses it, draws it out and bids it speak, implants it in reality and enjoins it to tell the truth: an entire glittering sexual array, reflected in a myriad of discourses, the obstination of powers, and the interplay of knowledge and pleasure.'[16] Foucault rebuts the notion, or myth as he sees it, of repression of sex by Western society, rather it is constantly being painted onto society in every conceivable way, and the homosexual movement and its discourses are part and parcel of this much wider process.

In terms of an appreciation of authority in Western society, Foucault appears to have extraordinary insight, insight which opens up the sociology of, or ideology of, sex. Western society is indeed coated with sexual discourse both sombre and wild, serious and flippant. The myth of Victorian repression and taboo, says Foucault, is needed as a foil to the development of sexual rhetoric, that which we must overcome in order to be free. This plays directly into the ideology of the gay Christian movement and its discourse of sexual liberation, of overcoming cruel repressive superstitions or taboos. In fact, says Foucault, Western sexual discourse is the modern version of preaching:

> A great sexual sermon – which has had its subtle theologians and its popular voices – has swept through our societies over the last decades; it has chastised the old order, denounced hypocrisy, and praised the rights of the immediate and the real; it has made people dream of a New City. The Franciscans are called to mind. And we might wonder how it is possible that the lyricism and religiosity that long accompanied the revolutionary project have, in Western industrial societies, been largely carried over to sex.[17]

---

[15]Ibid., p. 61.
[16]Ibid., p. 72.
[17]Ibid., p. 7–8.

Sex has become a dominating message or sermon in western society, infiltrating every cranny of life, as can readily be seen in the advertising industry.

Foucault's book seeks to get at the sources which have issued in this deep and widespread discourse about sexuality, with the repression theme woven into it as a foil, as the sour sauce heightening the flavour of the evocation to confess and 'bring out' the supposed 'inner truth' of ourselves and desires and the power structures in society which serve this complex process. Foucault performed a similar analysis of madness: some behaviour was deemed such as to require the incarceration of the individuals, it was 'medicalized' and turned into an illness by the forces, influences and powers at play in that process. For our purposes we need to note how power and authority has this deep-seated mode of operation affecting people at the most profound levels. Foucault's fascinating suggestion is that since the end of the sixteenth century,

> the putting into discourse of sex, far from undergoing a process of restriction, on the contrary has been subjected to a mechanism of increasing incitement; that the techniques of power exercised over sex have not obeyed a principle of rigorous selection, but rather one of dissemination and implantation of polymorphous sexualities; and that the will to knowledge has not come to a halt in the face of a taboo that must not be lifted, but has persisted in constituting – despite many mistakes, of course – as science of sexuality.[18]

Sex, or rather talk about sex, has as it were become a power, an influence, permeating society and institutions.

Who could deny Foucault's point that sexual discourse reigns as an authority in Western civilization, penetrating every area of life and into younger and younger age ranges, as the Archbishop of Canterbury has recently lamented.[19] Sex, or rather the logic of sex, today explains everything. 'The West has managed not only, or not so much, to annex sex to a field of rationality...but to bring us almost entirely – our bodies, our minds, our individuality, our history – under the sway of logic of concupiscence and desire.'[20] Sex has become a way of thinking: Foucault is almost suggesting an Orwellian notion of thought crime controlling human Western rationality, with sex the driving theme. As Orwell knew, discourse, control of language, affects how we think. Given this discourse we will identify ourselves accordingly: 'Whenever it is a question of knowing who we are, it is this logic that henceforth serves as our master key.'[21] We know who we are according to the range of ideas

---

[18]Ibid., p. 12. We might note here the effects of state sex education as 'an incitement', following Foucault.
[19]Rowan Williams, *Lost Icons*, London: Continuum, 2000.
[20]Foucault, *The History of Sexuality*, vol. 1, p. 78.
[21]Ibid.

on offer in our cultural surroundings, we take our cue about our identity from 'scripts', or roles suggested to us by society and the state, on offer. Foucault says that the all pervasive discourse of sexuality now very much affects our self-understanding and self-identification. Indeed we are now told by the great sexual sermonizers that we should choose how to classify ourselves, that we should search our hidden secret depths and confess to the public our real 'sexuality'. The sexual preachers have an increasing authority in this classification process and increasingly press the binary division upon us: there are two classes of people, homosexual and heterosexual, gay and straight, with a very few people having both capacities. Therefore you must choose which class you belong to and so how to conduct yourself in society according to the sexual lexicon of life.

Foucault regards this classification process as part of the nineteenth century's concern with ordering and defining species, with taxonomy. Whereas previously homosexuality had been 'a category of forbidden acts', 'the nineteenth century homosexual became a personage, a past, a case history, and a childhood, in addition to being a type of life, a life form…Nothing that went into his total composition was unaffected by his sexuality…Homosexuality appeared as one of the forms of sexuality when it was transposed from the practice of sodomy onto a kind of interior androgeny, a hermaphrodism of the soul…The homosexual was now a species.'[22] This development in sexual discourse and sexual reasoning has had immense influence on Western civilization and state policy, unquestioned and even given power to warn off those who do question this binary analysis of gay and straight persons. Such is the depth of this doctrine and its power in Western societies today that to disagree on moral grounds with homosexual activity is becoming itself a legal offence, since it infringes the rights of homosexual persons. Sexual discourse now represses those who dissent from the gay agenda, forcing them into 'the closet'.

This is precisely where religion and secular theory clash, and the move from seeing homosexuality as act to being is crucial in the attempt to persuade Christian ethicists to break with the traditional view discouraging such activity. The argument is that this dominating and controlling homosexual nature or being necessitates homosexual activity as a law of nature, which must be accepted as the primary characteristic of this identified, or self identified, people group.

---

[22]Ibid., p. 43.

Postmodern flexible identity

But 'postmodernity' seems to be rejecting such fixed and necessary
ways of looking at people and pointing to far greater flexibility in how
people understand themselves. Identity in the contemporary world is
not, according to Stuart Hall, 'a stable core of the self, unfolding from
the beginning to end through all the vicissitudes of history without
change.'[23] Bauman is probably right to suggest that identity now might
best be spoken of in terms of 'identification', an ongoing open-ended
activity which we are have to undertake, surfing the waves of life as they
sweep unexpectedly upon us. Flexibility for Bauman, as for Sennett, is a
catchword for this process. We need recognition and identification and
to be prepared at short notice to switch not only jobs but lifestyles and
'partners', an unstable precarious situation. As with the economic context
of work and its new 'virtue' of insecurity and flexibility, so in the context
of sexuality postmodernity discourages fixed forms of sexual activity and
identity. The gay or straight 'binary' divide is criticized for offering a
wooden procrustean bed rather than a genuine description of the range
of sexual affections and desires in the breasts of most human beings
who are multi-faceted and who also change in different circumstances
and under different influences. This movement goes with the grain of
Foucault's own line of thinking about discourse of sexuality and his
exposure of religious and scientific classifications or 'medicalizations' of
sexual behaviour.

Bauman quotes Mark C. Taylor: 'desire does not seek satisfaction. To
the contrary, desire desires desire'. Bauman elaborates: 'When (seldom
and in whispers) voiced before, such claims were classified as the heresy
of libertinism and exiled to the Devil's island of sexual disorder and
perversion. Now the self-sufficiency of eroticism, the freedom to seek
sexual delights for their own sake, has risen to the level of a cultural
norm, changing places with its critics.'[24] Eroticism, says Bauman, is a free
floating cultural 'substance' let loose, with no taboos attached. Christian
theology would add, free from being shaped and formed (by a moral
tradition) and in reality now a chaos. Sexual identities are loose and to
be rearranged at will, like postmodern eroticism calculated for maximal
impact and instant obsolescence.[25]

'Postmodernity' resists 'essentialist' self-understandings and tends to
regard social constructionism as a more likely way of describing who
we are and how we behave. The core identity, including that urged on
us by the sexual preachers of our day as 'homosexual' or 'heterosexual'
at the very root of our being, is likely to be less frozen than we are

---

[23]Ibid., quoted in Bauman, p. 152.
[24]Z. Bauman, *Postmodernism and its Discontents*, Cambridge: Cambridge University Press,
1997, p. 223.
[25]Ibid., p. 229.

told. Matthew Parris, a proudly homosexual British journalist, does not go along with the fixed and necessary understanding of sexual identity, regarding people as far more flexible in this direction:

My evidence? Direct experience and personal observation. I'm the type who calls himself totally homosexual, but I know from dreams and from occasional involuntary physical responses that some small heterosexual part of my nature, though elbowed aside, is still there. My sexual sample is less prolific than I would once have wanted, but I reckon about a third of the men I've slept with were what you might call "viable heterosexuals" — in the sense that they wanted and got girlfriends, believed themselves to be more straight than gay and in many cases ended up (unforced and happily) married. I've also known a fair few men who seemed quite contendedly gay, then changed their lives and went straight. And, of course, vice versa. We all know that plenty of married men dabble in homosexual behaviour; but plenty of gay men have flings with women too.[26]

Parris replaces the two box theory with a spectrum understanding. Jeffrey Weeks, another writer who describes himself as gay, very much backs this understanding and resists the 'binary' gay or straight template.[27] History and society play a critical role in shaping human sexual desire, behaviour and identity, in Weeks' view, and he insists on a very careful observation of the difference between these three aspects of being human. Homosexual *behaviour*, according to Weeks, is quite widespread and often engaged in by people who do not identify themselves as 'gay'; *desire*, which may be very specific and may well have biological causes; and *identities* which are always social and historical, because identities are made in particular cultural milieux. Today there are openly gay identities, fifty years ago there were not; things change, we need to take an historical perspective in our thinking on this complex matter. Biological and other factors in our makeup, says Weeks, take meaning only in the light of our social contexts, and these contexts shift and move in time with its changing concepts and categories. Weeks therefore identifies his view as 'social constructionist'.

'Categories like homosexuality and heterosexuality are categories of the human mind', Weeks points out, 'they are invented by us, they don't exist in nature, we read nature through these categories, the concept did not exist a hundred years ago, they were invented in the course of the last hundred years and had an impact in the course of the last hundred years in particular milieux, particularly in the West.' Here Weeks is very much with Foucault. These categories do not exist necessarily in that way in other parts of the world; we are very culturally specific in trying to

[26]Matthew Parris, 'Are you gay or straight? Admit it, you are most likely an in-between', *The Times*, 5 August 2006.
[27]I am here citing his contribution to the Dana Centre Symposium, http://www.danacentre.

find to explanations for homosexuality and heterosexuality as we know them. It is always very important therefore to start on the basis of seeing human sexuality as a potential spectrum of different behaviours, the way we divide them up depends on a whole series of different cultural and historical influences.

The West for the last 100 to 150 years, says Weeks, has been determined to divide homosexuality and heterosexuality dualistically, a binary divide which looks like the absolute last word of nature. Weeks robustly denies the reality claimed by this binary system, this binary categorization is something we invented and if we invented it we can deconstruct it; we can, he says, 'dis-invent' it and we can forget about it and instead we can look at the real diversity of human sexual natures and ask about the ways we conduct ourselves socially. Parris wishes to move from the 'necessity' claim, or 'I can't help it', to a gay claim based on freedom of choice alone. His stance is set out in his review of Andrew Sullivan's book *Virtually Normal*:

> Sullivan thinks sexual orientation is fixed early, finally, and unambiguously. For my, part I believe that we are all placed somewhere on a scale between other-sex and same-sex attraction; and that it is human conditioning which "herds" us towards the most accessible pole. If it is true that any who call themselves bisexual are actually homosexual, it is equally true that any who call themselves heterosexual are actually bisexual. If so, then homosexuality can indeed be promoted, just as heterosexuality so relentlessly is. Why do we gay men resist the thought so angrily? If we are easy with what we are, why is it important to us that "we couldn't help it"? Does a Jew, a Catholic or a red-head need to protest that the condition is involuntary? This is to cop out of the requirement to mount a principled defence of our moral right to embrace these conditions. "We can't help it" is a demeaning argument, intended to foil the finger-waggers. But it doesn't, anyway. We can help our actions, if not our inclinations. I do not feel the need to settle the question whether a pederast can help feeling attracted to children, a kleptomaniac to shoplifting or a yob to assault, before I decide to outlaw the act – not the impulse.[28]

Weeks and Parris point to the deep cultural conditioning of our self-understandings in terms of sexual affection and practice, which is not a matter of necessity or 'nature' or being, but a complex of individual and social possibilities and their realization, objectively and subjectively. Just as the perceived restrictions imposed by the church have been rolled back, so also should the idea that each person is 'gay or straight' and should behave accordingly. The truth, they think, is that sexual desire and potential is far more fluid. The authority of traditional Christianity has been wiped away in Western society, but a binary fundamentalism

---

[28]Matthew Parris, 'In a waste of shame, spare no expense', *The Times*, 19 October 1995.

of sexuality grips Western society, even so far as being written in legal statutes. The 'discourse of sexuality', rather like the fog described by Dickens in the opening of Bleak House, has spread as far and as deep as the statute book and the courts. Now the 'repressors' are to be hunted down and made to repent, as dissent from the new moral code is deemed to infringe 'gay rights' and be 'perceived to be offensive'.

Foucault may have his vindication at this point in cultural history, since there clearly is no actual 'repression' now of any kind against any sort of sexuality, save paedophile activity, but still the spectre of reactionary repressive forces somehow remains presupposed, despite the triumphant special status accorded to people who have 'come out' as 'homosexuals' as public signs of the normality of homosexual activity. Foucault's linking of this process with medieval Christian confessional practice and repression remains deeply suggestive. Society has constructed a sort of new initiation process, the command to 'come out', to be reborn into society with a new identity which declares one's true self defined sexually through and through. Western society now knows of no core mode of sexual bonding from which others differ as minority tastes. Marriage declines as the 'bedrock' of social structures for child rearing and sexual management. The authority of the Christian ethical tradition has gone, certainly in the UK and much of Europe, replaced by a pluralism of equally valued sexual practices and bondings, probably soon to include polygamy as Islamic demands are increasingly asserted. 'Minority' identities, asserted as needing recognition and equal rights, entail a kind of authority in themselves since society has to accept their practices as of equal worth and validity as those of the non-minority. What was the 'mainline' tradition of authority and meaning in the UK has been fragmented in thoroughly postmodern fashion.

Postmodernism and Christianity

Mark C. Taylor – Erring

The intellectual project of deconstruction has indeed been taken up by theologians such as Mark C. Taylor as a way of deconstructing theology, indeed as the new matrix of theology or 'A/theology'.[29] Very much along the lines of Derrida and Turkle, Taylor wishes to do theology by playing with words – by 'tinkering', to use Turkle's term for multiple game playing and interaction. Taylor deconstructs the four key theological foundations 'God, self, history and book. By following deconstructive procedures, I

---

[29]Mark C. Taylor, *Erring: A Postmodern A/theology*, Chicago and London: University of Chicago Press, 1984.

seek to solicit the inherent instability and covert contradictions of these foundational concepts.'[30] He then seeks to set out a 'deconstructive a/theology' by reformulating these notions – 'God as writing, self as trace, history as erring, and book as text.'[31] His project reinterprets God as a process of all manner of possible meanings, rather than a transcendent being or even 'being' itself, a view of God totally different to the traditional Christian one which is taken to be oppressive, closing down variety and creativity. He rejects the divine Logos over against and spoken to the created order separated from God and obedient to God. God is not the truth of things nor the depth of things, there is no transcendent realm nor depth to plumb; the surfaces of things are all we have, and – as Sherry Turkle so usefully put it – we are playing around on these surfaces, surfing the programmes available, tinkering and fiddling, negotiating the slalom on skis as we can and wish. God is not therefore 'present' to us, rather he is absent and we glimpse ambiguous traces of the absent presence. Postmodernist deconstruction dissolves the notion of God and truth. For Taylor theology is erring, wandering, surfing. For him:

> The inescapability of erring calls into question the notion of truth that lies at the heart of the Western theological and philosophical network. Whether implicitly or explicitly, truth and God are usually identified: *Deus est Veritas* and *Veritas est Deus*. The dominant theological position in the West is of course monotheism. This monotheism is both directly and indirectly related to the notion of truth. Insofar as God is one, truth is one. From this point of view, the true is never plural, multiple and complex but always unified, single and simple. This unity, singularity and simplicity lend truth its abiding character. In contrast to ephemeral temporal flux, truth is believed to be eternal. Truth does not change. The opposition between eternal verity and timely fashion is generally described in terms of the difference between reality and appearance.[32]

Postmodernism rejects these dualities of reality and appearance, inner and outer truth, eternal and temporal, changeless and changing, and Christianity is taken as assuming the Platonic or Kantian dualisms of the phenomenal and the real. The quest for truth and for this God is a 'futile effort to escape the world of appearances', and 'when time and eternity are regarded as exclusive opposites, the affirmation of one is the denial of the other'.[33] Final truth is never found, the final meaning never reached, rather we move from sign to sign and appearance to appearance, there is no transcendent Logos, no 'depth reality' sustaining all the realities, no 'Being' behind beings. There are no foundations to discover, 'Truth

---

[30]Ibid., p. 13
[31]Ibid.
[32]Ibid., p. 175.
[33]Ibid., p. 176.

is never totally present'[34] and we shift from ambiguity to ambiguity. It is of course strange that Taylor never applies his own deconstruction to his own theory: the one 'truth' we are bidden to accept is that there is no truth, only ambiguity and playfulness – but does this not reduce his own interpretation to one of many surfaces? The fate of reductivist philosophy is always to undermine itself, and this is not addressed by the post moderns who curiously lack as sense of humour at this point of their own sermonic rhetoric, summoning us to a conversion of thought.

But postmodernist deconstruction undoubtedly affects Christian claims to authoritative revelation of the truth of God in Christ. Scripture is of course radically deconstructed so as to provide nothing more a text repeating and sharing in other texts, taken up by later texts, not referring to truth external to the text, not with any final meaning. So it cannot be authoritative in any sense, even its narrative and narratives will be deconstructed and emptied of any intentional message by authors and editors of the texts composing the Bible. The postmodern condition of multiple human being rather than centred self translates into this a/ theology of wandering, erring and straying like lost sheep, not finding any guide. Texts are denied authorial intention and are opened up to all kinds of differentiating springing forth as the human reader 'navigates' through them, collecting those most appealing or stimulating, but deconstructing even those. Postmodernist analysis therefore renders the Bible and its narratives, its witness beyond itself, a sea of relativity – no kind of secure authority whatsoever rather an invitation to swim around in the floating seaweed. This is 'post liberal' since the swimmer cannot even appeal to innate morality or religious sense to help make sense of the currents and shapes and temperatures in this sea. Postmodernism has also deconstructed the 'centred self' and any ordering conscience or morality. The authority of God, of history and tradition, of scripture, have been melted down in the heat of deconstruction.

The one sure foundational rock, curiously enough, is the one truth that this deconstructive theory itself is absolute, indeed the process of deconstruction is the absolute truth to be gained by all this erring and textual meandering. There is no 'closure', no hope of 'sabbath rest', there is this purposeless movement across the surfaces of things, rather like snails leaving a 'trace' of our absent presence and listening to voices anonymously patched into texts upon texts. Death likewise is not to be taken seriously, not a 'matter of ultimate concern', but the trace of our life we leave in the text we surf and weave. Our death however does not have a quality of rounding off a life and its meaning, rather like a Buddhist view our decentred self gives its straggling ends to other lives also interweaving in the texts. Without that truth that this process is the truth – a deeply Hegelian point that the absolute is realized as

---

[34]Ibid., p. 176.

the process itself – presumably the radical postmodernists would have surrendered the capacity to speak meaningfully to one another and to engage in argument, even criticism. There would be no distinction between the sane and the insane – as Foucault teaches – and rational discourse would seep away.

The truth of the process of intratextual life seems to be revealed in the event of Jesus' death, according to Taylor, for whom the death of Jesus symbolizes the uniting of finite and infinite, history and meaning, God and sinful reality. 'The main contours of deconstructive a/theology', for Taylor, 'begin to emerge with realization of the necessary interrelation between the death of God and radical christology.'[35] Here we again note the authoritative tone of the 'necessary relation' when Taylor's insistent message is to deconstruct all such necessities of reading a text. He continues, 'Radical christology is *thoroughly* incarnational – the divine "*is*" the incarnate word.' For Taylor this means a permanent state, not a moment or event happening once, not an advent of God into history from eternity, since he has abolished this duality. 'Furthermore' he goes on,

> this embodiment of the divine is the death of God. With the appearance of the divine that is not only itself but is at the same time other, the God who alone is God disappears. The death of God is the sacrifice of the transcendent Author/Creator/Master who governs from afar. Incarnation irrevocably erases the disembodied logos and inscribes a word that becomes the script enacted in the infinite play of interpretation. To understand the incarnation as inscription is to discover the word. Embodied word is script(ure), the writing in which we are inscribed and which we inscribe.[36]

Taylor argues that this deconstruction of the word 'God' does not, like the older atheistic arguments, lead to a displacement of what 'God' stood for into the human self, the deification of the individual ego, since the postmodern 'a/theologian welcomes the death of God and embraces the disappearance of the self.'[37] Ludwig Feuerbach, in the nineteenth century, had famously asserted that God is a human projection, a word encapsulating human desires and aspirations. For Taylor on the other hand the word 'God' refers not to the human self but 'refers to the word "word" and the word "word" refers to the word "God"'. Taylor says that radical Christology means the word is forever embodied, always already inscribed, incarnation or inscription is a continual process.

Writing is not about something, it is that something itself, and writing inscribes the disappearance of the transcendental signified, the 'real'

---

[35]Ibid., p. 103.
[36]Ibid., p. 104.
[37]Ibid.

God. Perhaps we could try to explain this understanding as teaching that the incarnation, or the doctrine of the incarnation, wakes us up to the fact that the word is reality, we are already living in writing and rewriting of meaning – indeed the word is meaning and truth. Does this mean that words are meaning and truth, 'God' or the 'Spirit', 'Geist' or 'Mind', no matter how the words are aggregated together, what system of grammar binds them into lines and paragraphs and blocks? Taylor slips from 'word' to 'words' and 'writing' quite easily. A major point he denies is that words need a speaker or a writer, a self expressing human individuality through these words – the self is not an insulated entity or logos or mind issuing words, rather the self is integrated into the word system or flow. The self is rather a complex word or paragraph, whose meaning if any is provisional and never to be finalized. God is writing, the process of meaning and reality in the world, certainly not some finished product of the process which has not overarching meaning and no given goal, it just is this loose Sargasso sea of slippery words. This is what there is, there is no authority to decide what is true in this alphabet soup, since truth is the soup itself.

This a/theological appropriation of postmodernism means the end of authority as we have conceived it, given by God in creation and covenant, actualized supremely in the life, death and resurrection of Jesus, present now in the Spirit. We are committed to the sea of relativism, and need to embrace this fact. The deep irony of this of course is that we are told this is the case – authoritatively! This standard point about the self-undermining nature of all reductivisms and relativisms, that they relativize their own theories as well as their opponents', is amusing and ironical, and yet not taken by our postmodern preachers of their new world of writing. They may claim that this point derives from 'logic' and old fashioned reason, which itself must be deconstructed – but no more or less than the assertion of deconstruction? Authority in Western culture has been deconstructed, with the associated realities of truth, beauty and virtue, and God becomes the text in which we find ourselves.

This intellectual relativism chimes in very well with Western cultural consumerism, shallowness, individualism and rootlessness. God once was the accepted source of authority, then the rational self usurped the divine throne in secular modernity, and now there is what there is – a culture of clashing meanings and nothing beyond or above or below. God is not to be worshipped, virtue is not to identified, truth is now – but will differ tomorrow. The cultural hypermarket is all there is, and Western worship at this cathedral of the shallow, disposable and dispensable, rebranding way of being now our life context. We are this life, this life is us, and there is nothing else. The word, the idea, is and always was embodied, never separable from the stuff of life. To Mark C. Taylor this is great news, to many others it is a matter of despair. Theologically and religiously Taylor seems to present us with a kind of monism in which the self has been dissolved along with the transcendent God. Authority cannot be received from outside this sealed system and does not exist above or beneath the signs and language. That would be to find the imprisoning Ontotheological Logos, preventing freedom with a freezing form of rationalism and legalism.

Crucially, this Christian adoption of postmodernism destroys any claim to the universal truth of the Gospel of Jesus. Indeed, for the Church of England, postmodernism and multi culturalism are pressures against any calling of people back to faith in the Gospel, since the Gospel is to regarded as only applicable to one particular 'community', not in principle to all. This pressure is growing temptation for the established church of England, and a critical one for any institution claiming to be a church.

Part II

6

Jesus – Divine Authority Revealed

Freedom and form

In part one we have tried to describe the consecration of diversity in church and society, the pressures for relativism and the fragmentation of truth and morality in the secular state. This has pushed Christianity out of the public forum and left a vacuum of values and a state left with trying to manage competing claimants to rights, without any compass to use. We now turn to see what Christianity has to offer by way of resources to address this crisis of authority. We will argue that it offers a unique blend of freedom with form for society, and that rejecting it leads to these two poles moving to chaos or control.

Rejection of authoritarianism, deadening form, was one of the key moves made by the shapers of the Enlightenment, thinkers who were not prepared to take the teachings of the churches and the Bible on trust, without critical scrutiny, rational and moral. Postmodern rejection of authoritarianism does not accept the possibility of an authoritative voice or text or institution, however rationally or morally its case be made. Likewise the Romantic movement, accompanying the Enlightenment tradition of reasonable testing, rejected authority over the individual free spirit in the name of the nobility of the soul and its aspirations towards the sublime and the beautiful. The figure of Byron, breaking with restrictive moral conventions of society, or Rousseau's noble savage as yet untainted by social conditioning, illustrate this individual pursuit of the heart's desire in the face of any constraining authority. Authority belongs to what is reasonable in the eyes of the Enlightenment, to the call of nobility and beauty for the Romantic, with both movements rejecting the summons of any institution to be obeyed on the basis of a claim to external authority. Rejection of authority as authoritarian and oppressive, if it cannot vindicate itself, is not an invention of the postmoderns by any means. They have gone further by deconstructing the very reason which the Enlightenment trusted, and the noble self of the Romantic movement likewise is not treated as an enduring or unified reality let alone authoritative voice. Cynicism towards all claims to authority whatsoever, seems to be where we end up with the postmoderns. As Gillian Rose put it, the essence of postmodernism is the 'despair of reason'.[1] Thinking has thought away rationality and morality, even the thinker doing the thinking.

Mark Taylor's unqualified adoption of postmodernist 'erring' and a/theology is not, however, the only engagement with this powerful and highly influential Western movement. It would be a curious irony if postmodernism itself became an iron law rather than a catalyst for discussion and disagreement! Critical but constructive engagement with postmodernism in relation to theology has been undertaken by theologians such as Anthony Thiselton.[2] Thiselton accepts the importance of the theological challenge posed by postmodernist deconstruction of meta-narrative and meaning, but he does not accept the postmodernist agenda that we are consigned to the shifting, sliding phenomena as reality and truth. Thiselton accepts that postmodernist criticisms of Christianity can hit home, but argues strongly that the faith understands the human condition more profoundly and realistically than these critics. Yes, Christian history has been tarnished with manipulation and authoritarian abuse of power, but this is by no all there is to be said.

Jesus Christ – True Humanity

Christianity brings us both freedom and form, uniting to bring about true life; diversity is essential to life in its glorious freedom, but chaotic diversity ceases to be diversity at all but serial disconnected units, without a unifying factor within which there can be no diversity and differentiation. While of course church authority has too often been authoritarian and oppressive, the Jesus way itself, in the Spirit, is full of freedom and diversity and life itself. The very doctrine of God as Trinitarian means diversity in unity, continual pointing away from self to the other, mutuality and the reverse of insulation and sealed units.

---

[1]Rose, G. *The Broken Middle: Out of Our Ancient Society*. Oxford: Blackwell 1992.
[2]Anthony C. Thiselton, *Interpreting God and the Postmodern Self: On Meaning, Manipulation and Promise*, Edinburgh: T & T Clark, 1995.

Postmodernism is helpful in its critique of foundationalism and in its critical stimulus, but as Thiselton says 'an adequate account of the self and of personhood cannot stop with its situatedness in some instantaneous moment within processes of shifting flux. Selfhood discovers its identity and personhood within a larger purposive narrative which allows room for agency, responsibility and hope.'[3] Thiselton points to the narrative structure of human experience, individual and corporate, and links this with the Christian story leading to the promised goal. 'Even if postmodernity fragments the self and society into multiple role-performances, and dissolves truth into the conventions or power interests of different competing communities, the future may nevertheless hold out the possibility of reintegration on the basis of promise.'[4] Christian promise of hope and healing, of knitting up what is broken and finding one's true self in dialogue with the other, such themes are born of the life and death and resurrection of Jesus.

Moreover Jesus of Nazareth and the identification of God with this life means that God is not at all the oppressive Logos, freezing out human freedom and life by its terrifying presence. Thiselton adduces the Trinity, drawing on some of the great twentieth-century theologians such as Pannenberg and Moltmann, to show that Christology and Trinity can encompass much postmodern criticism and go beyond it. The Christian faith has the resources to embrace unity and plurality: God is no dictator or monadic first principle, rather God is love, behind, before, alongside, nurturing and healing. Moreover the church similarly is not an authoritarian loveless institution handing down edicts from a hierarchy, but is the 'Body of Christ', knit together in mutual support and care ultimately. This insight is not new, for example we can find a theologian of the early twentieth century speaking of social personality and personal society in respect of humanity and by extension of divine being.[5] Thiselton speaks of Nietzsche's 'will to power' being 'de-centred, transformed and re-centred in promise and love.'[6] We find ourselves in those who love us, and the Trinity makes good sense in the light of this most profound and humane experience – although as Austin Farrer put it, we would not have invented the doctrine of the Trinity beforehand, we are 'wise after the event'.[7] We could add that the Christian notion of salvation embraces acceptance and trust, we are bidden to trust God as revealed in Christ, notwithstanding our sins and wickedness – the shifting sands of postmodernity leave us in a lonely desert, the Christian hope gives us a network of love and care.

---

[3]Ibid., p. ix.
[4]Ibid., p. ix.
[5]A.E Garvie *The Christian Doctrine of the Godhead,* London:Hodder 1925.
[6]Ibid., p. 158.
[7]Austin Farrer, *Saving Belief,* London: Hodder and Stoughton, 1954.

Thiselton also makes the very interesting point that the postmodernist thinker can leave us no guidance for social improvement, we are left in distress and despair, or in a whimsical state of 'erring', unable to get beyond being passively situated and resituated, no earthly use to anyone else – let alone to ourselves. Marxism at least, with some deep roots in the biblical eschatological tradition of future justice, sought to locate individuals in a purposive social system – while freezing individual freedoms and creativity to the bone, thus becoming a target for postmodern deconstruction. Postmodernists not only leave themselves in the bleak world of unmeaning with no purpose, but they consign society likewise to this fate. And when all truth and purpose is gone the controllers of society are left to manipulate and manage people and their expectations, an Orwellian future indeed. Ironically, of course, the postmodernist critics do believe that our politicians and institutions are only that, agencies of power play imposing themselves on individuals with no moral shaping or purpose at all. The deep cynicism and suspicion adopted by postmodernism towards all authority structures in fact leaves the way open for violent confrontation as pillars of trust and shared values collapse.[8] Authority is an impossible notion for postmodernity, unless deconstructed into a power claim. In fact, the summons to deconstruct is itself absolute, and itself subject to deconstruction.

Thiselton reminds us that the deconstruction of reason and morality can only lead us into the darkness, and MacIntyre had said much the same, fearing a turn to fascism when the liberal experiment had splintered into pieces and no longer shaped an agreed social mores. It seems that authority, rooted in something more than pragmatism, is needed to preserve freedom in society. There is a strong argument to be made that the secularist attack on the old Protestant social tradition – which was the root of Western liberalism, a universal metanarrative of reason and morality – has led to this dangerous situation. Certainly postmodernism emphasizes pluralism and difference as an absolute good and rejects any 'shared value system' beneath diversity or any common goal uniting different cultures. For the intellectual postmodernist, authority itself is to be rejected and diversity embraced, a recipe for chaos and indeed possible communal violence in the future. Authority which is accepted, which does not crush individual liberty but nourishes it, and which promotes mutual acceptance rather than tribalism and vendetta, is necessary for a healthy culture and society. It seems that this has arisen from Christian soil, but is now being quickly eradicated with dangers not apparently realized by those who are so enthusiastically digging up the soil of the Christian moral base. The well being of Western liberal democratic society may depend on the well being of Christianity. The

---

[8]Thiselton, op. cit., p. 134.

Jewish philosopher Leo Strauss credits Nietzsche 'with having seen with unrivaled clarity that the morality of modern liberalism derives from and depends upon biblical faith,'[9] and that consequently the erasure of that faith would mean the hollowing out of liberal society. Judeo-Christian faith has proved to be the bedrock of the political achievement of the West, and the removal of the bedrock is seeing growing chaos and confusion morally. The question of authority for the good of the state is inseparable from that of the church.

For Thiselton, hermeneutics – the study of meaning of text and person – involves empathy with the 'other' not some detached observational stance but an interrelating and listening, opening the way to mutual understanding and transformation. The Bible is to be read in this light of respect and mutuality, neither imposing alien patterns onto its text nor allowing the brain to become a mere copy of the text and its victim in some unthinking way. With Paul Ricoeur, Thiselton argues against 'the self interpretation of the postmodern self as mere flotsam, driven by the surface currents of the power interests and language worlds of society',[10] proposing instead 'a theology of promise' beckoning us forward towards new hope and purpose. Indeed resurrection promises the same but new, a deconstruction perhaps of the present imperfect self to be healed and taken forward, centred but radically open to God, the God of love and joy.

Autonomy is banished, so is heteronomy in this theology of promise, but so is the individualist vision of postmodernism. Postmodern theories of signs and language do not wish to offer any thought of a convincing or probable meaning of a text, rather the reader makes his or her meaning within the world of language, an all-embracing world since there is nothing outside the text. There is no 'closure' of meaning, each sign points to the next, no text being independent of others let alone authoritative or reliable as a guide or witness to truth. The self is itself deconstructed and pluralized, so that the existence of the human mind as there to 'read' and do the deconstructing is itself in principle denied – the attack on the mind as dominating Logos, a technological entity rather than a humane moral intellectual person able to love and respond, destroys too much which is then presupposed. And for deconstruction to happen others need to be able to follow the process and join in the party at the text's expense, so a community of selves would seem to be presupposed.

---

[9]'Nietzsche's criticism can be reduced to one proposition: modern man has been trying to preserve Biblical morality while abandoning Biblical faith. That is impossible. If the Biblical faith goes, Biblical morality must go too, and a radically different morality must be accepted', Leo Strauss, *Jewish Philosophy and the Crisis of Modernity: Essays and Lectures in Modern Jewish Thought*, Albany: SUNY Press, 1997, p. 99.
[10]Ibid., p. 78.

Derrida and theologians taking his track – if his track remains traceable in the shifting sands of his text world – leave us no possible authority, good or bad, from which to take our bearings or to which to travel through life. Mark Taylor, and his equivalent Don Cupitt in his final intellectual phase, embrace this a/theology with enthusiasm. It is evidently an individualistic take on reality, connected to others through textuality, taking up and reconstructing text or meaning from the past and projecting it ahead for others to do likewise – but with no participatory community of learning or sharing of wisdom in a tradition. Thiselton much prefers the hermeneutical approach of Gadamer with his emphasis on conversation as the 'non-manipulatory mode of apprehending truth without predetermining what counts as truth in advance.'[11] Derrida's deconstructive approach depends on the individual rewriting and remaking meaning in the textuality of life, but not together with others while negotiating the problematic ambiguities of life, which he is right to stress. Derrida does not seek to dialogue with his contemporaries nor listen to voices of the past in pursuit of wisdom; such voices are fragmented into shards of meaning and suggestion, not partners in a common human cause or quest. The lonely postmodernist reader reinscribes meaning onto and from what he finds already possibly there, not in dialogue with others. Gadamer on the contrary regards 'conversation' as the open context in which something new and unexpected, can emerge 'which does not reflect the prior manipulative interests of one or more of the speakers.' This respectful listening and conversation involves 'being transformed into a communion in which we do not remain what we were.'[12] Gadamer's hermeneutic looks far more personal and less individualistic than the postmodern proposal, which is often regarded as nihilistic.

But Gadamer and Thiselton may be embracing a key Derridean point, that we have never got the truth 'tied down' or formulated or objectified, we need constantly to reformulate and try again. As Pannenberg puts it, all such claims are provisional and open to being broken into new syntheses emerging from the future.[13] The truth is personal and communal; that is a very Christian insight found at the heart of Thiselton's constructive engagement with the postmoderns and their desperate distrust of authority. His theology of promise for textual and personal meaning surely includes concern for continual improvement of our understanding, never settling for 'freezing the frame' here and now, a Derridean imperative, likewise his claim for emerging transformation as we read and converse as readers and listeners, but this is a deeper form of change than Derrida's playful puns and shocks in meaning change, with no possible moral shaping or improvement.

---

[11]Ibid., p. 70.
[12]Ibid., p. 71.
[13]W.Pannenberg, *Basic Questions in Theology vol 2*, London: SCM 1971.

This theological engagement with postmodernism, we must agree with Thiselton, holds out a much more humane and hopeful way of maintaining the need for continual questioning and probing while accepting the tacit tradition and authority of Christ, who brings church, sacraments, the Sabbath, scripture and the revelation of the divine nature with him. In terms of the current secular world, this Christ-like pattern is precisely what state and nations are rejecting in favour of the chaos of thought and reality described by the postmodernist thinkers. Politicians of the West are desperately scrabbling around in the barren dust bowl after Eden for 'shared values' as a bandage to bind up the many wounds and cuts now deepening in the body politic. The state cannot itself produce 'values', only management policies and these soon will provoke resentments and even violence with no moral common ground.

Thomas Hobbes' analysis of the state's role as violently imposing peace if necessary is the fascist threat in the face of chaos. But Jesus did not leave a political template for society: his legacy was the Holy Spirit, his life as a model for ours, and the Hebrew Scriptures' testimony about God and the goal of history. Freedom and form are indeed part and parcel of the Christian faith, but a society shaped by this faith will be one that has space for reform, improvement, questioning, and change, it will not freeze the frame with a rule book, deadening the minds, frightening people into submission with threat of punishment, and quelling exploration and originality. The Trinitarian view of human being, revealed in the grand narrative of biblical history and gathered experience culminating in Jesus, provides a far more convincing account of the human potential, predicament and way forward than the bleakness and banality of life as 'erring' as Mark Taylor puts it.

Moreover, this Trinitarian spirituality, going beyond the duality of autonomy or heteronomy, lies at the heart of the Christian faith, and this faith gradually came to influence and so shape the development of liberal Western democracy, law and social ethics. 'God has sent the Spirit of his Son into our hearts, so we cry Abba, Father!'[14] The authority of God is not imposed as by a human dictator, but reaches into the heart of responsive humanity in what John Oman called 'the omnipotence of love'. Western civilization with its distinctive democracy and social welfare systems has its roots in this imperative of transcending tribalism and loving one's neighbour as oneself. The authority of care, or charity, wove itself into societies and nations in different ways, through indirect influence and not through the imposition of a legal or social code left by Jesus or the Apostles. For state as for church it is the Spirit at work through all manner of political and social reformers which has borne

---

[14]Galatians 4:6.

fruit in representative democracy, educational and social care systems[15] as individuals have been led to campaign for humane change. While the state cannot create virtue or compel good behaviour, it can damage it as it hacks at the roots of Christianity in hostile fashion.

Narrative

The more the influence of Jesus and his way of life spread, the more compassionate and less tribal society became. This way cannot be enforced – that is not the mode of authority of Jesus who sought to evoke free personal response to divine grace. The postmodern rejection of authoritarianism is part of properly Christian theology, the postmodern rejection of all authority is not. The crucified and risen Jesus, the one who was put to death by the most powerful political empire of his day, gradually came to shape and form the political order of the Western world over two millennia through the faith and practice of his disciples. It may well be that only a renewal of Christianity can fuel a recovery of a social order in which freedom and order can coincide, rather than either chaos or authoritarian rule.

The authority of Jesus is a unique kind of authority, a revelation of divine holiness and love as this impacts on human behaviour, a revelation which empowers when accepted. This is a personal authority rather than an institutional authority, and it broke open a new history from the history of the life, death and resurrection of Jesus. We have already heard Professor Thiselton's powerful point that the resurrection of the dead Jesus points to the theology of hope and promise, to newness of life, to breaking open old horizons of bondage, to deconstructing fixed and imprisoning ideas about ourselves and the human condition which lead us to despair. In terms of dialogue with establishment postmodernism, Jesus subverts the power and manipulation of state and hierarchy by his decision to go to Jerusalem and unmask the truth of the situation. Or again, in Derridean vocabulary, Jesus 'inscribes' on the Hebrew text he belongs to a loving and trustful 'sign' pointing to God, and hoping in God alone.

The resurrection of Jesus not only points to a meaning of the whole of the text of history, but affirms that this end meaning now challenges and judges the experience of current texts and meanings. This truth and reality also shows that personal truth exists in temporal and 'textual' meaning, and that the transcendent is 'personal', self-accommodating to finite freedom and giving it purpose. The Christian story is that Jesus in

---

[15]The UK National Health Service is described as the "model of health care as a secular church", leglislated by Aneurin Bevan" (Rudolf Klein, *The New Politics of the NHS* London: Longman 1995.

his life, death and resurrection has deconstructed the text of human sin and granted a new thread of meaning from the old, corrupted, sclerotic and dying condition of self-obsessed humanity.

Theological interpretations of the resurrection of Jesus as a mere story are not part of the New Testament's own understanding of this crucial event. Those who understand the resurrection as a myth find themselves in the curious position of affirming a myth whose meaning is that the resurrection actually happened in space and time, a myth being precisely the opposite of an actual event. Or to put in terms of postmodern textuality, as Francis Watson pithily says with reference to Luke's Gospel,

> But if this risen Jesus is *purely* the creation of the narrator, then he is a being not of flesh and bones but of words, incorporeal as a spirit. In other words, to read this narrative as self-enclosed is to fall prey to precisely the docetism that it so emphatically opposes…The corporeality of the risen Lord implies his refusal to be bound within the constraints of textuality.[16]

The resurrection of Jesus, as Pannenberg argues, anticipates the end time finale of history, giving its meaning and revealing God as triune, confirming Jesus' identity as divine, revealing divine self-giving at the heart of God's very being. The resurrection of Jesus is interpreted in the light of the Jewish hope of apocalyptic final judgement, marked by the resurrection of the dead. Jesus' resurrection, for Pannenberg,[17] indicates this end time in advance, a final vindication of the meaning of history and of God's purposes in all the ambiguities and problems of history. While Pannenberg, no doubt, would come under the postmodernists' attack for adducing rational evidence for his view, his understanding of history as producing ever new horizons of meaning, breaking open the existing understandings, seems to satisfy postmodern demands – the difference being that God is behind the new understandings rather than simply an insulated human deconstructive mind.

Pannenberg argues that Christians believe in Jesus' resurrection on the grounds of historical evidence and probability that there is a real intellectual claim to accept the resurrection of Jesus as an event that did happen, and that therefore the authority of divine revelation has been declared, the last judgement announced in the life and death of Jesus. While Pannenberg's historical arguments can obviously be debated, his overall theology of Jesus' resurrection as confirming Jesus' intimacy with God and his assertion of Jewish apocalyptic as the key context for understanding this event, is convincing. He could emphasize more deeply the significance of the crucifixion in the apocalyptic expectation of resurrection and vindication: the crucifixion of Jesus, as P. T. Forsyth

[16]Francis Watson, *Text, Church and World*, Edinburgh: T & T Clark, 1994, p. 292.
[17]W.Pannenberg *Revelation as History*, New York: Macmillan 1969.

put it, was the last judgement come in advance.[18] The ongoing 'textuality' and its rewriters do not have the potential to save themselves, to bring history to reconciliation and healing, but such salvation and healing must be integrated into this vast flow of textual reality to have effect: judgement and grace is given by God in Jesus, a judgement which gives hope and forgiveness from the end of the story back into its centre. The whole object of the Christian witness to the meaning and authority of history is that it needs divine redemption and has not the power to save itself, eschatological coming to humanity in Christ is the simple and powerful reality able to heal the human predicament, a new non-dictatorial transcendence is revealed as the source of reality and truth in this saving act of God in Christ and the Spirit. Divine authority has been revealed in and over history as Jesus and the kingdom he inaugurated by dying, rising, and leaving nothing but his disciples, the Spirit, and the Hebrew tradition from which Jesus came and against which he interpreted his life and work.

As we read the text of Scripture we, rather than it, are deconstructed and rewritten, since the Spirit promises to touch us in our reading, listening, preaching, and repenting in the house of the texts. As baptised people we read as dying to our old selves and rising in Christ afresh, broken and remade. 'Reading Scripture', says John Webster, is best understood as an aspect of mortification and vivification: to read Holy Scripture is to be slain and made alive. And because of this, the rectitude of the will, its conformity to the matter of the gospel, is crucial, so that reading can only occur as a kind of brokenness, a relinquishment of willed mastery of the text of the encounter with God in the which the text is the instrument.'[19] As for Barth, the reader ends up as the object of the text mediating the Word to us: as we read in faith and patience, we are judged and deconstructed, not the text. On the other hand, the Word has made himself known in the narrative that is Jesus Christ.

The free and liberating Word

Jesus Christ, then, is the supreme authority in, with and under human history, an empathetic authority of love, an authority supporting freedom and creativity, a purposive authority seeking fellowship and acceptance. This is no paralysing or dominating Logos, freezing and unifying the diversity of creation into pure mind.[20] The Christian Gospel uniquely

---

[18]*The Justification of God*, London: Duckworth, 1916, p. 205 passim.
[19]John Webster, *Holy Scripture*, Cambridge: Cambridge University Press, 2002, p. 11.
[20]See John Zizioulas, *Being as Communion*, New York: St Vladimir's Seminary Press, 1985, p. 72, for a criticism of platonistic 'Logos' theology which fails to register the incarnation in the actualities of history.

defines this as God's authority revealed and accommodated in human historical conditions, an authority attracting recognition from ordinary people of Jesus' time – 'he spoke as one with authority'. (Matt 7.29). His life was unique for its honesty and care for the unfashionable and unregarded, women equally as men, refocusing his own Scriptural tradition, a major factor in his self understanding and the identity yielded up for him by his death and resurrection. His prayer life, as Pannenberg stresses, disclosed a close intimate trust of God, called Father by Jesus, and opened the way for the radically new insight into God's very being that there is relational 'structure' or form to God, a giving and receiving, a sensitivity of love and responsiveness in the very divine nature. God has not fully revealed himself in text or rules or feelings but in a life: when we see the life of Jesus we see the divine and the divine response to human thought and act.

God the Creator and author of all things is so transcendent as to be free to enter the creation and the 'text' or the play of life, to enter space and time and meaning. Divine authority, in other words, desires acceptance by way of free assent and glad response, not by way of enforced of terrorized 'submission' – *'mysterium tremendum et fascinans'*, a terrifying divine presence reducing its object to paralysed fearful obedience, is not the Christian revelation or insight. 'God is Christlike, and in him is no unchristlikeness at all', said Archbishop Michael Ramsey. The God of Israel and of Jesus Christ is the judge of all the earth, to whom all are responsible for their lives and deeds, to whom all should look as the way, the truth and the life, the great divine authority who has enacted free acceptance of this creative authority in human history. This authority is not divorced from those summoned to obey, calling across a vast gap as a dog owner to a dog. Rather this authority empathetically enters into the life of those who need to hear and obey: authority is redefined in Christ and the Spirit, as the Father loves and sends the Son to his own created order.

The Christian Gospel of God is strikingly unique. For Islam, as Cragg says, God is supremely great – a conviction common to all the theisms of Hebrew lineage. The issue that divides them is precisely how this divine supremacy is to be understood. What makes God great? Cragg contends patiently that Islam misunderstands the greatness of God when it deflects the issue of human perversity into the political dimension, where rejection is subdued rather than redeemed. Cragg argues that Muhammad's recruitment of the political wing was a necessary corollary of his belief that prophethood exhausts the divine resources for dealing with human sin and rebellion. God has warned through his spokesmen; men disregard and ignore, and need to be taught a lesson. When divine warning fails to cure perversity – the pen runs out of ink – the sovereignty that has no richer resources than law must opt for coercion. For God must succeed; and yet God's Party – Hizb Allah, in Qur'anic terminology – has run out of the only arsenal allowed to the truly faithful. If the prophet sticks to his guns, so to speak, the message is not merely taught but enforced. The sword then becomes mightier than the pen. In that sense, God and His Messenger do indeed have the last word. But the Christian Gospel entails divine sovereignty acting through human freedom and so evoking free response by grace. This also reveals the life giving character of God.[21]

This is the Christian gospel, however much it has been distorted and reversed in the history of the church: Jesus Christ, the divine Son, the divine way of being of comes sacrificially to those in need of salvation. Jesus is an Israelite as a matter of human fact and act, his tradition and context, cannot be separated from his very identity and being. This is critical to the Christian portrait of Jesus and his authoritative message: he is not a figure to be torn from his context and repackaged to suit contemporary tastes, however convenient that might be to many current movements and campaigns.

Witness to Jesus – Theological and historical

In the history of Christian faith the figure of Irenaeus of Lyons helped develop this key point over against the groups called *'Gnostics'*. These groupings believed that human beings need to escape the material world, which is fundamentally evil and the product of an evil god: the Creator god of the Old Testament. A greater deity sent Jesus to rescue us from space and time by giving us special knowledge, gnosis, to enable us to detach from the created order, escape its evil taint and attain the higher, purer realms of the true deity of Jesus, not the Creator of this world. This Gnostic gospel was widespread and attractive in an era of many religions, cults and philosophies, a syncretistic age in which elements of different religions were mingled with others. In many ways this era of the Roman Empire resembled our own 'postmodern' era intellectually and spiritually, with its jostling sects and claims, appeal to experiential novelty and rejection of old fashioned Roman moralism and rationalism. There was also a deep cynicism about truth claims and human virtue. Roman citizens had rights, slaves had none; the absurd cult of emperor worship was colluded with at the expense of moral seriousness.

The Hebrew faith was tolerated, although often subject to bouts of scapegoating persecution, and its monotheism and moral code was deeply attractive to many gentiles. Bread and circuses for the poor worked well, as consumerism and football today distract many from any serious moral life. Postmodern despair in any purpose to history, postmodern failure to engage with the brutalities and immoralities of

---

[21]K.Cragg, *Muhammed and the Christian*, Oxford: Oneworld 1999.

culture, all these connect with Western relativism, hedonism, and quasi-religious superstition. Alongside this was Platonistic philosophy and the attempt to find meaning in the universe in its transcendent stable forms, philosophy often mingling with the Stoic moralism long attractive to serious minded Roman republicans who disliked the banality and kitsch of the new Imperial Rome of the Caesars. A kind of despairing postmodern relativism matched today's mood: everything is permitted, each group and sect has its own ways and customs, none is universally valid.

Irenaeus, originally from Asia Minor, rebutted Gnostic interpretations – we might say 'deconstructions' – of Jesus with a mixture of robust theology, history and practice. The Hebrew Scriptures did not teach a different god to that of Jesus, he in fact fulfilled the purposes of the Creator God attested by Israel and he constantly pointed towards the God of Israel as his Father. The Creator God of Israel's Scriptures was the God of Jesus, there was no divorce between them. The kingdom of God ushered in by Jesus fulfilled the divine plan, healing what was broken, putting right what was torn and wrong, and revealing God as present to his people. Irenaeus united what the Gnostics put asunder, creation and redemption, first Adam and second Adam, Old Testament and New Testament. Christ restored what had been marred by the human race, restoring creation to what it was intended to be by God, the great act of obedience at Calvary reversed the act of disobedience by Adam in the Garden of Eden.

Irenaeus rejected the Gnostic gospels and accepted only the four gospels, albeit with some reasons being rather strange to us today, but his theological instincts towards salvation history and against Gnostic magic were evidently at work in this judgement. The ministry of Jesus implements God's creative intention and his kingdom is relevant to all mankind, not just to a special interest group, the authority of God applies to the created order and the human race. The death and resurrection of Jesus, for Irenaeus, are a cosmic victory over evil and a recapitulation of the human race, reorientating it from its wayward disobedient state. This is for all people, not just an intracultural group, the linking of Jesus with the Creator's work of healing what is torn and wounded underlines the universality of the gospel. Jesus' moral victory at the cross is shared with all who have faith in him, offered to all human history so as to fulfil the creative intention of God.

Christ's influence is here by the Holy Spirit's presence: the Word or Son is not suddenly absent, but present differently – and not in the mode of 'presence' so feared by the postmodernists, the dominating and paralysing presence, not authoritarian but loving and creative authority weaving the spiritual way of Jesus into the heart of disciples. The kingdom of God is instituted by Jesus and constituted by the Spirit in a Trinitarian interlacing. Again the key text from Paul compels itself on the Christian

mind, 'God has sent the Spirit of his Son into our hearts, so we cry
Abba, Father' (Galatians 4:6) – worship is the truest response to divine
authority, worship and joyful gratitude and the Holy Spirit, according to
the promises of Jesus and the teaching of the prophets and apostles found
in the Bible, is the way of God's being making Jesus Christ 'yesterday,
today and forever' in human time. We might say that grateful and joyful
worship in the Spirit – being taken up by God to praise God, a heavenly
eschatological worship involving participation and identification with
Jesus way of being – is the deep antidote to cynicism about life as it
affirms the sheer worth of God and all God's creation.

The Spirit's way of being catches us up and orientates us toward the
Father in the passion and energy of the Son. In our worship we share
in and fulfil the worship of Israel, and the earliest church knew this as
it placed the threefold 'qadosh' at the heart of the practice of the holy
communion, the eucharist – 'Holy Holy Holy, Lord God of Hosts, Heaven
and Earth are full of Thy glory': the vision of Isaiah in the Temple as the
angel carried the burning coal from the altar, symbol of divine holiness,
to touch the unclean lips of the prophet Isaiah, thus cleansing and calling
him. Isaiah's response, the threefold cry of worship to the holy God, is
the cry of one taken up into the sacrificial love of God, the 'eucharistic'
worship of thanksgiving for God's pure gift of forgiveness.

The Hebrew origins of Jesus, in terms of his being and his being
known, are at the centre of the church wars on sexual ethics and
multiculturalism, and also at the centre of the gathering storm of moral
chaos in Western civilization. The medium and the message cohere in
the strongest way as the divine Word made flesh unites Creator and
creation on the stage of history, in the blood, sweat, toil and tears of
Romano-Jewish politics, and this event gains recognition and memory,
enacts a deep and wide human movement of behaviour and hope, gains
a witness in the immediate disciples and apostles and textual impression.
The gritty fact of the incarnation, of witness in the Spirit by disciples, of
craggy texts before and after the life, death and resurrection of Jesus, Old
and New Testaments, this all holds together in content and form, a living
complex of 'good news', the fulfilment of God's purpose for humanity as
a gift which needs only to be received, but needs to be received. The Old
Testament's many and various texts directly and indirectly point to the
incarnation of the Word.

Gerhard von Rad discusses the prophets Ezekiel and Jeremiah, both
called to speak the word to their communities – often words highly
unpopular and rejected by their hearers, words of judgement and
predictions of impending disaster. These strange bearers of the word found
their calling almost impossibly painful, preaching 'against' their own
people for failing to heed the word of the Lord and now summoned to
repent and face the horrors of military defeat and enslavement. Jeremiah
at one time is thrown down a well shaft in Jerusalem to shut him up

and perhaps kill him, suppressing the word. Von Rad comments that this is getting close to the incarnation of the word,[22] the identification of the word of God with the life of the prophet who suffers for his faithfulness to this word – Jeremiah suffers for his identification with the word he must deliver. Moreover Jeremiah remains with his people pastorally, he cares passionately for them and remains with them whatever the cost to himself. Ezekiel engages in prophetic symbolism of his message, sometimes in painful mimes, such as lying on his side for days on end, again in a weak sense 'incarnating' the word. Yet neither Jeremiah nor Ezekiel 'are' the word; there is a distinction between their human persons and the word they speak and enact – with Jesus this distinction dissolves, he 'is' the Word.

We can see a definite continuum, consummated in Jesus the Word lived out in actual human life. Words spoken, enacted, effective, evocative were written down and copied; Jeremiah and Ezekiel became recognized as speaking the message from God, Jesus was recognized as the promised one, the Messiah or Christ. The traditions handed on by oral and written means were accessible and public, not secret, open to all to hear and consider. Their authority came from their substance and content, found by many to be powerful and life changing. That this rich content was later accepted as imbued with the divine is the pattern of the canon of Scripture: the message compelled itself on the community who kept it and sought to live by it, becoming a strand in the mediation of divine authority, and a very rich complex strand comprising all kinds of literary forms. Scripture came before the canon of Scripture, as Shakespeare's plays came before the canon of those plays, their quality impressing and convincing the community, causing their collection and preservation. The gradual process of collecting and keeping the texts did not create their authority, but recognized them as authoritative in their content, reflecting divine wisdom and truth.

This process was not a systematic one, far more of a river than a canal, far more reflecting the divine purposes working through human free will and historical conditions not blasting artificially and mathematically through human historical granite. The Old Testament ranges through millennia, and ranges through all manner of literary types, from almost 'neat' historical lists and genealogies to heavily interpreted history, to poetic stories pregnant with meaning, to prophecy, moral teaching, cultic instruction, sayings of a very pragmatic kind, all 'random' and arising from historical circumstance of this covenant people in all their faithfulness and waywardness – something that is definitely not airbrushed away. The early Christians were Jews who accepted what we now call the Old Testament canon,[23] and the writings of the New Testament gradually

---

[22]G von Rad, *The Message of the Prophets*, London: SCM 1968.
[23]For example Romans 9–11 and the claim that the Jews are the keepers of the Old Testament covenant writings.

came to be accepted as the complement to that, Revelation and Hebrews being the last to be settled. The witnesses and disciples of the Jesus, particularly the Apostles, initially played the role later played by the New Testament, seeking to hand on a picture of Jesus' life and teaching, his death and resurrection, against the background of the Old Testament. The New Testament writings are born of the intensely practical situation of missionary and pastoral work, for instance Paul sending letters to churches to encourage them in their faith and practice, and in so doing unfolding the implications of Jesus, laying down doctrine for Christian discipleship. The Old Testament is constantly drawn on in the New, to show Jesus as the climax of the purposes of God for all humanity and indeed all creation, revealing the heart of God as love.

The Christian Gospel arguably outdoes the postmodernist deconstruction of text with the claim that the text's message is lived out, dies and rises, taking the text to a new level of life and meaning, rescuing it from the ocean of everlasting deconstruction and rewriting, bringing it to relate to us in a way beyond mere meaning and significance.

While there clearly are complex strands beneath the written texts and fierce critical debates on the face of the texts – prophetic denunciations of merely cultic religion alongside moral indifference, for example – there is not the quixotic rewriting desired by Derrida. Questioning, lamenting, perplexed puzzling, irony and complaint, are all very much part of the Hebrew tradition of engaging honestly with God. It may perhaps be the case that texts were written contradicting the tradition, but that these were discarded, likewise that prophecies were declared but proved somehow hollow, and again fell away from the collection. The New Testament canon, as Irenaeus' work shows, developed with no little struggle and argument, the Gnostic gospels failing to convince the Christians and proving contradictory to the clear pattern of creation, redemption, and eschatology of the divine purposes for humankind.

Derrida's point that nothing is ever said in final form, that there will always be loose ends, always more to say and bring out, does mesh with the 'already-not yet' shape of eschatology in Christ and his resurrection, since the full significance and richness of this can never be pinned down as if in some definitive summary. Scripture is authoritative and essential for all Christian practice and teaching, and is far from 'frozen' in form and content, which is why the Bible is read our loud in churches and its texts used by preachers as they seek to allow the text, the voices behind the text, to speak now so we are addressed by the apostles and prophets and sages. The Christian Gospel envisages authority as the living Word of the creator, revealed in Christ.

In fact the text comes to life – or lives in the lives of those today – in many ways: the eucharist, baptisms, praises and laments, gathering people together on the Sabbath day. This is far from a mentalist 'understanding' in the mind, but a concrete embodiment of the text by communities. Nor is this just an obedience of inscripted rules, nor a memorizing the text onto the mind to repeat word for word, it is a freedom and form coming together in a transformative life act of reception and thanks, essentially a kind of baptismal pattern.

Just as theatre-goers will return to new performances of the same play and gain new insights, so with the biblical texts. This, again, is in line with the postmodern insight against 'closure' and the idea that nothing new can come from the text, that truth is extracted from texts as juice from an orange which then has done its job. The Scriptural texts do contain propositions and truths referring to historical, moral, aesthetic and theological facts, but the texts communicate afresh and need to be read and heard. Scripture's authority in church life is embedded in the formal documents of all denominations, but practically in all congregational worship, and in such matters as ordination of clergy adherence to Scripture is always a prerequisite for ministers, priests and bishops. The grand narrative of Scripture is integral to the deepest grammar of church life, the very air the church breathes, inhales and exhales. Text becomes voice in sermons all round the globe probably hourly, readings, expositions, interpretations, performances, hymns, prayers, eucharists, all root back to God in Christ told in words to the churches today, as a basis and yet a living basis shaping and challenging life today.

The life of the Word

Richard Bauckham points out that the particularity of the biblical texts, narratives and letters, for example, written about specific times and situations, is a key factor in considering the nature of Scripture, a factor acknowledged by the postmodernists as against 'modernism' of the Enlightenment rationalist tradition. The rationalist tradition gave no regard to actual lived customs and traditions, narratives of particular peoples, seeking instead an absolute rational and moral ground-plan to fit all situations, abstract principles implemented on actual life. The French Revolution is taken to be the archetypal secular rationalist revolt against custom and irrational privilege, in that case overthrowing a regime perpetuating injustice – but producing mass bloodshed and suffering on a still grander scale. The goddess 'reason' proved to be a cruel substitute for the ancient regime, and indeed unreasonable.

As Bauckham says, the scientific model cannot be applied to all aspects of human life, as if everything can be 'cut and squared' and organized like a chemical process. Human life is bedded into contexts, histories and customs, some of which are indeed in need of reform, some not. Rationalism is not reasonableness: the former has a much narrower scope, the latter will encompass wider aspects of humanity such as the moral, the aesthetic, the historical, the customary. In terms of our secular law, the problems now emerging over 'rights' is very much related to this point: rights in the abstract do not in fact exist – they depend on duties being performed by others and are thus rooted in social contexts. A 'right to a job' does not exist if there are no jobs to be had, that 'right' depends on the actualities of life.

Bauckham rejects the rationalistic notion that a text can be filleted of its meaning, so as not to need to be consulted ever again, as if the meaning can be extracted once and for all given a proper application of the scientific principles of interpretation, rendering further readings of the text redundant. This kind of approach is very much a scientific one and no doubt excellent for solving quadratic equations, but quite irrelevant for reading texts such as plays, poetry, essays and literature generally, nor for historical documents, nor texts with any human cultural dimension. Shakespeare's plays will continue to be read and pondered, Mozart's operas to be performed over again, Wordsworth's poetry, Spinoza's philosophy, and countless other such texts and scores, likewise. We have never got such texts 'taped'. This is the important point in Derrida's work. Bauckham also points out that the old 'quest for the historical Jesus' conducted in the nineteenth century assumed that scholarship could probe beneath the texts to get at a more real history, and so again peel away the skin to get at the fruit lying beneath. This is an attempt to extract a history that is observable and controllable, in the same way as a biologist seeks to identify a gene within a cell under a powerful microscope or computer technology.

This questing, for Bauckham, imposes a modernist grid on the text with all sorts of assumptions entailed, notably the idea that raw 'fact' can be got at and that 'meaning' can be wholly peeled away. He says that postmodernity is right to reject this mode of approach with its universalizing template in favour of accepting the particular and culturally relative aspects of historical narrative as very important and meaningful ways of communicating truth. The problem with the postmodernists is that they swing too much to the equal and opposite mistake of making their subjectivity the dominating template imposed on the text. Postmoderns, he says, reject the idea of any fixed universal meaning, rather the reader is the authority to find meaning in the text and so dominate it.

> Postmodernism represents a radical reaction against universal reason in favour of the particular. In that sense, it may look more friendly to the biblical tradition. But postmodern relativism favours the particular only by reducing all truth claims to preference. To the authority of the Bible's claim to truth which is valid for all people postmodernism is probably even less hospitable than modernism.[24]

---

[24]Richard Bauckham, *Scripture and Authority Today,* Cambridge: Grove, 1999, p. 9.

Modernism at least agrees that the text refers to something objective, postmodernism regards the texts as the interlocking sign system with no reference possible outside this textuality tapestry, and no controls or criteria as to an agreed or established sense in the text. Postmodernism seeks to reject external authority of any kind in the interests of making space for individuals to make up their own mind and not be pressed or deceived into obeying a power imposed on them. This is clearly a worthy aim, upholding human freedom to think and decide for themselves, but this aim alone is insufficient to avoid a radical individualism equivalent to intellectual consumerism and moral relativism, a bleak value-free world.

And a major question arising must be the quality of the interpretation of texts woven in a very, very different context to this Western cultural consumerism. The 'moderns' at least can use their historical critical scholarship to gain a picture of the culture of biblical eras, however loose. In fact gospel historians such as the Jewish scholars Geza Vermes and Martin Goodman think that the synoptic gospels give a very accurate picture of the world of Judea some two millennia ago, and that the critical Christian scholars are far too sceptical in their reading of these texts.[25] The moderns are surely right to seek Jesus as a historical figure, which the texts intend to assert, but wrong in going about it with a single approach, looking past the voices of the textual writers and contributors as if they were irrelevant, and as if form and content can be sharply split apart.

George Tyrrell famously said of this liberal quest for the historical Jesus that it resembled a middle-class scholar looking down a long well and seeing his own reflection, that what he expected and assumed would be the result of paring away ancient ideas and testimony rationally by modern techniques. One might say that such scientific scholars seemed little aware of their own cultural relativity, and obsessed with evaporating away cultural features of the text, whereas postmodernists are so overwhelmed by awareness of cultural contextuality as to fall into total relativism and thereby scepticism of truth and meaning as objective at all – truth is the individual's truth, nothing wider or longer lasting.

The rationalist liberal approach of the enlightenment and the mono-textual approach of the postmodernists each have their points. The latter bestows freedom on the readers to be allowed to find meaning in the texts, not to be browbeaten by the 'experts', who claim to have distilled out the proper and allowable substance from the texts. One might even say that the postmoderns have something of the Reformation on their side there: as Tyndale said, he translated the New Testament to put the Scriptures into the hands of everyone, including the boy who drives the plough; they are not just for the professionals. But, as Bauckham indicates,

---

[25]Geza Vermes, *The Religion of Jesus the Jew,* London: SCM Press, 1993, chapter 1.

the postmodernists make a wrong move in thinking that the texts can mean whatever the individual thinks, that there is no possibility of any misreading, or less plausible reading. The texts are about something beyond my subjective ideas and emotions, and yet of course these are crucial in any reading and understanding. There is freedom in addressing the texts, and yet there is form, bringing about historicity as our free selves, in Christ, are energized and illumined in the Spirit.

I suspect we need to embrace the widest possible view of truth here, using the widest possible array of examples and parallels to illustrate this. Coleridge, the great poet and thinker, said of Scripture that is 'inspired because it is inspiring', seeking to move from a rigid fundamentalism of text and truth as wooden. Yes, Christians do find Scripture often inspiring, sometimes perhaps healthily challenging, or temporarily depressing, if they have sinned and find divine demands to repent and engage with the processes of holy life? The question for Coleridge then is why is the Bible inspiring, what quality has it to inspire – or does the Spirit use it, as a kind of magic text, lighting it up as we read it? Far more likely it is the substance, the content, of the texts that moves us and inspires us, as well no doubt as the matching forms. 'When I survey the wondrous cross, on which the Prince of Glory died, my richest gain I count but loss, and pour contempt on all my pride,' wrote the poet and hymn writer Isaac Watts in 1707, encapsulating supremely the spirituality of the Christian faith, expressing the essential content of what the core message of the New Testament says, 'rewriting it' – and there is this enduring content, substance, 'Sache' as the German theological lexicon might say to repeat, represent.

The Jewish philosopher and Bible translator Martin Buber asked in a lecture, 'Meinen wir ein Buch? Wir meinen die Stimme': Do we mean a book? We mean the Voice. The living nature of Scripture, the dynamic word coming through the written words, was to him the essence of the Bible. He continued his questions by asking 'Do we mean that one should learn to read? We mean that one should learn to listen.'[26] The word of the Lord mediates itself to us as we listen to the voice of God coming to us in and through the texts. This is the same kind of mediation as the sermon by the preacher, seeking to bring the word of God to the congregation today, through a meditation on the historic texts of the community. Karl Barth developed a very similar view of how the 'written word' dynamically points us to the revealed word, who is Christ, and our task is to listen and attend to this revealed word and be at one with it in the Spirit. This listening and responding happens in all sorts of ways, from personal reading to listening to sermons to conversations and to church practices such as sharing the eucharist, baptisms, and worship.

---

[26]Martin Buber from a lecture delivered in 1926, 'Der Mensch von Heute und die juedische Bibel', *in Die Schrift und ihre Verdeutschung*, Berlin: Schocken Verlag, 1936, p. 45.

All this is steeped in Scripture and in the living Word present in the Spirit. The presence of the Word is in the Christian nurse's kind hands in her care for the sick, and in all kinds of other ripple effects in church and society. She acts as the Wisdom of the universe there and then, for that patient's comfort and healing, she is a sacrament of Christ's care.

We conclude this description of God's authority revealed in Christ by emphasising its personal character. God does not compel his creatures by coercive power, rather true authority is revealed in Christ as working through freedom, through the omnipotence of love. Service is perfect freedom, freedom is true freedom in the form of Christlikeness. Authority confers liberty and form which is not imprisoning but fulfilling. Here we see true authority, freedom rather than chaos, form rather than control. This is personal truth and authority at work in the real world, moral but not legalistic, objective but not inflexible nor irrelevant to new situations in the future. And God's authority is universal, for everyone, not a select few. To privatise this truth is not Christian, but by its very nature it cannot be compulsorily enforced, as Jesus reveals. To the dismay of secular politicians and bureaucrats, they cannot purchase altruism nor compel it. It is a Christian virtue.

God has revealed his authority as loving kindness and holiness in the man Jesus, made present in the Spirit. God is Trinitarian in being multi dimensional, being in creation and yet beyond it and creation rests in divine sustaining. We find authority in God as Father, Son and Spirit as this divine life addresses and inspires us. Referring back to Part 1 above and the needs of authority in society which brings together both freedom and form, liberty and framework, objective and subjective, morality, feelings, reason, and beauty - the doctrine of the Trinity holds these together in the divine life. Here is the core of a Christian view of authority. We now continue to explore this reality as it affects our life in history and creation.

7

Responding in Christ to Divine Desire

Worshipping God – Freedom and form

We now move to consider the human response to, and participation in, divine authority, will and desire. This is a free response, formed in Christ, to the Father, empowered by the Spirit. The Christian believes that we live in the created order sustained constantly by the surrounding love of God, whether acknowledged or not. The primary Christian response to this divine love is worship, being taken up with Christ in the Spirit to praise God as Father. I would like to begin with worship as the core response of faith and praise. Worship authoritatively cures all cynicism about the value of creation and the point of life. The ordinary hymn, for example, taking us out of ourselves, directs us to God, the giver of all creation and its possibilities.

Hymns are personal poetic responses to the text and its divine subject, and they reprise and resonate the gospel message – through individual circumstances, very honestly and with profound power. Content and individual space: the great hymns and psalms incorporate and rewrite what the moderns and postmoderns seek – we have never said the last thing about Christ, there is always a new expression, and indeed also rediscovering old and deep insights perhaps forgotten. The slave trading sailor, John Newton, encountered Christ and accepted judgement and grace as he renounced his sinful life and became a clergyman, most famously writing his hymn 'Amazing grace how sweet the sound, that saved a wretch like me'.[1] Scottish pastor George Mattheson had gone blind, and his fiancée had left him in the process, and the night before his sister's wedding he felt utterly bereft as he was reminded of his own loss and about to lose his carer, his sister. In five minutes, during his deep pain, he wrote his hymn 'O love that wilt not let me go', containing the verse: 'O joy that seekest me through pain', expressing the way of the disciple in Christ's death and resurrection. Mattheson writes his own experience of desperate pain and perplexity, into the gospel of Christ. In terms of the postmodernist analytical grid, Mattheson's hymn is no praising of a dominating and repressive deity who has meted out suffering and demands unquestioning submission, rather this is a radical engagement with God about the experience of suffering and faith, a dialogue finding its core in the eschatological hope of Christ crucified and risen. Christian spiritual response, at its most deep, combines the tears of the Calvary inside the joy of resurrection hope, banishing despair, cynicism and sentimentalism.

This Christian hymn stands in the same narrative as the Hebrew Psalm, often calling on God in the face of unjust suffering, protesting to God, protesting against God – this is the covenant giving God of relationship and dialogue, of honesty and reality, not a remote dictatorial divine authority whose has willed events and demands, submission and resignation. Watts, Newton and Mattheson related their own personal unique stories of life in faith and doubt to the grand narrative of God the Creator and redeemer, the narrative with the sharpest of focuses in Jesus. Jesus himself is God in microcosm, the stories of the hymn writers share in this Jesus story, the crucible of the covenant of God and man; they are free and have space to tell their stories in the gospel story, and in singing their hymns Christian congregations gain encouragement, meaning and insight into the message of God's love in Christ, a love brought home to us in the Spirit – not for 'closure' and deadening fixity but for endless differentiation in the Trinitarian movement of love and response. The hymnbook is a symphonic testimony to the multiplicity of human responsive engagement with God in Christ, to the amazing flexibility of its relevance through centuries of time and across immensely different cultures. The authority of God is real and relevant, not frozen in any one cultural form. The narrative form of revelation, reflecting divine reaching out to us in history, ensures this continual capacity of the Gospel to be re-expressed again and again, while remaining the same, pointing to the same Jesus Christ, crucified and risen.

History has its hope alone in Christ and the Spirit rather than the letter of the law is the dynamic of the Church. As we go through life we look to Jesus Christ in his earthly ministry, and ahead to the future hope,

---

[1] John Newton, c. 1765.

trusting in the presence of the Spirit now. Our freedom is shaped by the Christlike form through the changes and chances of life. Divine authority is at the same time divine love and truth, freedom, form and true life.

Such hymns are not summaries of the Christian message, as if creeds, rather lived and living incarnations of the reality of that message, the message experienced in the jagged edges of life, the same experience no doubt as that of disciples in the boat with Jesus as a storm threatened to sink it, and of Peter in the depth of his grief at betraying Jesus when the cock crowed, of Thomas in his doubt met by Jesus keeping faith with the doubter. The phenomenon of the hymn is not that of developing a spirituality from 'experience' and projecting a portrait of God from that, rather it arises from experience matched to Christ's total self giving for the disciple. The 'feeling of absolute dependence' spoken of by the great German theologian Schleiermacher[2] as core to Christianity, must be that of Jesus – and his victory at Calvary, his whole faith act of life for his Father. The more apostolic way of making this point is Trinitarian; to cite the key text from the letters of Paul again, 'God has sent the Spirit of his Son into our hearts, so we cry Abba Father!' – we are caught up in the arms of God to be brought to the place of worship and adoration. The Christian consciousness entails a deep sense of gratitude to Christ for the suffering he endured for us along with the sense of a responsive self-giving into his self-giving on our behalf. Christian joy goes through the cross to the resurrection sense of victory and security in Christ. The dying and rising of Jesus embraces us and calls forth our deep joy at sharing in his life victorious through redemptive suffering and death. And such response in song to God for this spiritual life through suffering and death is supremely fitting, singing being the quintessential creaturely way of expressing joy and gladness. True freedom, true realization of the relationship of humanity with the generous Creator God, takes place in glorification and praise in hymns addressed to God the Father in the Spirit generated by the Son.

This spiritual reality makes all talk of measuring Christianity in terms of modernity or postmodernity pale into academic aridity, but this spiritual fact of our unholy lives being taken up by God in love, mercy and forgiveness, does include the postmodern subjectivity – yet never an independent subjectivity glad to be free of God for its own 'space'. Rather this space of gladness, freedom and joy is gained only by sharing in the love of God, a holy love made present to us through suffering at a particular time and place. God as present is a fearful prospect for the postmodernist a/theologian Mark Taylor, implying divine repressing and removal of space and freedom, but this fear is unfounded, ignoring the new space, 'spiritual space' or 'grace space', opened up for us by

---

[2] F. D. E. Schleiermacher, *The Christian Faith*, trans. H. R. MacIntosh and J. S. Stewart, Edinburgh: T & T Clark, 1928 (1830), pp. 76–93.

God in Christ. The presence of God is the presence of the Father, Son and Spirit, a whole new spiritual-moral dimension, transcending entirely the below-above two dimensional model. Facing the Father in joyful free praise entails the grace of Christ holding us, and the Spirit indwelling us – fulfilling our freedom, not diminishing it. This postmodern fear of God seems deeply strange to the Christian ear, for which God, as Wesley's great hymn puts it, brings 'life and health and peace',[3] and also the awakening to true and real life from the dark dungeon of sin and death: 'my chains fell off, my heart was free', 'I rose, the dungeon flamed with light'.[4] Here Wesley describes Christ's saving act in his own life, an act performed 'once for all' decisively at Calvary and yet made real in the spatio-temporal lives of countless disciples down the centuries, evoking the kind of echo of praise found in Watts, Newton, Mattheson and Wesley, each speaking from their own 'particular' spaces, times and circumstances.

For them the passion of Christ is crucial in restoring true life in the Spirit, whose 'absence' would be the very reverse of blessing and freedom. The Father is precisely the Father – not 'Nobodaddy' of Blake's dire theological warning – because he is loving and caring, interested in the fall of a single sparrow and therefore far more in the sufferings of a person. God is present, and present in many and various ways since he is the God of Jesus Christ. Perhaps the postmodernist fear of divine presence as spoiling their party as autonomous selves, free from any responsibilities to others, may be adjudged juvenile, and in danger of repeating the dangers of creating God-free zones in which humans enact their own will to power – inevitably at the expense of others. Of course, as Blake preached, the churches can and have regressed at times into forgetting the self-definition of God as the triune God of Jesus and the Spirit and reinventing the single entity 'up there' gazing down with no love at us 'down here' – and this seems to be deity perhaps rightly feared by Taylor and postmodernity – but it is not the God of the Christian Gospel.

I am suggesting that the hymns of the church down the centuries join the chorus of worship going back to the earliest disciples, to Jesus' own prayer, and back to the Psalms. They are free expressions of worship to the living God of the Old and New Testaments in the ever changing contexts of life. As an Eastern Orthodox church building will always have its walls painted with a crowd of disciples, saints, martyrs and mystics queuing back to the Apostles, then to Jesus, then to the the Trinity on the highest point of the cuppola, so hymns likewise form a chain of apostolic worship back to God – while being inspired by the Spirit in every age.

---

[3]Charles Wesley, *O for a thousand tongues to sing my great redeemer's praise.*
[4]Charles Wesley, *And can it be that I should gain an interest in the saviour's blood.*

The whole burden of Scripture's narratives builds up to this climax, Christological, Trinitarian, always focused on the crucible of Christ's passion, the crucible which remakes us fit for this communion of praise. This reality is pointed to in the texts, but comes to us enabling us to respond aright as the Spirit bringing the letter to life, a bringing to life we alone with and in textuality could not achieve, this is grace, pure gift of Good Friday, Easter Sunday and Pentecost. This embrace of our lives by the Trinitarian life of God, is enacted in the sacraments where the past event of redemption is made present now in the Spirit: the form of Christ crucified and our own free personalities meet as the Spirit moves. At the heart of the Christian eucharist we are taken up into God with his own act of self-giving, into which we give ourselves for his mission in the world. This dramatic picture of atonement, renewal, worship and commitment to God's mission gives us another portrait of the gospel, and of grace coming to us not so much to remove us from the textuality of history but to reorient us to engage in its struggles in faith and hope. God's authority is that of holy love, it evokes repentance, a sense of our own distortedness and need to be untwisted. Divine authority in the world is that of Christ and so is redefined from the terror inspiring deity making continual demands and criticisms as we only fail to meet them: this authority is multi-dimensional grace and holiness, purposive and healing, actively calling and actively inspiring. The authority of God desires the response of love and thanks, it evokes not the obedience of a slave, rather of a son or a friend, God's authority is creative, regenerative, fatherly, loving and holy.

Responding to creation as gift

The Christian view of creation is that it is a gift of God, continually coming to us, meshing together all manner of physical, aesthetic, relational and moral aspects. The doctrine of creation is more than 'protology', the consideration of the initiation of all things outside of God, it considers 'the world' now and to come, our own personal worlds including our relationships and our intellectual questioning and probing of things. Many sources contribute to the theology of creation, from within faith and outside it. The ancient texts of Genesis, the Psalms, Prophets such as Isaiah, and Proverbs, for example, all speak of the divine bringing the world into being by majestic word and sustaining it through divine wisdom and the Spirit, conferring beauty, freedom, purpose, love and truth on his creatures. Divine desire to work with creation fruitfully, to work in covenant with us in creation, is a basic Christian view of how things are and should be.

Ingolph Dalferth[5] explains the doctrine of creation by distinguishing it from science and philosophy. He says that science gives us an empirical description of reality, that philosophy gives us a view of what could be true, and theology's doctrine of creation gives us an account of reality as God's gift as it comes to us and evokes our response of wonder, love, and praise. The best analogy for divine creation is poesis. He writes:

> Confessions of creation are confessions of hope, and as such they have relevance for the practice of life. They do not only talk of what is but of what should be and will be. They do not ignore the difference between good and evil, what serves life and what threatens it, but recognise good as good, evil as evil, wickedness as wickedness. And they do not weigh equally everything that is and may be, but seek those traces of the new by which the goodness of God's creation makes itself seen and signals its presence. They are constantly going beyond what is – not to explain but to discover it as the good gift of God or to demonstrate its opposition to that gift. In all of these respects they are different from scientific statements about the reality of the world.

For the Christian to affirm creation is not simply one human interpretation laid onto reality, an arbitrary act of subjective interpretation from our minds, although of course reality must be interpreted by us; it is the creative principle active in the maker expressed in the work of art, which includes us. The poetic creativity that holds all reality together, we can call it the creative Word or Wisdom sounding through the universe, this is the heart of what creation says about reality. Dalferth tells us that

> the principle to which a reality owes its unity is not itself a part of that reality. Correspondingly, the principle to which the world owes its unity as creation is not itself some part of the world that may be grasped by observation and imitation of the world; it is rather the style of the creator that is on display throughout the world because it draws all the phenomena together into the unity of creation.

Confessing creation is hopeful and itself creative, 'a creative act of grasping the creative', and this is always becoming, interpreted in the light of the Christ-like God whose judgement we share as disciples to enable us to discern what is good and healthy for creation and what negates it, and God the giver of this gift. God and his activity cannot be domesticated or classified. This will always surprise us and render us full of wonder. Dalferth stresses the dynamic quality of creation. It is not a static copy of a divine prototype from a Platonic transcendent realm, a reflection of a perfection reflected, albeit brokenly, in this changing and material world. Creation does indeed embody a security and continuity,

---

[5]Ingolph Dalferth, 'Creation – Style of the World', *International Journal of Systematic Theology*, vol. 1 no. 2, 1999, p. 132.

but also a newness and creativity. God creates creation as creative, his act of creation being like that of the artist, a 'poesis' pregnant with potential and new possibilities. 'Theological description does not therefore deal with an additional aspect of reality and possibility, but sets all reality and possibility together in a different perspective and horizon in which they are determined in relation to God'. God creates creation to be free, yet with its destiny of shape or form which is revealed in Christ.

The analogy of a home or household may be useful in illustrating the many sided nature of God's caring authority in and for the world. Children in a family home feel safe and secure, they know what their parents desire of them in terms of behaviour, they take for granted the whole ambience of life, the fact of water to drink, meals, heat and light. That background security – with its implicit authority shaping behaviour to cooperate, to enhance and not damage the home – echoes the always positive authority of God the Creator. Parents shape children's development in more particular and complex ways as well – although keeping the home warm, paying the electricity bills, and ensuring food is always there is a costly personal commitment however little noticed or taken for granted. Costly love is the mode of authority pervading the home, where rules implicit and explicit, such as not putting fingers into electric sockets, are from care and not a desire to dominate, and are obeyed in cooperative mutual family goodwill.

The parental desire is wholly for the security and development of the family, including the provision of freedom and 'space' for the thriving of growing personalities. The older the child, the more particular and individual interactions take place, the more intellectual and moral and aesthetic discussion, disagreement, argument, and angry confrontation – followed by apology and reconciliation in the healthy family household. But the background work of the parents in maintaining the home and its facilities at cost to themselves is still 'personal' commitment to the children, while not 'face to face'. Perhaps only later in life might a child realize the cost involved to parents of sustaining the home life and providing the security and context for thriving.

The authority of God is really the desire of God for our best; this is revealed in the created order, however little Western culture acknowledges the wonder, richness and security of that ambience, however much it is taken for granted and transferred to the creature's authority structures alone, reflecting and badly distorting the divine creative intention. This same parental divine authoritative desire for us is supremely revealed in Christ, mediated by the Spirit through the texts of Scripture and retellings of the narratives. The life act of Jesus given to us in the gospel stories make it quite clear that he relates his ministry to humanity in the created order: his healings are acts of mending creation, putting together what has been torn apart, ordering what has become chaotic, and on the Sabbath – the great symbol of the rest and gladness of the divine creation at its completion. Death itself is the terrible jagged edge for humans, effecting a final individualization of the self, sealing off of the person from others, a becoming 'natural' as the personal finally evaporates as the consequence of our selfish ego-centred desire – death is the fulfilment of our desire and the rejection of the divine desire.

And this too is underwritten by God in Jesus: restoring communion, enacting divine life humanly, and so undoing death as the final solipsism, bringing us to fellowship with the divine. Parental sacrifice for wayward children is of course a major literary theme, and a reality known to countless parents down the centuries. The analogy of the household may help open up the nature of divine authority as really divine desire for the very best for his creatures, a desire implemented in creation and covenant in many and various ways, backgrounded and foregrounded, but all rooted in holy love, purposive and evoking responsive love, not terrorized submission. The whole context of love is, to use the postmodern vocabulary, woven into the divine desire, care and authority, and in many ways this authority touches us, calls us, invites us to respond in glad loving obedience and to participate in the kingdom it evokes and promotes. This is the authority of parent and child not slave owner and slave – as John's Gospel so clearly announces, and as Jesus' prayer shows plainly at its very beginning, an authority of love and holiness, the loving father desiring only the best for the beloved child. And of course this model of authority takes us to the Christian insight of God's very richness of life, love and outward reaching care, the love of the holy God.

The divine Word to creation, in short, is Jesus Christ and his history, not any other word contradicting the reality and truth of Jesus, the way, the truth and the life. This is the authoritative word of God to us, about us and the world given to us. This authoritative word is also the divine wisdom of God the Creator. There is a pattern to the cosmos, or better a whole symphony of patterns of all kinds, patterns unfolded by science for example, patterns harnessed and deployed by musicians and singers, patterns of beauty and goodness – wisdom is a word perhaps capable of gathering such patterns into one. We might say that the most terrible disasters caused by human beings come about when a single narrow concern, even truth, is made to dominate all others and subject them to itself. The Stalinist terror tried to rationalize humanity for the sake of some originally worthy idea of strict equality, the 'cutting and squaring' of millions of humans as if pieces of polystyrene; modern Western culture at the other extreme treats people as 'free' consumers, with little regard to the overall shape of society and our mutual responsibility one to another. No doubt we will never, in history, attain to a perfect social way of being, but Christians do claim to know the overall shape and patterning of human destiny in the light of divine wisdom, a shape not a precise programme or code of regulations, but a shape allowing for and encouraging freedom and space for the particularity of personal individuality, and openness to the future as new cultures develop with new problems to be addressed. God is Father, Son and Spirit: freedom, form and historicity.

The Western world seems intent to refuse all manner of paths of peace and health, intent on creating its own authorities and wisdoms, indeed locked into a hatred of God.[6] It is important to note that God allows us this freedom not to receive his authority and love, and this looking away from God has negative consequences individually and socially, akin perhaps to the pollution of the environment, the model we find in the epistle to the Romans. A Christian theology of authority affirms the persistence of the wisdom of the divine authority through the cosmos and history, despite human cultures ignoring and denying it, illustrated by Western consumerism and hedonism, old but powerfully present idolatries banishing the wisdom of God. Yet as the Apostle Paul insists, 'they are without excuse'; no matter how corrupt a culture has become, however powerful the culturally conditioning influences on behaviour patterns, still the claim of the holy Creator God remains authoritative, notwithstanding humans 'repressing the truth'.[7]

Here the Freudian theory of repression can be inverted to suggest that humans in the grip of pure consumerist hedonism are suppressing what they really know to be true, that there is a creative wisdom of the universe summoning them to a nobler way of life than a kind of reduction to a purely animalistic level. Donald Baillie spoke of this moral or spiritual repression in modern society, arguing that it is deeply damaging to the person failing to face up to the divine imperative and preferring to mask it and look the other way.[8] Freud's theory is that we repress our sexual urges and desires, and this causes psychological damage, a theory itself evidently culturally relative to the late Victorian era and hardly applicable to our postmodern, deeply sexualized, Western culture, for which the sexual imperative is so dominating as to cause worry and guilt if it is not being regularly served. The theory of repression advocated by the Apostle Paul is now certainly a far more persuasive one and encapsulates a real response to divine authority as it is felt through the moral order of the creation. We can push away the creative intention, bury it and go with the ethos of the day, whether the human race can finally push God out of their horizons, permitted to do so by creaturely freedom, is an interesting question.

Bonhoeffer spoke of the God of Jesus Christ allowing himself to be pushed out,[9] as happened at Calvary, but this insight cannot be extended

[6]Hardy and Ford, *Jubilee: Theology in Praise*, London: Dartman, Longman, & Todd, 1984.
[7]Romans 1.
[8]D. M. Baillie, *God was in Christ*, London: Faber, 1948, p. 163 f.
[9]D. Bonhoeffer, *Letters and Papers from Prison*, London: Folio Society, 2000, pp. 247–8, 319–24.

to mean that God leaves himself without witnesses in the world at all levels of his creativity and authority, whereas it does mean that we are free to repress this truth if we so choose. God however continues to seek out his own, does not accept rejection as do human beings with resentment and 'closure', and does not shut down the structures of wisdom in the universe which make life worth living – despite our attempts at depersonalizing uglification in so many dimensions. This indicates an ongoing struggle or dialectic in history between the creative wisdom of God and human attempts to displace that with new focuses of adoration, ultimate loyalty and authority. The Apostle Paul teaches that Christ surpasses and conquers all authorities and powers, a reassertion and enactment by God the Creator of his authority in, with and under the created order. Our 'hearing', or 'seeing', this divine glory is muffled and darkened by our own sin and by the cultural constructs in which we live and move and have our being in societies which move further and further away from wanting to heed God's summons and ways of ordering life. The Christian theology of created order plainly understands the universe to embody truth, beauty and right, and the very notion of sin and fall means that there is this standard to sin against and to fall from, that we prefer darkness to light, that we collude with what is evil to greater or lesser degrees.

That strange final book of the New Testament, Revelation, clearly teaches this ongoing struggle between light and dark, the kingdom of God and the rejectors of this kingdom, the Lamb on the throne and the persecutors of the disciples of the Lamb, the rule of the new power of love and the continual lust for dominating depersonalizing power. The Christ and the Antichrist, noted by Hendrikus Berkhof, are the two poles of this ongoing clashing dialectic in world history. Victory has indeed been won by the wounded, slain and risen Christ, whose cross has absorbed all negativity towards God, rendering it temporary and absurd, indeed irrational and without foundation, 'the nihil', as Barth calls it.[10] Revelation, in its craggy and strange way, tells of the praise of the persecuted, believers under pressure to conform to the ways of the world, in those days of course the ways of the pagan empire of Rome, praise to the holy God being the response of those 'in Christ', in the wounded and slain 'Lamb in the midst of the throne', the great authority in history – however lacking in worldly power he seems. This gospel authority is heard in Christian preaching, summoning the hearer to the point of self giving response to grace, is heard in the resistance of evil and the telling of truth against oppression and lies, is heard as a great penumbra in the created order, a penumbra whose brightest burning light is Christ crucified and risen, at the heart of cosmos itself is this

---

[10]Karl Barth *Church Dogmatics* III/3, § 50 Edinburgh: T&T Clark, 1960, pp. 289–297.

reality, the peace brought about by the blood of the cross, as Colossians puts it (1: 15–20). In Him all things hold together, the epistle tells us, ultimately through this dying and rising of Christ, the ultimate effect of negation of God, itself negated and confirming the creative will of God the Father, the Creator of all things for covenant with himself.

Response to the authority of God finds its sharpest focus in Christ's response to his Father, a response into which we are drawn by baptismal faith, dying into Christ and rising to his new life, and a response drawing together all positive responses towards the multi-faceted goodness of the creation. For example, caring for the sick and the poor is extremely evident in the life of Jesus, and all altruism in human life has to be linked to the creative intention in some way. Jesus was not a philosopher directly referring to all the goods in the created order, Jesus was no aesthete for example, although of course the beauty of his life and self-giving transcends and takes up, even purifies, the beauty attractive to the dilettante or to the sensualist, Kierkegaard's picture of the modern aesthete. The creative work of God and the redemption in Christ cohere wonderfully, as Irenaeus and Justin knew. Jesus healing of the broken and sick on the Sabbath reasserts the goodness of creation, Jesus' obedience in going to Calvary in faith and hope, restores what Adam lost for us in the story of disobedience at the tree in the Garden of Eden. Authority in creation flows to and from authority of Christ, who is the fulfilment of the created order and also the creative Word.

As well as pointing to the rejection of divine authority by so much of modern culture we must of course point to those aspects which resonate with God's creative intention in all sorts of ways, in particular today we notice the growing concern for 'the planet' and its delicate eco-system, the criticism of damaging practices on such a vast scale as to imperil the environment for human habitation. A sense of what 'ought to be done', however vague and at times confused or selfish, surely accords with the divine authority in one of its many modes in the universe, and trying to act on that new eco morality in some way answers the call of the divine wisdom and its authority. Altruism, caring for others, again is a response to the summons to treat everyone as made in the divine image, as worthy of our care. The 'moral argument' for the existence of God has a long history in philosophical theology, seeking to move from the human sense of duty to a source for that sense, which seems so common among human beings according, for example, to cultural and religious historians.

C. S. Lewis was a popular exponent of this argument, that 'the ought' is not simply to be gained from 'the is' or from raw facts and events. Kant, the great Enlightenment philosopher, had made this move earlier, but not to a deity who could be somehow 'known' but rather to a postulate of God, alongside freedom and immortality, a postulate all must make in order to account in moral reason for our sense of duty, a rationalistic move. Indeed the Christian experience of morality is given more deeply by John Baillie, for whom the moralist is led to the point of realizing that his best efforts to live the good life lead him to understand his need for grace, for support and strength beyond his own, to reach out to God.[11] John Macquarrie uses this point in his theology in terms of human beings and supportive Being, or God, to whom we open ourselves as we feel threatened by fear, doubt, anxiety and guilt, and find to be the generous ground of all beings.[12] A Christian theology of this moral experience must lead to and from divine grace, not to and from a rigid moral grid, or template, as if without love and empathy.

Anglican theology has preferred a theology of morality, rationality, and beauty, or God making sense of our wide human experience of life, rather than stressing a 'knock down' kind of argument from any of these routes.[13] The authority of the Christian God is always Christ-like, the divine wisdom of holy love, reaching out to evoke response from the depths of the human being. Indeed God's desire is to achieve human self-transformation and enrichment in this response, a self-transformation contemporaneously empowered by the Spirit in what D. M. Baillie called 'the paradox of grace', the human self being most truly itself when attuned to the Spirit of God. The revelation of humanity to us in the humanity of Jesus confirms this insight, that divine authority, like parental authority, desires the formation of free and particular persons, not template individuals conditioned to obey a set of rules and rituals by an external power – this is surely the message of Jesus' parable of the Pharisee and the Publican. God's authority calls us to relationship, we are called to be 'sons, not slaves', we are free and this free response is what God desires.

God's personal authority

This divine desire to form 'covenant' with his human creatures, a covenant of the heart and not just a moral rule-book, keys in with the multiplex Trinitarian creative action, providing the secure context for human life, reaching into human will and enabling the fulfilment of our creation in the divine image. Coleridge argued that our reason was not simply of the scientific, observational, mode, which is better described as understanding, but has a far wider scope including the moral and aesthetic realities of the created order. Reason is ultimately rooted in the divine Word and shares in that life, hence has a moral dimension and this accounts for conscience in humanity. While secularists will seek to

---

[11]John Baillie, *Our Knowledge of God*, London: Oxford University Press, 1949, pp. 75ff.
[12]John Macquarrie, *Principles of Christian Theology*, London: SCM Press, 1977, chapter 3.
[13]For example, O. C. Quick, *Doctrines of the Creed*, London: Nisbet, 1963 (1938).

account for both rationality and morality in purely reductionist ways, which is not an easy task, the Christian theology of human response to that call to what is fair and decent is rooted back to God the Creator, to the perpetually sounding voice of holiness in the cosmos, a voice sustaining and upholding all things good. Coleridge's most interesting reflection on human perception and response to the divine focuses on our imaginative capacity to probe and gain new insights by our creative artistic work. This is no abstract mental activity, and no passive waiting for inspiration, but a responsive working in and with the real world, a rising above surrounding cultural expectations to produce what is new yet related to what we already know and feel. A great poem or play or novel might illustrate what Coleridge is trying to express, and this creative imagination is in tune with the divine self-existence. We might add that the desire of this 'I AM' is communion with those created beings capable of responsive love, and this again leads us to the Trinitarian God as the source of all things.

The authority of God in the created order is an authority rooted in the good and holy Creator's desire for the best, however much human beings may feel otherwise, and may feel mere pawns in a cosmic game of chance or even cruelty – as Thomas Hardy clearly felt, for example at the conclusion of *Tess of the D'Ubervilles*.[14] The Christian believes, come what may by way of misfortunes, that the heart of the universe is one of 'I AM', of personal self-existence and love, revealed most deeply at Calvary, not 'IT IS', a law of nature and necessity. Yes, of course the world of nature is real and conforms to regular patterns discernible and discoverable by rational empirical science, and of course our physical nature is part of this dimension of being: but the cosmos is created by the divine will and desire, not of a necessary force, and this divine will and desire is reflected in human beings and their relationship to the dimension of 'nature'. Divine authority in creation is primarily revealed to humans calling for free covenant response of gratitude and joy, not simply submission to a divine natural law impregnated into the cosmos, a kind of impersonal DNA of the world which we have to discover, or find revealed, and submit to.

The character of God and his authority in with and under the created order is of course the reason there is space for sin, for God's authority and love to be resisted, leading to distortion of what we and the world should be. God's authority is personal, bestowing freedom and space to allow the 'omnipotence of love', the kingdom of God implemented by God in Jesus, to inspire and evoke the human response of love to God as Father in the Spirit. This is the nature of the 'covenant' God desires with us, and the nature of the authority he exercises in his kingdom,

---

[14]The final page contains the bleak conclusion 'the President of the Immortals had ended his sport with Tess'.

his rule revealed in Christ. He calls us to love God and our neighbour, to reach out to the poor, to overcome tribal hatred, to heal the sick and be merciful. This reflects the character of God as 'merciful and gracious, abounding in steadfast love', or 'full of grace and truth'. The authority of God then enfolds the created order in love and desires the best for it, desires to bestow freedom and potential and to evoke the fulfilment of this potential towards personhood and loving kindness. The evident and also revealed fact of human resistance to this divine desire and rejection of its authority is the reason for most human suffering – for 'man's inhumanity to man' – when so much pain, illness and famine could be solved rationally if 'neighbour love' were the orientation of the human race. We are created to personhood and its ultimate realization in love for God and our neighbour, the Christ-like kingdom or rule of God in history, disclosure and fulfilment of divine authority, a personal and corporate fulfilment, participation in holy divine love, not merely obedience towards an unknowable first principle, cause, or deity which has issued moral orders and punishes or reward accordingly, rather as a dog might be trained.

The competing claims of the functional and personal were probed in a famous experiment conducted by a psychologist, Stanley Milgram. He asked a random sample of people to join in an important experiment concerning pain thresholds. A white-coated 'doctor' sat the subject at a desk with a dial attached to wires and a machine, facing a screen. Behind that screen, the subject was told, was seated a person connected to the wires. When the subject turned the dial it sent pain into the person behind the screen according to how far the dial was turned. Milgram began by telling the subject to turn the dial just a little, to inflict minimal shock and pain. Then the instruction was for more to be administered, eliciting cries of pain from behind the screen. The white-coated doctor emphasized how important this experiment was, and instructed the subjects to turn the dial to the full, eliciting screams of pain. Nearly all the subjects went along with the instructions and as far as they knew inflicting dreadful pain on a fellow human being at the authority of the 'doctor' in the white coat. The authority of 'science' and technology had triumphed over that of common humanity, the duty of care we have to our neighbour. At the debriefing later, most subjects were alarmed at themselves for being so uncritical and biddable in turning the dial and hearing cries. One subject only refused to turn the dial to inflict pain, a lecturer in Old Testament theology. Presumably that subject used a higher criterion or authority in deciding what to do, an authority higher than science and technological expertise represented by the white-coated 'doctor'. The experiment revealed the willingness of apparently normal people to act in cruel and violent ways under the authority of the expert, overriding their normal everyday morality. The subjects could quickly be moved into a mindset treating people as 'it' and not as persons. This experiment was carried out not long after the end of World War II and the disaster of a whole – apparently civilized – nation colluding with a genocidal criminal and mass murderer. Christ's way opens the prison bars of selfish desire and enables us to regain our conscious desire in the divine desire, to live in the authority of God's kingdom. This form is true freedom to be human and bring about true life and history in the Spirit.

God's Holy desire for us

Divine authority then is more than some iron law in the universe detached from divine desire and the will of divine character. We inhabit not a 'penal universe' but a creative one shaped for the divine intention and desire for holiness and love, beauty and truth. Law is from and for grace, for personal response and goodness in relation to God; the 'laws' of natural science, discovered by human reason and experiment on the physical world to give the most accurate account of the matter and events of the world, are rules of thumb fitting in with the current state of experimentation and mathematical projection. Scientific laws presuppose and reflect the order and stability, along with its dynamic energies, and indeed presupposes the human mind's ongoing stability and rationality in relation to the world. Christian theology regards this as sacramental of divine blessing, that the universe is stable, structured and that humanity has the intellectual gifts to probe, describe and explain it, taking this wonder as a pointer to the Creator and also as a moral reminder of the goodness of the universe, its worth and summons to respect rather than being simply an object for plundering. The universe itself, in its scientific description, bears this divinely given stamp of worth, witnessing to the Creator's goodness and purpose. Reality as examined by science can of course be regarded atheistically and bleakly, as a purposeless accident to be shaped rather as can be plastic or polystyrene into whatever we choose to make of it.

The authority of the Creator is found in the universe as described by physics, chemistry and biology and in our human capacity to undertake such describing and questioning. The world is stable and wonderful, not quixotic and unreliable. We find ourselves healthiest if we fit into the patterns of the universe. Theology sees this as akin to the stage on which we humans live out our lives in history, or as the house built by the parent, with all its capability of keeping us warm, clean and safe. Such facilities seem not personal, and they are not so directly in our experience, but since they flow from generous free divine purposive will, they are related to the personal authority of God, as is all else. Kant spoke of 'the starry heavens above' in relation to this point, the wonder of the universe to faith, and also of 'the moral law within', referring to the human sense of duty to do what is right. Kant divided these two facets of human reality and experience sharply, but Christianity connects them both to the Creator and to the divine purposive desire – to the giver of all goodness, whose gift of the universe is a whole. Moral sense, attributed by atheistic evolutionism to a curious accident buffering the survival of the fittest and strongest, has been regarded by theology as part and parcel of human shaping in the divine image of holy love. Nietzsche was probably right to say that morality is essentially religious and that Kant's view of duty was far more religio-cultural than anthropological, shaped by the Protestant tradition. Theologians such as Newman and Coleridge have argued that the conscience is a mode of divine communication or signal conferred on us and guiding us into what is right and good. The Apostle Paul teaches that we do know what is right, but that we have 'repressed the truth' of God and goodness, preferring to be our own gods and creating our own worlds around the devices and desires of our own hearts. Clearly Nietzsche was right to point to cultural conditioning, but still basic moral imperatives do seem universal across cultures, for example that murder is wrong. Perhaps Kant here might trump Nietzsche if he were to reply that culture is itself shaped by moral sense.

Moral sense is, to the theologian, a mode of divine authority flowing from the creative purpose of divine holiness. Theology understands this to be felt by human beings across cultures and that cultures can be judged by their adherence to such broad moral ideals, indeed the whole 'human rights culture' might be attributable to a basic version of traditional Christian morality and its view of human life as precious. The sense of goodness behind all things, the worth of the world, stems from the Creator, as the Apostle Paul teaches.[15] Indeed he goes on to teach the paradox that our attempts to fulfil the moral law autonomously, by our own strength alone, fails and this leads us to acknowledge our need for divine grace. Luther's monastic experience led him to a very strong endorsement of this, as later the Danish thinker Kierkegaard was led to advocate the moral law as driving us to 'the leap of faith'. Christian experience has accepted the fact of our moral responsibility, and also the need of grace to enable us seriously to get through our inability to enact this morality.

The strange Christian doctrine of 'original sin' speaks of a cultural conditioning away from goodness, a pull we find around us in society, which we can resist but with which we so often collude. Psychologically this rings true with the human moral situation; we are not simply independent selves but rather in and of our surrounding social context and tradition. This context contains elements of the good and healthy,

---

[15]Romans 1.

and yet elements of the opposite, a negativity or dark side pulling us from our better selves, from what we really should do and be. Our conscience, yes, is no doubt formed in part by our cultural context, as Nietzsche claimed, but on the other hand we are in a tension between what we know to be right and a tempting easier path which includes wrong. And the more we take that path the easier it becomes to 'repress the truth' and habituate wrong, to become addicted to the negative, to dull our conscience and sensitivity to the divine desire for us, to the divine authority.

Covenant

This theological understanding of divine loving authority – in, with and under the created order – is expressed through the Bible as the 'covenant', the divine relationship of God with the created order, with humanity, and with Israel, enacted and revealed supremely in Jesus of Nazareth. The covenant is rooted in God's gift, bestowing security and care, seeking a response of trust and loyalty. Barth very simply teaches that creation is the stage on which the covenant is played out, for which it is made, and the covenant is the inner basis of the created order, its reason and aim. They interweave, divine loving care is the authority woven into creation, and humanity holds creation in trust on the basis of this authority and intention.

Creation comes with God's covenant promise of grace, and the covenant is focused several times through the history of the Old Testament, we move from the covenant promise to Noah regarding the whole created order, to Abraham and his descendents, to Moses and the giving of the law, to David. The covenant relationship continues, re-expressed and modified, through the narrative tradition of this people, in sharper focus. And all the time the tension of the goodness of creation and the capacity of humans to ruin it, goodness and sin, runs through this covenant theme. Noah's flood stands for the divine anger at wickedness and malice unleashed in the good creation, a wickedness bringing destruction and judgement, a new start being needed but yet out of the old. The law, the Ten Commandments, are given as a gift, not as a harsh rule-book, then Moses coming down from Sinai sees his people cavorting round the golden calf in thoroughly twenty-first-century fashion, and is not happy. The prophets rail against the disloyalty of the people, their shallow love and commitment, always in terms of breach of relationship rather than merely rule breaking, a symptom of lack of love for God. The human race is given this covenant relationship with the Creator, is given special responsibilities and privileges, enters into the very purposes of the Creator as co-Creator. Humanity has authority over the creation, bestowed by the Creator. Humanity is guided by divine authority and intention, but yet is given freedom and space freely to shape and develop creation. Jesus's parable of the tenants and the vineyard let to them by the owner speaks of just this kind of role of mankind and of Israel. St Paul's Epistle to the Romans speaks of humanity, given freedom and responsibility, veering away from loyalty to the Creator and worshipping dimensions of the created order, including greed and lust. The outcome of this was a spiralling downwards into deepening decadence and abuse. Paul connects this phenomenon with the Old Testament narrative of Adam and Eve, again a story of covenant in the wonderful creation being taken for granted, usurped and abused, an abuse which wounded the abusers to the core of their being and relationships. Covenant love and loyalty, entailing holiness and worship, this is the biblical theological shape to divine authority.

This covenant is often illustrated through biblical literature as a marriage relationship. Israel is portrayed by prophets as a bride beloved of her husband, but she seems to lack loyalty and strays to others – deserving of rejection and yet treated with grace and forgiveness. Hosea in particular expresses his prophecy in these words, and indeed in his own life experience, buying back his wayward wife from the slave market where her faithlessness has finally deposited her. 'How can I give you up, O Israel', says God through Hosea's words and life. Husband and wife are united 'as Christ is united with his Church', is a New Testament teaching in the same tradition. In that cultural context the husband is the giver of security, the authoritative figure, who loves his wife and expects a response of gratitude and loyal love in this covenant. The Christian marriage liturgies use the term 'covenant' between man and woman, a coming together to form something deeper than a contract. The idea of covenant deepened with the history of the prophets. Jeremiah looked forward to a covenant on our hearts, 'But this is the covenant I will make with the house of Israel after those days, says the Lord; I will put my law within them and I will write it upon their hearts; and I will be their God and they shall be my people' (Jer. 31:33). The law is to become personal, not just a set of heteronomous laws to be obeyed. Relationship between the covenant giver and accepter is the core to this. The covenant comes with the summons to holiness and the promise of holiness that Israel might be a royal priesthood, a holy nation, and that all people globally should be included in this destiny, Israel being the first fruits or messenger to the nations. God's holy love is for all creation, his authority is within a covenant, akin to marriage, Christ calls his disciples friends, even sons and daughters and particularly not 'slaves'. This covenant authority is to create a loyal and caring people, a holy and virtuous people, who love their neighbours and even their enemies, within the love of God.

The creative intention of God is then a matter of this Christ-like love, working for us, fostering what is good, and supremely disclosed in Christ.

God's love for humanity is as that of a husband for his wife, of cherishing and loving, bestowing all that he has on her, desiring responsive love. Christian theology knows one basic distinction within the human race of any significance, that between men and women. They are to shape their relationship by way of covenant, becoming one flesh, a new entity, one out of two, not just contracted together but bonded in love and faithfulness. Creation and covenant could not be more integrated in this reality: human beings are different in one respect only, they are men and women, they are 'other' in that and in nothing else. Barth argues that this otherness and relation reaching across the difference in love reflects the divine Trinitarian love and constitutes the image of God in humankind, male and female together. Here is the one great distinction and union, sacramentally sealed in sex. Sexual purpose and behaviour, how our sexual impulses are deployed or realized according to the creative intention of God, is faithful covenant love between one man and one woman, not several, not with other species, and not with the same sex.

The deeply positive message of creation is that human sex is a gift, and a means of co-creation with God in bringing forth children, to be held in trust by a man and his wife for each other. This covenant is so deeply important and clear that it is used as the analogy of Christ's love for his church. Creation and covenant merge in the difference and union of men and women, human beings are all men or women, their union sexually is the way the race continues, and co-creation with God is surely at its most heightened form in the procreation and care of children. Sex divides the human race into two complementary halves, and bridges the distinction in fruitful union. Sex is physical union, pregnant for procreation, in the context of covenant love and care: it bears the hallmark of the Sabbath rest and joy, a completed pattern rooted in divine creation, not merely an invention of human culture. In marriage a man and a woman, with all the and strangeness of being of the 'other' sex, come together and in a task to remain faithful together while undertaking the raising of children for the good of society. Sociologist Helmut Schelsky sees the normative status of this ideal of marriage because 'in a monopolising of sexual relations in marriage it puts the partners above the striving for personal and especially sexual satisfaction', it is a set goal of inviolable life partnership, and the shared faith in Jesus' eschatological message underlying this task blends human sexual union with life in the Spirit.[16]

Today's theology has to take account of the developmental aspect of organic creation in particular, the process of evolution stretching out the pattern of creation through interaction with and adjustment to physical contexts. As in all things, God conducts his purposes like a river, not like

---

[16]Cited in W. Pannenberg, *Systematic Theology*, vol. 3, trans. G Bromiley, Edinburgh: T&T Clark (1993) 1998, p. 362.

a mathematically engineered canal blasted through the rock; he works through the natural conditions, opportunities and obstacles, as clearly happens in the history of Israel, Jesus and the Church. Men and women, one human race, face each other as the same and yet different, having to trust each other and entrust themselves to the other in co-creating the world, as well as being its steward exercising oversight and care. The creation of the human race as men and women, the one and only division, a division for the sake of creative covenant in union, bestows and shapes the gift of sexual partnership. Here the realities of creation and its covenant pattern gain a particular and unique focus, here is the deepest anthropological and social fact about the race, a fact pregnant with value and purpose, a fact determining parenthood and childhood, the generations of mankind. As Barth puts it, men and women reach across their otherness and find union as they trust and love each other in the great creative adventure of covenant partnership sealed by sex and fruitful. This is part of the creative intention of God, not a reality to be overtaken by development and evolution, with this pattern God is 'well pleased'. The human race comprises men and women who are given 'space' and freedom by God to care for creation in covenant. This is their trust and destiny, and it is a joint one, as Barth rightly emphasizes.[17] This union bears the mark of divine authoritative intention, pregnant with the divine image itself, and sealed by the mark of the Sabbath rest, the completedness of the structure of the created order. This differentiation for union is 'the Magna Carta of humanity'.[18]

Creation and covenant entwine inseparably in this ultimate union in distinction, the mystery of woman and man, together in their different similarity, a union sealed by sex for procreation of the race, co-creation with God. In both the creation narratives of the Old Testament Adam and Eve, man and woman, are at the pinnacle of the completed creation.[19] Their mutuality, their covenant together, stems not from a human cultural construct but from the creative intention of God at the wellspring of all culture. Here is the authoritative shaping of sexual union, stemming from this foundation of men and women in covenant, the purposive gift of God, to be faithful, loyal and caring, mirroring the covenant of Christ with his church. Man and woman differentiated and united at the head of the race and for the future of the race physically, morally and emotionally, are not faced with a set of rules about themselves and their relationship, they simply are what they are, men and women fitted by creative intention for this union. The divine authority intends this great gift in creation and bestows it with love and for love, a sacrament of fruitful creative union, a gift calling for loyalty to God and loyalty

---

[17]Karl Barth, *Church Dogmatics*, III/2, p. 289.
[18]Karl Barth, *Church Dogmatics*, III/2, p. 286.
[19]Karl Barth *Church Dogmatics* III/1 Edinburgh: T&T Clark, 1958, pp. 228–329.

of man to woman in covenant – human beings fitted for each other in God.

The life of Jesus signals the other mode of human being and relationships, deep friendship and commitment to others, and again brings out the message of diversity in creation, freedom and form. God the Trinity created and creates in the Spirit, sustaining all things in the relationality of care, rather like the love of parents always 'there' even when absent, in all sorts of ways, desiring the best mature destiny for their family. The freedom and diversity of creation, shown in the covenant form, is rooted in the divine life of freedom and form, persons and essence. We are not isolated individuals, nor are we absorbed into a necessitarian corporate whole: the Trinitarian revelation maintains freedom and form, diversity and unity, precisely what we see in the created order at all levels of life.

The command of God

Karl Barth speaks of the authority of God revealed in Jesus Christ, the gospel of grace which contains law and command, uniting them and not allowing 'law' and ethics to be defined separately, as if ethics could have a different basis. In particular he is deeply critical of church and theology for encouraging a separation of ethics based on some neutral ground rooted in secular values rather than in Christ. For Barth, in Jesus God is both the giver of the command to holiness and the one who has obeyed this command in its true manner of love, in Christ God has lived out his own authority, and has been shocked at our hardness of heart. Barth's insistent emphasis on Christology as the way to sharp focus all dimensions of Christian truth is both epistemological and ontological, a distinction worth bearing in mind here. For Barth we can know the true authority of God only in Christ, but the reality of the cosmos is in Christ whether or not we know this fact – creation is elected in Christ. This ontological fact means that the universe exists in grace; it is claimed insistently by the God of grace, who intends that its destiny is fulfilled in Christ. This accords fully with the New Testament affirmation that the cosmos at its very heart finds its core in the cross of Jesus, whose shed blood makes peace and reconciliation for all time and space. The authority of God through the universe and human history is given in Jesus, with the whole depth and breadth of what he did and means and is. The creative Word of God, the Logos, the Son in Trinitarian theology, calls and claims all people to his way of love and care, a vision seen in the Old Testament prophets and in many secular yearnings, for example Marx's hope for a final just and mutually caring society. This creative Word has come among us in Jesus, initiating his kingdom in the historical conditions of sin and hostility, setting up a struggle between the kingdom of Christ and idolatries of self-rule negating and usurping divine authority.

The command of God is a command of grace and revealed in Jesus Christ as the reverse of dominating and coercive. The gospel entails law, the command of God: what God desires for us and what human response we should make. But this response is to be made freely, we 'may' make it, we are given space and permission to act for God, to act as covenant partners we are trusted to be. Barth therefore concludes that what we 'should' do is a matter of what we 'may' do. Our true freedom is serving God, 'whose service is perfect freedom', and whose service is never compelled. Our freedom in creation and the covenant is a gift from God. The command of God is permission to act freely, permission we should use by choosing God's way, freely. This of course is Jesus Christ's very life act, free obedience to his Father, even unto death. We may respond to the grace of God as God desires, and so we therefore should: this is the nature of divine command and authority in the world. The law of God is gracious and not the dictatorial statement of harsh commands; it is not 'heteronomous', nor does God leave us in the dark to make up our own pattern of life autonomously. Rather we are in covenant with God.

> The command of God 'will not compel man, but burst open the door of compulsion under which he has been living. It will not meet him with mistrust but trust. It will not appeal to his fear but to his courage. It will instill courage and not fear into him. This is the case because the command... is itself the form of the grace of God...the easy yoke and the light burden of Christ...the assumption of which is in every sense our quickening and refreshing. This is what God prepares for us when He gives us His command.[20]

As children in a family home, we obey out of love and loyalty, responding to the caring love given us, directly face to face, or indirectly through all the structures and facilities supporting our existence provided and sustained by our parents. We behave as children of loving parents, or again we behave as spouses in the covenant of marriage, responsible to and for the other. For Barth the command of God, divine authority, focuses in relationships, these are the field in which divine authority regularly meets us, linking individual to social ethics. The authority of God, for Christian theology, is supremely revealed at the cross, and deconstructs the authority of 'Nobodaddy', Blake's oppressive dictatorial God who is 'nobody's daddy' but is a threatening giver of rules and punisher of transgressors of that law.

Religion based on rules and laws alone can result in a febrile state. This is because the fiercely religious uphold and state the rules strongly, but people cannot keep them, indeed nor can the zealots. A

---

[20]Karl Barth, *Church Dogmatics*, II/2, p. 586.

kind of dissonance ensues from repression and denial, a dishonesty of form at odds with reality, resulting in a fanaticism for the rules as if their ever-stronger affirmation could help their observation. Jesus is, for the Christian, the divine giving of this divine command and the true human way of fully observing God's authority. For Jesus the law given in the covenanted created order authoritatively shapes human life in relationship with the God of grace, the law and the prophets give decisive orientation to human relationship to the Creator and each other. This orientation of holiness and love patterning human action has a clarity and is to be enacted with free and glad obedience, not the obedience of mere submission to a higher power and will. Men and women are 'in the image and likeness of God'; they owe all they are and have to the grace of the Creator and their true destiny is to inculcate personally and culturally this divine authoritative pattern of life. Our freedom is most real as we live out the creative intention and desire of God, focused so sharply in the life of Jesus – for he is the image of the invisible God, first born of all creation, in him all things hold together. The supreme authority over the world has plumbed the depths of world suffering to give all things their meaning and final judgement, the risen Christ crucified, the interweaving of holiness, love, truth and beauty. Supreme authority is revealed as majestic and free yet incarnated into space-time and personhood, reaching across heteronomy and autonomy, divine wisdom at work on many levels and in dimensions known and beyond our knowing.

The creative Word has created the cosmos as an artist creates: the work of art is characterized by the artist and bears his signature in all manner of ways. Creation speaks of this Creator, and the human race, 'made in the divine image and likeness', has the gift of realizing this and having the inside story. In all kinds of ways, ways not necessarily chartable by human science or theory, humanity 'knows' the goodness of creation and of itself, knows its destiny and finds itself frustrated and in disease it contradicts itself by going into denial. Divine authority is at work in this process of self-judgement, is at work in conscience and culture, in the disasters of human pride and greed, in human failures to attend to those at risk, in collusion with human grabs for power. The authority of God is not merely over creation, but runs through it like the grain through wood, in ways sometimes more like laws, sometimes like personal engagement, sometimes like a combination. The analogy of the family household is worth mentioning again. Authority in the home is multi-layered and experienced variously, indirectly or less so, over a course of time, through other people or cultures. Through all manner of codes, messages, practices, customs, the desire and authority of the loving and nurturing parents home intend to shape and affect the children.

Creation needs covenant to cherish and understand it, to arise from it and wonder at it and its Creator, to take the challenge and opportunity to engage positively in the covenant at every level. The 'non-brute' fact of our being men and women protects our materiality and saves us from forms of idealism, forms of life denying the radical significance of our being space-time, people rather than feelings and ideas discarnate from the actualities of history. Our bodily selves creatively interact and bring forth a future in freedom and form. The actual structure of creation is vital in Christian theology for the shape of our relationships and for the good of the world in the good pleasure of God.

This physicality of the world and ourselves can of course be taken as if a kind of polystyrene by a purely functionalist, secular view of the world, a substance to be shaped and formed as 'we' may wish – 'we' being the cadre of 'experts' who get to do the cutting and squaring of our human nature. Such a view plays down the value of the physical, which in fact becomes 'value free', of no 'worth' beyond its usefulness to whatever project currently requires it. The rapidly advancing technology of genetic engineering and reproductive techniques show how far we have come in this respect. In the UK now it is becoming legal for human foetuses to be 'grown' just to be destroyed and used as genetic tissue. It is even now being considered ethical to mix human and animal DNA for such processes. The sacramental value of human life must be downgraded by such technologies, the means justifying the ends. But not only is the physical dimension of humanity 'de-valued' in such genetic engineering, the 'covenant' aspect of the world is also abolished. Reproduction by test tube methods, bypassing human love and togetherness in the adventure of procreation, was predicted in Huxley's *Brave New World*, where technology ruled, sex was detached from permanent relationships and childbirth, and the purposelessness of this bleak utilitarian world as softened by the drug 'soma'. It is remarkable how creation and covenant are so core to human well being and how the relationship of men with women stands at the centre of human thriving. Undoing this relationship, relativizing it, breaking up its constituent elements into all manner of other techniques and relationships and experiences, seems to be a secular agenda. The very identity of man and woman can now be melted down and reprocessed by way of changed birth certificates, re-registering the sex of a person retroactively, by government decree and personal preference. Yes, there are hard and rare conditions and cases to deal with, but hard cases make bad law, and if such reconstructions erode the givenness of men and women, along with the other changes mentioned above, then creation and covenant, sacramentally stated by men and women existing as such, is being resisted and the divine authority ignored.

Cultural construction, of course, plays a part in conditioning how we understand ourselves, but we remain men and women, clearly formed to come together in covenant as the way of expressing sexual desire and fruitfulness. The man and the woman stand at the centre of the race, and it is only in the light of their covenant relationship that other forms of sexual deployment can be assessed: Adam and Eve are the creaturely building block of humanity, and the given for any practice and theory of human sexual behaviour. Cultures moving away from this are in a sense departing from their creaturely basis and future destiny, are moving towards confusion and fragmentation. Cultures likewise which treat human physicality as material for experiment and resources similarly move away from the creative intention and desire of God for the cherishing of creation and the supporting of covenant relationship at the heart of what it means to be human. Humans are 'made in the image and likeness of God', according to Christian theology, they are precious however aged and infirm, however young and defenceless and unwanted. The desire and authority of God tells us this in all sorts of ways, that we owe a duty of care to each other, that we are created with a value and purpose, that God confers this gift on us all.

This orientation of the cosmos towards the good, the positive, an orientation given to us all somehow as human beings, is recognized by religions generally, as C. S. Lewis argued[21] using the term 'Tao' to describe this very general pattern of the world (perhaps 'wisdom' might be the more biblical term). 'It' seems to endure across cultures and to resist efforts to annihilate it, bubbling up even in conditions of savage persecution as in the USSR or Nazi Germany. Deconstructionists, of course, deny this as an underlying reality, 'ground of being', in fact 'it' is a great target since it is assumed to be oppressive, a dominating 'logos' suppressing freedom and personhood. But this wisdom or creative word is revealed as bestowing freedom, absorbing violent wrong rather than administering it, and able to 'speak' in many languages and cultures rather than destroying them in its wake. The divine authority is creative, is given to the creation, does not repress but enables freedom, and without it all would be mere determinism. How does this divine word of authority make itself felt in space and time? 'It' just does, and subtly subverts all efforts to crush it out, efforts that entail crushing people and freedom as collateral damage, as for example in the Soviet Union or radical social experiments such as Cambodia where attempts to reconstruct the deep grammar of human patterns of life and relationships have been catastrophic.

Western consumerist hedonism, on the other hand, apparently supporting individual freedom to the hilt, may seem to have more success in distracting people from the divine desire and authority in the world – surely just the picture painted parabolically by the sages who wrote Genesis 1 – 11, depicting humanity walking away from the creative intention and desire of God in the household of the universe, a pathway

---

[21]C. S. Lewis, *The Abolition of Man*, London: Fount (1943) 1978. 'Only the Tao provides a common human law of action which can over arch rulers and ruled alike. A dogmatic belief in objective value is necessary to the very idea of rule which is not tyranny or an obedience which is not slavery' (p. 44).

leading to malfunction and chaos. God allows this free action, and so allows the consequences to occur in the form of judgement, a judgement calling us back to our senses and the common sense of creation and covenant. The authority of God in the universe does not override human freedom. Divine omnipotence is the omnipotence of love which does not conquer by external victory but glad inner assent – there is no victory otherwise.[22]

True authority is for the people, open and reasonable not manipulative and coercive, not a means to control and make use of others. True authority fosters the potential and differences in people, while not opening the way to chaos and evil. Freedom and form, diversity and unity, love and truth, all are upheld and not fudged or polarized: the Trinitarian description of God, in whose creative parental care we all exist, makes dazzling sense of our experience in the world.

We now need to consider authority in the world in its institutional modes set in the context of the creation, and to pursue the theme of freedom and form, emerging as the key factors marking out authority for Christian theology: avoiding chaotic quixotic freedom, seemingly espoused by the deconstructionism of postmodernism, and also the deadening weight of form which crushes out freedom and individualism and diversity. The interweaving of these in the Christian Gospel has arguably led to the richness of Western civilization, where freedom is encouraged but with form and shaping to avoid chaos and oppressive control.

---

[22]John Oman, *Grace and Personality*, Cambridge: Cambridge University Press, 1925.

8

Political Authority:
Democracy, Law, Capitalism

Democracy – a fruit of the Gospel tree

The Christian view of authority in wider society cannot but start with the figure of Jesus, the incarnation of the creative Wisdom and Word, his life, death and overcoming of death. The one behind the cosmos enters the drama he has created to heal and mend it, to give it its true pathway, to enable creation to create itself anew. As we have said, this involves not clamping some legalistic grid onto humanity but to set it free for the glorious diversity of the meadow of creation and to root this freedom in the plurality and unity of God. As theologians such as Pannenberg[1] have pointed out, the sheer multiplicity of creation has to be grounded in the Creator, the pluralism of the cosmos and of humanity comes from the creative will of God inseparable from the very being of God. The doctrine of the Trinity makes increasing sense the more one ponders the sheer fact of unity and differentiation as the very fabric of the world, of all reality mental and material, the energy pulsing through it, the ongoing making and remaking of what is new and different. This also ties in with the Trinitarian idea of freedom, form and historicity or authentic life, which is also a rich conceptuality through which to understand authority through the Christian lens. Authority increases our freedom by shaping it along the lines of the divine desire, avoiding chaotic freedom and deadening formalism. We can see this precisely lived out in Jesus of Nazareth. in

[1]W. Pannenberg, *Systematic Theology*, vol 2. Edinburgh T&T Clark, 1994 p. 62.

132

the power of the Spirit. Western democracy uniquely achieved the richest synthesis of freedom and form working out the ethos rooted in Jesus.

How should we envisage Christianity affecting society and the authorities of a society? It was born into a very hostile environment and existed for centuries under conditions of persecution. Forsaking violent means, it absorbed this hostility, and so became the moral driver of Western civilization for two millennia. This has not been as a result of a direct template, or specific political constitution, for the running of a society by the church, but rather indirectly as Christian moral and spiritual impulses gradually took hold of individuals and then became principles of social and political communal life, at higher or lower intensities. For example the hospice and hospital was a Christian institution born of the impulse to care for the sick of any tribe or race, basically the working out of the parable of the Good Samaritan. Abolishing slavery was a major socio-economic reform enacted by the Emperor on the clear Christian moral impulse of loving our neighbour.

But there was no specific political or social manifesto for organizing a society left by Jesus, as there was by Mohammed. The Christian influence worked by the Spirit through all manner of circumstances and events and characters freely acting to help the will of God to be done in Christ-like fashion. And this process has had 'booms and slumps', for example the Eastern Orthodox Church having to live under Islamic domination for centuries, and then Soviet rule. And the Church itself has fallen into the sin of abusing power all too often. The Christian impulse is to seek a caring social order, justice and peace, freedom of thought and worship, recognizing all people as valuable, developing a fair and honest system of law. The authority of Christ must be Christlike: crusading in the name of Christ is a contradiction in terms, as is the inquisition. Christians look to Christ as the criterion of reform and change, and this self-criticism must occur often in this sinful world: this is a vitally important principle of Christianity, and has been the basis of the capacity of self criticism and reform, however long the process. This has been a slow development, but a definite one: the way of loving our neighbour has transformed structures as it has found them, and evolved as time has changed things. Newman's vision of the development of Christian doctrine[2] might apply to the development of social values and politics – although Newman's own papacy in fact hindered liberal democracy developing!

Going back to our analogy of creation as a home or household with all its multi-layered influences at play, direct and indirect, can be put to further use in the case of a society and nation. Structures of authority will be explicit and implicit, local and national, formal and informal, accepted gladly and accepted with difficulty. Christian theology acknowledges Christ as the supreme authority over all things, the church and also all the

---

[2]J.H Newman *The Development of Christian Doctrine* London 1845

created order including human history and society. This does not mean that the church should be governing society or controlling its rulers, as in the medieval doctrine of Hildebrand.[3] The church must be allowed to govern itself, and has a responsibility to try to influence the government of the world into Christ-like ways, such as care for the weak, poor and oppressed. But the church now has learned over the centuries that it is not an agency to compel anyone nor to coerce or threaten governmental systems into structures or policies: the Gospel mode of authority is to work by free personal consent. Hence democracy itself is thoroughly compatible with, as well as historically a product of, the Protestant Christian influence on culture and politics[4] with the message of even the poorest person being precious to God and therefore important in how society is run.

'The divine right of kings' doctrine gave way to the idea of the people all having a say. This development of practice and thought illustrates the way that the logic of Christ works itself out in history, over time, in the guidance of the Spirit. The notion that God anointed the king who ruled as a Christian monarch, not as a brutal dictator, retains a residual place in the British Constitution; but this royalist idea was superseded by the democratic ideal which must be said to have a deeper basis in Christian truth and practice. But democracy itself can become corrupt, the *'demos'* can turn savage and vote in a murderous regime as it did Hitler. This democratic ideal in fact depends on a morally good *'demos'*, it arose on Christian soil and it needs a moral framework to function as we assume it will. Democracy depends on the winners respecting the losers of elections and vice versa: if not then tribalistic violence occurs and insurgency by the minority against the majority. The mutual acceptance of election results also depends on rigorous honest and fairness in the electoral process, again something that depends on honest people and officials, a moral population. Secular political analysts forget this, assuming that honesty is just a law of nature, rather than a moral achievement to be nurtured. Democratic government is supported by Christians on the grounds of humans being equal in the sight of God – but any democratic vote to persecute minorities would of course conflict with any Christian political judgement.

The economic dimension of liberal democracy, capitalism, similarly needs the Christian moral framework to ensure that the 'unacceptable face of capitalism' – the idolization of greed and profit at all costs – does not 'trample on the face of the poor'. Capitalism has to be qualified by strong systems of public care for all, and again this is a structural

---

[3]Pope Gregory VII from 1073-1085, he asserted the sovereign right of the church and dominated secular rulers through the power of excommunication.
[4]Protestant specifically. Roman Catholicism rejected democracy into the 1930s, fearing socialism.

evolution driven by the realization of the logic of neighbour love and the Jesus way. The Gospel rejects the notion that the poor deserve their fate, rather they are to be helped and cared for. It is also bad business practice to lie and cheat and deceive, to bribe and corrupt contractors for personal gain. That is wrong, and ultimately the spread of such a culture will bring an economy down: sin becomes endemic and destroys what it infects. A moral framework is needed here as elsewhere in Western society, which tacitly presupposes such trust and honesty. But again also, Jesus left no economic plan for the world; he left the power of his love and goodness and trusted the Spirit and the Church to unfold this logic of love and care in and through societies and their evolving structures.

Secularism is a new experiment,[5] still trading upon Christian ideals in the form of 'human rights' as enshrined by the United Nations in 1945 to protect individuals against rogue states. But the overall tendency of secularist society is one of an increasingly functionalist view of human life, and a crisis of altruism – which is fast disappearing and has no basis in secularist ideology. The authority of liberal government and of human rights is supported by Christians – indeed it arose from the Christian Gospel – again because it values individuals against possible abuse, although the wooden application of rights to those who plan to murder others raises complications. Freedom is to be encouraged and protected, not deadened by 'form' as with the communist system, but chaotic freedom threatens everyone. The Christian ethos indirectly influencing constitutions, governments, legal systems and global international rights has arguably produced the best synthesis of freedom and form for thriving of societies. Breaking down of tribalism and hostility by 'truth and reconciliation' seems a core ethic behind this phenomenon. Christianity as a power base or ideology ceases to be Christian: the old South African 'Apartheid' regime fell into this category, and the present Russian regime and its use of ecclesiastical power and jurisdiction in seeking to gain suzerainty over nations formerly in the USSR likewise can hardly be deemed Christian. That is authoritarianism, rather than Christ like authority.

Society needs authority, but good authority, so that human freedom and diversity is maximized and yet order given to preserve safety for the space needed for freedom to be exercised and indeed preserved for the future. Some options taken now might foreclose options in future generations. This major merit of the Christian theological and spiritual way of 'indirectness' helps to shape structures and institutions, rather than impose or claim to an institutional framework for society and its structures. Authority is needed, but we need to prevent its abuse. Attacks

---

[5]See Grace Davie, *Europe: the Exceptional Case. Parameters of Faith in the Modern World*, London: Darton, Longman and Todd, 2002.

on authority itself can lead to loss of faith in institutions and cynicism,[6] which in turn is dangerous for democracy, as the history of Europe in the 1930s shows when 'the strong leader' was applauded over against the petty minded and corrupt bureaucrats and elected bodies getting in the way of efficiency. This is a reminder to Christian people to get involved in the authority structures of government at all levels, to try to maintain the Jesus way in social structures, and not leave other values to dominate.

It is a vital distinction that the church itself should not directly govern the world as a power structure, but Christian principles should be continually mediated into the structures in order to mitigate wrong and bring about the good. These structures will of course be affected and reformed as this process goes on, but that does not mean rule by clerics or church structures over society: that is rather the Islamic vision. Christ's temptations by the devil in the Gospels include that of power over the world, a temptation that, alas, was not resisted by the church in history as can be seen in the Prince Bishops, Cardinals and their political and economic power. The 'Grand Inquisitor' in Dostoevsky's *Brothers Karamazov*[7] exercises total power in medieval Seville and arrests Christ when he appears in the city, accusing him of having offered the people a vision of authority and freedom combined. It was inhuman of Christ to do so, because the people cannot bear the burden of this combination. 'I tell you man has no more agonizing anxiety than to find someone to whom he can hand over with all speed the gift of freedom with which the unhappy creature was born.' The Grand Inquisitor is subtle, not arguing that voluntary servitude arose because people are lazy and consumed only by the desire for secure, petty pleasures. 'Man is born a rebel', the Grand Inquisitor says. Undisciplined, greedy, out for himself – a Hobbesian animal. Yet the rebelliousness is self-destructive; the Hobbesian animal cannot control even himself. It is mutually destructive: the animals will kill off each other, and no one will be left. Thus they go in search of some person or principle to stand above themselves, who will put an end to this terrible licence which is their freedom, the figures of Mohammed or Nietzsche's *Übermensch* come to mind, but the medieval papacy and hierarchy is clearly Dostoevsky's focus. In perhaps the most famous passage of the parable, the Grand Inquisitor declares:

> …Man seeks to worship only what is incontestable, so incontestable, indeed, that all men at once agree to worship it all together. For the chief concern of these miserable creatures is not only to find something that I or someone else

---

[6]At the time of writing British Members of Parliament are suffering from such cynicism as their allowances and expenses are put into the public forum. See the Archbishop of Canterbury's article in the The Times 23.05.09 *Humiliation of MPs must stop*.
http://www.timesonline.co.uk/tol/news/politics/article6344882.ece.
[7]F. Dostoevsky, *The Brothers Karamazov*, trans. David Magarshack, Harmondsworth: Penguin Books, 1982, Book 5, Chapter 5, pp. 288–311.

can worship, but to find something that all believe in and worship, and the absolutely essential thing is that they should do so *all together.*

Something incontestable and certain, something which brings people together: this is the bond of authority. The more people search for human relations which are solid like the stones of a church, the more people will abandon their freedom – and this, proclaims the Grand Inquisitor, is how it should be. Christ's sin therefore was to encourage man to develop in himself a better strength than the licentious strength with which he was born; it was a sin of nurturing man, of setting an example. But the Hobbesian animal cannot learn. Worldly authorities must do for him what he cannot do for himself. 'Miracle, mystery and authority' – that is higher, repressive authority – these are the 'only three forces that are able to conquer and hold captive forever the conscience of these weak rebels for their own happiness. 'Authority is founded on the illusions of miracle and mystery, and they are necessary illusions.' When freedom and science, which will lead humanity to disaster in the future, even to cannibalism, people will crawl back to the feet of the church hierarchy and give up their freedom, for this form, this total control.

Dostoevsky captures the distinctive characteristic of Jesus' authority: it seeks to set individuals free, not to dominate them and subjugate, his rule is the rule of love and he evokes the response of love, bringing about holiness and goodness which is authentic. And for Jesus 'the Hobbesian animal' can indeed learn, grow and fulfil his or her potential as created by God. Jesus enables people to be fulfilled as creatures, and so fosters the fulfilment of creation itself, its freedom and true form. Secular versions of the dominating power claim of the Inquisitor exist in Stalinism and Nazism with their associated 'cult of personality', 'Big Brother' in Orwell's *1984*, to whom even the resistant eventually submit their wills, in adoration – 'I love Big Brother' says Winston at the end of the novel, 'I do'. His freedom and critical thought has been surrendered fully and willingly, which is the requirement of that state. But Christ's authority, the revealed desire of God, brings about reasonable and moral transformation with no hint of manipulation and abuse of power.

Sennett points out that political leaders have drawn on different kinds of authority figures to cement their own validity.[8] Stalin, for example, projected himself as the father figure who should be trusted to look after the people if they obeyed him. George Orwell's 'Big Brother' suggests this kind of authority figure as important in the modern technological world of mass media reaching into the very soul of the people, even as far as to get children to disobey their parents and report them to the police for 'thought crime': Big Brother takes care of us, and the other side of the deal is our total obedience and conformity. He gazes, as a deity, into our

---

[8]R. Sennett, *Authority*, London: W. W. Norton, 1980, p. 194.

lives and controls us totally. Orwell's study of authority in the twentieth century probes deeply into the relationship of freedom and authority, the latter conditioning and shaping the former, and even defining what is 'rational'. Our Western culture has elements of this world, as of course does much non-Western culture, for example Iran after the Islamic revolution dictates what is reasonable in terms of Islamic doctrine, as do fully Islamic states such as Saudi Arabia, where to quit Islam for another faith is an impossible idea, since Islam is the truth about reality.[9] Today's equivalent in the West might be 'the market' and its logic, its own rationality which would be heresy to deny, it is the mental and real system shaping how we live and move and have our being and as such the great authoritative context or web of Western life.

Authority of the right kind is necessary for human thriving but can become deformed. Sociologically it is vital to knit human beings with their freedom together and to find ways of working from within the individual rather than to compel. The Western market appeals to individual freedom, but clearly unfettered capitalism, leaving the weak and poor vulnerable to inhumane exploitation, is not compatible with Christianity, as Newbigin points out.[10] But capitalism, duly regulated, is so dominant a culture as to qualify as an authoritative assumption in Western civilization, although as always there is opposition to this authority in the 'anti-globalization' movement, akin to the anarchists of the nineteenth century. No doubt MacIntyre's 'manager' – the high priest of contemporary society – is a figure of authority, an expert we need to need and want, someone who can organize things for us, and yet who tells us it is good for us to be flexible and dispensable, ready to be sacked and retrained. 'People turn to the managers to take care of their problems'.[11]

Emotivism reigns with particular power in the area of politics, where keen rational debate is almost a forgotten art and of little interest to the public. Voters are appealed to by the arts of the advertising industry; actual argumentation and consistency mean little. Politicians need the abilities of actors to be successful in gaining power. Fundamental principles, for example of democratic accountability, are of little interest to politicians nor electors. The media has a large part to play in backgrounding such matters, while foregrounding others. An example of this is the ongoing process of the transfer of power from the nation state to the European Community in the face of reasoned democratic protests in referenda and

---

[9]A legal ruling in Malaysia decided that a woman who had become Roman Catholic could not legally be deemed non-Muslim, and identity necessarily part of her being in that society (Lionel Beehner, 'Religious Conversion and Sharia Law', Council on Foregin Relations, see www.cfr.org/publication/13552/religious_conversion_and_sharia_law.html).

[10]L. Newbigin, *Gospel in a Pluralist Society*, London: SPCK, 1989, p. 206.

[11]R. Sennett, *Authority*, op cit., p. 153.

ignored election results.[12] This attitude entails an assumption in political managers that this process must go on for the common good, it is a necessary and misunderstood movement of history which the common herd will in the end learn to love. The political and moral criticisms will pass away as we 'move forward'. Marcuse's words fit curiously well:

> Just as this society tends to reduce, and absorb opposition (the qualitative difference!) in the realm of politics and higher culture, so it does in the instinctual sphere. The result is the atrophy of the mental organs for grasping the contradictions and the alternatives and, in the one remaining dimension of technological rationality, the *Happy Consciousness* comes to prevail. It reflects the belief that the real is the rational, and that the established system, in spite of everything, delivers the goods. The people are led to find in the productive apparatus [for which substitute the bureaucratic apparatus] the effective agent of thought and action to which their personal thought and action can and must be surrendered. And in this transfer, the apparatus also assumes the role of a moral agent. Conscience is absolved by reification, by the general necessity of things. In this general necessity guilt has no place. One man can give the signal that liquidates hundreds and thousands of people, then declare himself free from the pangs of conscience, and live happily ever after.[13]

This articulates the decline in the authority of reason and intellectual debate in the political forum today, in fact the erosion of 'the public forum' as a place where the polis orders its affairs. The bureaucrat – MacIntyre's manager – makes such decisions today, more and more. And the deeply penetrative power of public rhetoric in the hands of public service broadcasters shapes what is 'reasonable' to think. George Orwell was an employee of the BBC in his early career.

In general, democratic authority still reigns in the West rather than naked power or authoritarianism, that is to say the law is, broadly speaking, still respected and implemented, the government is still accountable, the press is free to speak, people are free to live their lives as they wish, the only proviso being that the exercise of their freedom should not harm others. Freedom therefore recognizes authority in the form of law and government as vital to peace and order in society. But the Christian moral ethos which was the cultural norm in society has now been rejected by the state as having any useful public role for the majority population. Authority as an essential good for the keeping of order and peace is a Christian teaching, gained from the apostle Paul, without the law we would be in chaos and disorder. And this idea in secular form can be seen in Hobbes' Leviathan where the power of the

---

[12]Referenda rejecting the European Constitution in several EU states, including France, were met by a repackaging of the Constitution into a Treaty, which itself suffered a referendum defeat; the clear will of the voters of Europe being ignored by 'the management'. See www.civitas.org.uk/eufacts/FSTREAT/TR6.htm.

[13]Herbert Marcuse, *One Dimensional Man*, Boston: Beacon Press, 1964, p. 79.

state is accepted to stop mayhem breaking out. This is the idea of a basic framework, without which life would be Darwinian jungle warfare, with the strong oppressing the weak. In his day, Paul of Tarsus taught that the state and magistracy were God-given to keep order and prevent chaos, despite their fallibility. This is a corollary of creation: we need peace and order to maintain life, however imperfect a state may be, and this order should provide for freedom of worship and belief and expression, freedom and form.

A fascist form of rule could conceivably satisfy the Hobbesian ideal, and the 1930s the dictators were supported by the Roman Catholic Church in many countries; as Christopher Dawson put it:

> there seems no doubt that the Catholic social ideals set forth in the encyclicals of Leo XIII and Pius XI have far more affinity with those of Fascism than with those of either Liberalism or Socialism. In the same way it is clear that Catholicism is by no means hostile to the authoritarian ideal of the State. Against the Liberal doctrines of the divine right of majorities and the unrestricted freedom of opinion the Church has always maintained the principles of authority and hierarchy and a high conception of the prerogatives of the State.[14]

Here we can note a major difference between theologies expressing how the Christian Gospel affects and influences the state and society. Roman Catholicism regards the institutional church hierarchy as the way Christianity should influence government, Pope and Holy Roman Emperor together, for example, acting in concert. Evangelicalism sees 'the church' as a movement of Christian disciples at work in society in many and various ways, indirectly shaping the future for the will of Christ, so that the likes of William Wilberforce, Elizabeth Fry, Josephine Butler, Lord Shaftesbury, and Florence Nightingale exemplify the impetus of the Gospel at work resisting evil and inculcating good.[15]

A Christian ideal surely assumes that human freedom is to be advanced in all ways, contributing to the common good, and that freedom to implement the ways of caring, of fostering truth and justice, of helping the sick and the poor, is the duty of the Christian citizen. The Evangelical movement of the nineteenth century took this message into every crevice of society and formed a national ethos, to which social

---

[14]Christopher Dawson, *Religion and the Modern State*, London: Sheed & Ward, 1935, p. 135.
[15]W. G. Ward exemplifies the 'high church' failure to grasp that the 'laity' is church in his criticism of the Church of England in mid nineteenth century for failing the poor: in fact the likes of Shaftesbury were actively passing legislation to improve conditions in mines and factories. See W. G. Ward, *The Ideal of A Christian Church*, London, J. Toovey, 1844 [reprinted Farnborough, Hants UK 1969], p. 414. Ward romanticises the state of the working classes in France and Roman Catholic nations, entirely forgetting their plight as shown by the enthusiasm for the Revolution of 1789, a few decades prior to Ward's book.

reformers in government could appeal and which could be appealed to by the public. Movements to abolish slavery, reform prisons, improve working conditions in mines and factories, education, reform of nursing, all sprang from this evangelical movement and its values which became normal. These of course built on the best of the previous centuries of Christendom. This movement pushed the widening of the franchise during the nineteenth century to include all men, and then women. The Liberal Party of the nineteenth century was essentially based on the broad Christian ethic of universal freedom and equality. Again it is interesting to note that Christopher Dawson points out the traditional Roman Catholic teaching 'is of course diametrically opposed to the liberal democratic ideal of absolute equality which ignores the very idea of status and regards society as a collection of identical units.'[16] The advance of democracy occurred in the nations with predominantly Protestant cultures, and this evidently was no accident.

The contemporary situation might bring in the Islamic social philosophy, much more akin to the traditional Roman Catholic vision, with heavy clerical influence and religious law and custom having a direct say in government and constitution. Liberal democracy and theocracy make awkward bedfellows. This is particularly true over freedom of critical thought and expression, which Protestant Europe through the Enlightenment came to champion as a good, since truth will establish itself and needs no shielding from any question at all, a development of the principle of *'semper reformanda'*, continual self-criticism and questioning. The Protestant Enlightenment tradition of Western Europe enabled freedom of thought its place, and maintained the Christian moral ethos believing it to be universal. Evangelical Protestant Christianity fuelled democracy and accountability, looking to empower individuals to have confidence in themselves as loved by God. Wesley's preaching led to poor people improving their lives as a result of their new-found faith in Jesus Christ, and building common life together; trade unions were the direct result of this movement, and these flew in the face of the laws of the day, using only peaceful means.

Wesley announced the authority of Christ for all, undoubtedly set the poor free from self-denigration, bringing them to see themselves as made in the image of God, precious and loved, not units of production in a factory or mine. Wesley's ministry can be seen in the context of the created order, restoring creatures to themselves in the midst of a sinful world, restoring freedom and form, in the way of Jesus, the true authority and ruler. Wesley's ministry and the response to it showed that 'the Hobbesian animal' can learn and indeed is not 'an animal', that a person is free and enjoys 'autonomy': the Gospel entails the 'law written our hearts', neither a chaotic freedom nor a heteronymous legalism

---

[16]Christopher Dawson, *Religion and the Modern State*, op cit., pp. 134–135.

gaining our submission. The household of creation has a clear voice running through it in many and various ways, crystallized in the person of Christ the creative wisdom of the cosmos, healing, restoring bring it to itself.

British Protestant Christianity, through the process of democracy, affected the structures and mores of the state at all levels. The Trinitarian and Christological imperatives of Christianity fed through indirectly, although of course by no means as fast as could have been desired ideally. The battle for the will of Christ to be done always needs fighting anew: in the nineteenth century by philanthropists and reformers, to Trade Unions through Methodism, to the old age pension through Lloyd George's Free Church liberalism, to the 'welfare state' in the mid-twentieth Century. And the professions were deeply coloured by altruism derived from Christian faith. Christ-like care for the weak, sick, elderly, women and children, is a simple model to follow and many did. The 'Nonconformist Conscience' fought against exploitation, alcoholism, prostitution, as did the Salvation Army at the start of the twentieth century. The Civil Service ethic of honesty and duty was rigorously promoted, and many examples of this religious impact could be given. And yet of course this society contained a wide diversity of views and much dissent, which became more and more prevalent. Women's suffrage is an important example, and the trial of Oscar Wilde for homosexuality and his imprisonment reflects an oppressive side of the culture that was reformed much later. Was it Christ-like to imprison Wilde for his sexual behaviour? On the other hand, today, is it Christ-like to encourage such behaviour and use of freedom? Form and freedom in the Gospel are not oppressive nor chaotic: society and state needed to reform in this regard in the light of the form of Christ, a change that did come gradually and indirectly. The ongoing process of self-reformation continues, in the church by the light of Christ and the unfolding of the logic of his Gospel.

Christians are not anarchists who want to attack structures; but as Newbigin sagely pointed out, we need structures in society to preserve life and enable it be more than jungle warfare. Nor are Christians conservatives who regard the structures as part of the unalterable order of creation.[17] They are called to work as Jesus worked, personally and humanely, telling the truth and promoting care for others. This is the way in which the European civilization, very slowly, developed into liberal democracy – but that is not the kingdom of God, it is not 'the end of history' as Fukuyama so hastily put it. Indeed Roman Catholic scholars are asking whether secular democracy is dangerous for Catholicism because it prevents Catholics speaking in the public sphere when their views are distinctively Catholic, pushing these views into the private closet: but who is to define what is private and public? If Catholic moral teaching is

---

[17]L. Newbigin, *Gospel in a Pluralist Society*, op cit., p. 208.

beyond the pale, not even allowed into the debate in public policy areas, then this is not pluralistic but the implementation of an alien ideology. Christians generally may need to be far more alert to what 'Big Brother' is telling them is 'reasonable' for public policy options.

Theology of law and the state

The phenomenon of law for regulating human behaviour points to the reality of human failure to live according to the grain of the universe, the way of being of our great cosmic home or household. We have failed to observe the balance of the gift of freedom and the gift of form, and so our relationships are fractured, we are alienated from each other in all sorts of ways. Through the ages, societies of all kinds have needed systems of law to prevent chaos and anarchy. The Eastern Christian tradition sees this as our failure to fulfil our potential and true destiny, with Jesus Christ being the remedy for this waywardness, since his life and work sets us back onto the path we should have taken. The Western tradition under Augustine's influence sees us as fallen from an initially perfect state into a state of sinful being, needing the grace of Jesus Christ as the only remedy. The human will has become corrupted and detached from the divine desire. This Christian assessment of the human predicament corresponds well with the actual confused and chaotic state we find in human history, ancient and modern. Law is necessary to order human violence and dishonesty, to control the will to power by those unconcerned at unleashing destruction on others. Law seeks to implement 'form', structure or stability in society, to control 'freedom' which has lost order and become perverse. Law is human authority in a sinful world, which yet has a root in creation and is now indispensable, indeed in today's contemporary world many lawless societies are desperate for 'law and order' to prevent criminal and militia warfare ruining life for the people as chaos reigns; and on the other hand tyranny oppresses and paralyses many other nations by corrupt violent government, some based on fanatical religious rule. Law, for a Christian theology, is to protect freedom for people by way of a fair and honest framework of order.

In the New Testament moral law is seen as given in creation to all peoples,[18] before the special covenant law given to Moses – that is to say we know right from wrong to put it at its most basic. The law is God-given as a way of an ordered life and of coping with sin. Societies need structures to prevent anarchy and the figure of ' the magistrate' in some form is a divinely appointed role to maintain order in society, according to St Paul.[19] To implement the law fairly in society is a good thing, to

---

[18]Romans 1.
[19]Romans 13.

use state power oppressively is not: and the state, whatever its form, can easily be corrupted, as the book of Revelation declares. Theologically the Christian message about law and behaviour is Trinitarian: Jesus gives us the 'way the truth and the life' and peace with God as the fulfiller and fulfilment of the law, the Spirit 'writes the law on our hearts' so that discipleship is not a question of mere 'law keeping' but of grace enabling love and obedience to God the Father. Any specifically Christian view of law has to remember this cooperative, participatory character of the divine life acting in human history.

The Gospel tells of ongoing human sin in history and the permanent struggle to achieve justice and peace in the world, which is not just an inevitable progressive process but a moral battle. 'The End of History' has not been reached, humanity goes down as well as up in its moral progress. The Church's role is to work for the kingdom of God in the world wherever it can, but it has no blueprint for managing society; it is not an agency to set up an earthly system of government, nor to validate any particular form of government. The Church seeks to bring the loving authority of Christ to influence any and all human activity, and the Church is under the authority of Christ and is not free to reshape her message in any other way. The Inquisition for example, and witch hunting, were ghastly wrongs committed by the Church in contravention of the way of Jesus, and they exemplify a kind of self-deification by church rulers in making themselves infallible arbiters and enforcers of the divine will on earth, with disastrous results, for victims and for the deep damage done to the church itself.

The Church needs to reform itself, and to help the state to do the same; the church does not have the task of setting up an earthly kingdom of structural state power. As argued earlier, history goes on, the church seeks to bring the way of Jesus to bear on political and legal structures, indeed on industrial and financial structures, on diplomatic and healthcare structures, as they develop. This influence has been indirect, not laying down a template of government, but rather influencing what is good and Christ-like in society and being aware of the dangers of power and suppressing freedom. People are equal before God and this has become a Christian imperative, as its logic has been realized, over time, starting with the abolition of slavery under the emperor Justinian – again not by a legal template left by Jesus but by unfolding the clear logical implications of his Gospel and life, indirectly bearing on state power and humanizing it. As Gibbon put it, it was the gradual effect of the waters of Baptism that changed the Roman Empire from the conversion of individuals, great and small in status.

Christian eschatology teaches that 'the end is not yet', that we live 'between the times' of the coming of Jesus and the final dénouement of history, and in our worldly history we have the Gospel to preach and enact, holiness and love to implement in our own broken and fractured way. Perfectionism is not an option for a Christian reading of law and politics, we remain on the way, we go backwards as well as forwards, as twentieth-century and now twenty-first-century history shows with its ongoing violent oppression and injustices. Law is a sticking plaster for human fallible societies, but it is a God-given, temporary bandage which we need – above all with the way of the Gospel of Christ. In particular Christianity brings a unique contribution to the development of western culture, the imperative of self judgement and criticism, rooted in the cross of Jesus. The institutional church stands under the cross and needs to repent, not to extend a power over others as if it were infallible and sinless.

Law, however informal or customary, is needed by all societies because of the fact that people do not all act rightly to their neighbours; it is an interim necessity until the final coming of the kingdom of God when 'the lion will lie down with the lamb' and the divine loving desire reigns supreme. Criminal law deals with crimes, civil law with disputes over property or broken contracts or damage done. In a perfect world we would not need contracts, prisons, remedies for fraud or deception, and the need for law interestingly points to this human fallibility and need for a system, ultimately based on force, to prevent injustice, harm and oppression. The authority of the law is not of ultimate eschatological significance, but is divinely authorized as a means of enabling the injured human race to manage its waywardness, greed, and lack of kindness to others. But at the same time the fact that we do, as a race, want to ensure that such evils are controlled shows that the created grammar of human goodness remains as an acknowledged ideal, although we now need institutions to cover our moral nakedness and provide a means of controlling the consequences of greed, domination, lust and abuse of others. The phenomenon of law illustrates the human situation interpreted by Christian teaching, that is with a fundamental goodness tainted and distorted by human self will and the frustration of not doing the good that we know we should.

For the Apostle Paul, as we noted, the magistrate is a God-given institution to keep social order. Indeed Paul teaches that the 'ruler is God's servant for your good'. He urges his readers to pay taxes and be cooperative with the law, 'Let everyone be subject to the governing authorities. For there is no authority except from God, and those that exist have been instituted by God'.[20] Paul regards the authorities as necessary and somehow instituted by God to enable humans to coexist in peace – albeit a peace enforced by the power of the magistrate's sword and so by threat and power. This is not the final deep peace of the kingdom of Christ, but the best humanity can achieve in this interim era, 'between the times' 'Render to Caesar the things that are Caesar's' says Jesus to

---

[20]Romans 13:1–8.

his interrogators, affirming the importance of civil government, however imperfect; and 'render to God the things that are God's', stressing that Caesar, civil government, is not ultimate. Christians believe that the gospel message can influence society and culture, including political life and law, for the good, pointing to such reforms as the abolition of slavery by the Emperor Justinian and the ending of such practices as infanticide, and the whole movement towards democracy and provision of health and education services. Of course the church itself has often failed to implement the will of its own Lord and fallen short of the kingdom of God, but it has a vocation to work for the values of the kingdom as taught by Jesus with its notable focus on the needs of the poor and helpless, a focus taken forward from the prophetic voices of the Old Testament and sharpened.

State law has a *prima facie* authority, whatever political system Christians have inhabited, beginning with the Roman Imperial dictatorship. But legal systems and laws vary. Nazi law, for example, inculcated all manner of evil in comparison with that of the liberal democracy: although as we will be pondering, it may well be that the early twenty-first century democracy is witnessing a definite shift towards a deeply secularist utilitarian form of law posing increasing difficulties to Christians. Human practices and institutions are corruptible, even those originating with the highest of motives. The book of Revelation burns with righteous indignation at the way the Roman Empire was then acting against the cause of right with its militarism, greed, violence and destructiveness, including its oppression of the faithful. The moral authority of law lessens to the degree that it departs from right and tends to wrong, but anarchy has no place in the Christian tradition and there will always be a *prima facie* duty to obey the legal authorities unless there is an overriding reason to disobey. Christian 'apologists', advocates of the faith to Roman Emperors, commended the gospel to rulers as being good for society and peace. The Apologists were very keen to gain freedom in the Roman Empire for Christian worship and faith, freedom from persecution, and this took some time to achieve.

Law, an institution found in all human societies, can be enacted for good or ill. Forms of government are all corruptible. Religion, as Barth points out, is another universal human institution or practice apparently as old as the human race itself that can be a human obsession of a very negative kind. Creation is full of potential for good as human freedom works with the grain of the universe for positive purposes, and yet this potential can be distorted towards the negative. Theologically it is important to note that this negative contrasts with the positive purposes of God the Creator for the created order; at the deepest level humanity has a vision of something good and a destiny to which the race should work and aspire, a vision and destiny signalled by the fact of our being made in the divine image. The further we depart from that image into viewing people as mere objects of our power, the less humane we and our societies become.

The more a culture incarnates Christ-like legislation and practices, encouraging Christ-like human living and relationships, the more it implements the desire of the Creator, the divine will, the authority of God.

The West has developed a system of liberal democracy and capitalism in order to try to implement fairness and represent everyone in political decision-making and law-making, and a deep dimension of this has been that winners of elections do not seek to destroy losers, who can campaign in the next election and whose views continue to matter. The secularization of Western democratic law has raised questions about the compatibility of secular democratic law and Christianity, and Roman Catholic theorists are particularly raising this as a question. An article entitled 'Is American Democracy Safe for Catholicism?'[21] illustrates this issue clearly, inverting the more traditional question as to whether Roman Catholicism can in fact support liberal democracy. The law in Western democracy is based on the majority opinion of the electorate, and this can clearly be deeply sinful in Christian eyes, as when the Nazi Party was voted in by the German people in the 1930s. But other systems can also produce wrong, and religious regimes have a poor record in this regard: as liberal democracy may be inclined to stress 'freedoms' over against 'form', fascist authoritarian Catholic regimes have clamped 'form' down on freedom of the individual historically. But elected majorities are not infallible, any more than Cardinal Archbishops.

The liberal democratic model does have the advantage of regular elections: if wrong is perceived to be done, then governments can be rejected by the electorate – a kind of negative value for democracy, and this via negative of democracy may be its most compelling attraction. After all, Roman Catholics can vote for parties reflecting their views, and form a party if they find one lacking. In the 1930s they did have one, the Centre Party, but the Pope fatally disbanded it in his deal with Hitler, by the 1934 Concordat[22]. As Roman Catholic scholars Gary D. Glenn and John Stack say, 'it seems historically plausible that Protestantism is somehow akin to democracy in a way that Catholicism is not. Furthermore, the Encyclicals of Pius IX (Syllabus of Errors 1864), of Leo XIII (Diuturnum 1881 and Immortale Dei 1885), and of Pius XI (Quas Primas 1925) considered democracy anti-Catholic.'[23] Democracy for the Vatican conjured up the works of the French Revolution and

---

[21]Gary D. Glenn and John Stack, in *The Review of Politics: Christianity and Politics*, vol. 61, 1999, pp. 5–29.

[22]See Klaus Scholder, *The Churches and the Third Reich*. London: SCM 1987.

[23]Ibid., p. 8. Compare the corroborating remarks of Christopher Dawson in the previous chapter.

'heretics', that is Protestants implementing democracy and liberalism in their nations.

The state, according to the decree Quas Primas 1925, should underwrite Roman Catholic faith and moral teachings. 'And as late as 1940', say Glenn and Stack, 'Father John Ryan, the distinguished Catholic liberal, wrote that separation of church and state and religious freedom were acceptable expedients when circumstances prevented establishing the Catholic faith as the state religion.'[24] The state was to be the instrument of the Roman Catholic Church, and this could be democratic in a sense if a large majority voted for this, although it does offend most Protestant views of the democratic nation state since this would give power over the state, in some form, to the Vatican, itself a state. Protestant views on religion and politics have been that tolerance is the best policy, but not tolerance of the intolerant. John Locke's Letter Concerning Toleration stated: 'That Church can have no right to be tolerated by the Magistrate, which is constituted upon such a bottom, that all those who enter into it, do thereby, *ipso facto*, deliver themselves up the Protection and Service of another Prince.'[25]

In terms of contemporary debate about culture and democracy in relation to the issue of loyalty to nation and state is the question of radical Islamic loyalty to the Umma and its welfare as more important than loyalty to a Western state and its democratic values.[26] The Christian view is that political structures should conform with the justice and fairness we would associate with Jesus, rather than create some structural institutions to control society. And as Barth might have advised, the Anglican Establishment, in its upper echelons, is bound to damage and weaken its full identity as a church of Jesus Christ as the process of secularization continues and it finds itself a chaplain to secular structures.

The law does shape assumptions as to what is acceptable or not. The changes in divorce law and arrangements over custody of children and financial settlements have been deep and are very contested by divorced fathers as unfair, no longer related to any moral fault and so a matter of amoral managerial administration. The declassification of cannabis, for example, sent a social signal, as did the banning of smoking in public places, as did the institutionalization of quasi-marital homosexual relationships in 'civil partnerships', the state thus signalling the equivalence of homosexual and marital relationships and putting up a positive invitation to young people to consider both pathways as a lifestyle.

---

[24]Ibid., p. 8.
[25]John Locke, *A Letter Concerning Toleration*, ed. James Tully, Indianapolis: Hackett, 1983, pp. 49–50.
[26]See Patrick Sookhdeo, *Faith, Power and Territory* (London: Isaac Publishing, 2008), for a magisterial treatment of this issue.

Here a clear departure from the Christian 'form' has been enacted, curiously with the help of votes of bishops in the House of Lords. A powerful influence of social construction is now in place in the UK encouraging some patterns of thought and behaviour, repressing others. H. L. A Hart argued that the law should not enforce 'morality', and should not seek to circumscribe liberty of action unless it harmed others – a dictum of course merely enshrining another, secularist, 'morality', and as pointed out above, and one not taking account of wider possible social harm. Western law has assumed this principle as its ideological guide in framing law since the 1960s. Although it has banned smoking in public places in the interests of promoting physical health and cutting health care costs, it does not see the same problems in alternative forms of sexual behaviour, the current limit being paedophilia, but on secularist terms there is no real reason for this boundary to be drawn, if a child's consent can be proven.

Law changes with cultural tides and new ideas and helps form them. Lord Denning was the classic example of a judge trying to keep pace with the times, or even to anticipate changing mores in society in mid-twentieth-century Britain. His decisions worked to promote women's rights being woven into British law during the 1960s and 70s, enabling women to claim a share of property on divorce. At that time there seemed to be an injustice which needed to be corrected. Today some feel this right has gone so far as to radically disadvantage divorced husbands, who claim that men are now suffering severe discrimination in secret family law courts. Divorce itself has become easy, free of 'fault'; moral judgements play no part any more in such cases. The taxation system currently disadvantages couples who are married in comparison with those who are not. Christian imperatives and practices, formerly of unquestioned authority, are increasingly discounted in secular culture, a culture which therefore chooses to ignore and distort the patterns of divine wisdom in creation, to the overall detriment of social well being.

So fast is the law now integrating formerly quite alien cultural practices that at the time of writing the public has been told that polygamy is to be accepted for the purposes of claiming benefits for wives, the crime of bigamy now being clearly downgraded by implication. In fact there seems to be no reason now, under our secular and amoral legal system, why 'marriage' or dual 'partnerships' of a man and a woman should be normative: why should polygamous or polyandrous domestic arrangements not be acknowledged as normal? There is no real answer to this question now, given the powerful detachment of law from any one moral tradition as its root. The Christian view of marriage is distinctive. Women and men are without question equal before God and each other, the tradition of women being akin to a chattel to be purchased is quite alien the Christian way, as is polygamy which demotes the personal link between a man and a woman in the loving relationship sealed with the sexual bond. Clearly men and women are distinct biologically and in some other more subtle ways, but mutual respect is the longstanding Christian emphasis in how each regards the other, and also mutual need. Each is a gift to the other, male strength and power is not an excuse for domination of women, and the traditional note of authority is really about protection and stable provision for the woman, 'to love worship and to cherish' not a claim to servitude and subservience, absolute human worth is attributed to the woman in the Book of Common Prayer marriage service. This a covenant relationship, rooted in the wider community, not questioning the equality of the spouses, and insisting on the total exclusivity of the union, there is no question of several wives. Polygamy is a crime in Western law, influenced by the Christian tradition, and is regarded even by purely secular writers as an institution reducing women to domestic chattels. 'Polygamy', says Bertrand Russell, 'can seldom be the general practice of a community, since there is not as a rule a great excess of females; it is the prerogative of chiefs and rich men. Many wives and children form a valuable property, and will therefore enhance the already privileged position of their owners. Thus the primary function of a wife comes to be that of a lucrative domestic animal, and her sexual function becomes subordinated.'[27] The Christian tradition has been unique in this regard in comparison with civilizations rooted in other cultures bringing women out of that classification and into the place of equal co-humanity with men. The feminist attack on Christianity seems to forget that it was Jesus, and his focusing of the Hebraic view of creation and covenant, that achieved this drastic reform.

Radical thinkers like Foucault emphasize this socially controlling purpose of law: why should anyone be stopped from behaving in thoroughly eccentric fashion, why does society have any right to prevent activity taken by some or even by many to be 'offensive' or immoral? Secularism, emerging from, and abolishing, Christianity as the Western basis for law, assumed the validity of Christian ethics and for a while shadowed them, for example in marriage laws, Sunday trading legislation, and treatment of women. The authentic Christian view of law is plain: it should reflect the desire of God revealed decisively in the gospel, support fairness and equality and ban cruelty and oppression.

As secularism tightens its grip, clashes of values will occur, as they are in regard to homosexuality – which is now not just permitted but actively encouraged by the state. Those who disagree with the homosexual agenda are themselves now under the frosty 'chill factor' of law and are being hounded by the homosexual lobby to be silent or face charges of 'hate crime' and discrimination. A radical new form has reversed freedoms, from the appalling treatment of such as Oscar Wilde we now find that

[27]Bertrand Russell, *Marriage and Morals*, London: Allen & Unwin 1972 (1929) p 69.

those who do not accept the gay agenda face criminalization. This new form will shape choices and behaviour, and removes the necessary 'grey area' in culture where people can have legitimate disagreement: the new secularism is not necessarily liberal.

John Milbank has identified this secularized state and culture as an oppressive regime of intolerant liberalism seeking to dominate culture with a secular state that acts as a kind of new religion, rather like that of the Roman Empire and the cult of the divinized emperors. The utilitarian managerial culture, combined with the power of the market to form the desire of citizens into a pure materialism, adds up to a culture that claims to exalt absolute freedom while denying it a religious form in the mainstream. Milbank does not deal with Islam, the religion that is deeply respected by the secular state and offers a distinctive form for human freedom. Milbank urges the recovery of the vision of a Christian modernity, which would underpin true freedom and not mere legalist religious morality imposed on the people. The Christian vision of law and state is fundamentally positive, seeking to create safe space for freedom to thrive and exploit the potential of creation for all that is good, and true and beautiful. That vision has led to a culture of arts and sciences, of welfare and caring. The secular attack on it seems to be proving deeply destructive and negative of the common good.

The authority of human rights

The whole 'human rights' agenda parodies this Gospel ethos of the sanctity of all human life, since that agenda is committed totally to protecting individuals and their beliefs without any discrimination as to what these may be. Human Rights, rooted in the UN Declaration of 1948, are accorded to individuals to protect them whatever their views, to uphold their right to autonomy against the social networks and values they currently inhabit. Their *individual* rights completely triumph even over the rights of large numbers of people who are their potential victims.[28] The absolute freedom of such people is safeguarded, despite the beneficiaries of such law seeking to overturn states granting such freedoms to others.

A remarkable American judicial decision upholding the right of an individual to define themselves and their meaning concerned women's right to abort as fundamental to the American Constitution: 'At the heart of liberty is the right to define one's own concept of existence, of meaning, of the universe, and of the mystery of human life.'[29] On this basis a woman's right to abort, because of her self-understanding in

---

[28]The case of Abu Qtada is an interesting example. See *The Times*, 18 June 2008.
[29]Supreme Court 1992, Planned Parenthood v. Casey.

the cosmos, was made constitutional, a right deriving from a subjective decision about the mystery of life. This really does in a nutshell capture much of the liberal secular enterprise, freedom and individual sincerity leading to objective legal rights. The source of the authority for this right is the self in sincere interpretation of meaning of existence. The same reasoning would lead to the defence of the rights of women believing the reverse sincerely, and could defend the terrorist sincerely believing that the Supreme Court should be bombed into oblivion with all its Western ways.

Today's relativistic Western culture implements the legislative power of human freedom uncritically, privileging it over against the 'community' or nation – the mid-twentieth-century view of human rights developed against the background of the Nazi state oppressing individuals and creating a need for international law to give protection. As has been said, these are 'abstract rights' conferred on individuals globally, to be enacted by any court in the world irrespective of race, culture, opinions, age, gender, criminal record and so forth. The rights attach to the individual who can enact them anywhere in the world, even in a location he may be determined to destroy. Chief Rabbi Jonathan Sacks, while desperately aware of the Holocaust and need for individual protection against state mass murder, thinks that Western culture's dipolar focus on the autonomous individual and global rights omits any connection or bonding with actual local community life, customs, provisions and problems.[30] Of course the framers of these rights would say that is exactly the point: the oppressed themselves were rejected by their nation and state cut adrift and defenceless. Democracy had failed the victims of the Holocaust: the 'demos' had voted in a government that proceeded to abuse its mandate and set about mass murder. Human rights give people protection against the state and against the demos or electorate, since that proved insufficient a means of protection for the vulnerable minority. Human rights therefore seek to deal with individuals by absolutizing their individual needs, just in case liberal democracy fails to protect them.

J.L O'Donovan argues that this human rights culture is extremely individualistic, giving individuals rights by charters and laws over against governments of nations. This reduces public good to private good, and progressively transforms society into a jungle of competing individuals, none of whom owes duties to it by way of building up the common good.[31]

The post-1948 UN Declaration of Human Rights clearly assumes the Christian ethical tradition, secular liberal politicians picking the fruit from

[30]Jonathan Sacks, *The Politics of Hope*, London: Vintage 2000.
[31]J.L O'Donovan, 'Historical Prologomena to a Theological Review of Human Rights', *Studies in Christian Ethics* 4/2 1996 p 63.

the tree of the Christian orchard. The sanctity of human life is upheld, the right to life and to practise one's religion freely for example, and the duty of the state to ensure the list of rights is enforced. The international community of states are committed to defending individuals from state brutality as an ideal, and no Christian theologian would have disagreed. In fact in 1945 the liberal secular lawyers and politicians will have generally been Christians of some kind. The duty of the state not to kill, not to oppress, not to discriminate may have been a better way of putting what was intended: a version of the Ten Commandments extended to the body politic.

Fukuyama, however, points out that complications arise when 'individuals' present themselves as part a particular community – usually religious – with all the customs of that wider group, which thus attract claims to human rights. Individuals are not only autonomous isolated selves, especially non-Western individuals, they are born with a strong religio-cultural community identity. The fear is that from the individual rights will flow communal rights and the growth of communalist groups in nations with their own sets of rights to protect their customs. If those customs included, for example, arranged marriages without the proper consent of the girl, this in fact establishes a breach of individual rights in the nation. This point is closely linked to that of 'identity politics' of the Parekh Report. The Western view is that we are all autonomous individuals with 'rights', but the religious cultures of the East regard the group as primary and as bestowing identity on the member of the group. The fathers of the 1948 UN Declaration were not considering this wholly different context in the days before mass migration from Asia to Europe.

Michael Ignatieff's book on human rights illustrates this tension and one striking example is worth quoting. Here he tells his readers that human rights activists

> need to attend to conditions in which individuals on the bottom [of society, the poor] are free to avail themselves of such rights as they want. Increasing the freedom of people to exercise their rights depends on close cultural understanding of the frameworks that often constrain choice. The much-debated issue of genital mutilation illustrates this point. What may appear as mutilation in Western eyes is simply the price of tribal and family belonging to women; if they fail to submit to the ritual, they no longer have a place within their world. Choosing to exercise their rights, therefore, may result in a social ostracism that leaves them no option but to leave their tribe and make for the city. Human rights advocates have to be aware of what it really means for a woman to abandon traditional practices. But, equally, activists have a duty to inform women of the medical costs and consequences of these practices and to seek, as a first step, to make them less dangerous for women who wish to undergo them. …Consent in these cases means collective or group consent.[32]

---

[32]Michael Ignatieff, *Human Rights as Politics and Idolatry*, Princeton and Oxford: Princeton University Press, 2001, p. 72.

The practice of suttee, the 'voluntary' burning of widows, in India was banned by the British – against the local custom – but Michael Ignatieff's new form of liberalism would reject this as a sort global moral imperialism. Old liberalism operated on a tacitly Christian base; new-style liberalism is now relativistic and tolerant of all manner of customs deemed violent and oppressive to the old version.

The kind of example prevalent in the UK is that of 'arranged marriage' as matter of group consent overriding or embracing individual consent, and this practice is reportedly on the increase in Britain in large and exclusive minority communities.[33] In the secular world where there is no moral basis for the rights, how can genital mutilation and forced marriage be denied as a right, surely the state has a duty to uphold such rights for minority individuals? And when the point is made that individual girls are 'brainwashed' by such close religious communities into accepting such treatment freely, the reply can be made that the same applies to girls raised in secular liberal contexts. Conflicts between individual 'rights', with which the 1948 UNDHR was concerned, and newly but fiercely asserted 'community rights', which can undermine individual rights, are a growing problem with which Western governments are alarmingly unwilling to engage. This conflict illustrates the thesis articulated by Samuel Huntington's thesis of 'the clash of civilizations'. Genital mutilation and forced marriage contravene the Western and Christian understanding of the created individual 'in the image of God', whose freedom is to respected and bodies to be kept from harm – this simple criterion from creation can be usefully applied to various moral situations: 'does this practice cause physical harm to the individual'?

'Human rights' as set out in the 1948 UN Declaration are clearly a noble idea, but depend on the content given them by the UN, and the passage of sixty years shows that changing contexts can cause all kinds of quite deep contradictions. The right to change one's religion has never been a UN human right, it has always been blocked by Muslim states, whereas the UN Human Rights Council in 2008 passed a very contentious resolution against 'public defamation' of religion, with the Islamic states leading a block of votes against Western nations.[34] The one religion mentioned was Islam, and the resolution sought to ban any criticism of it, a clear violation of the human right to free speech. This illustrates again the difficulty of producing 'human rights' without an agreed moral basis. Whose idea of absolute rights is to prevail? There is almost an anthropological conflict at work here: the individual for Islam

---

[33] See the recent UK Parliamentary report on arranged marriage and 'honour'-based violence now on the increase in the UK: www.publications.parliament.uk/pa/cm200708/cmselect/cmhaff/263/263i.pdf.

[34] See www.un.org/News/Press/docs/2004/hrcn1082.doc.htm.

is subservient to the Umma, microcosmically representing a whole culture and way of life, whereas the 1948 UN Declaration of Human Rights is predicated on individuals as individuals to be protected from the claims of a wider 'community' – a community which might be oppressive of individual freedoms, Hitler's *'Ein Volk, Ein Reich, Ein Fuhrer'* being the very specific case driving the Declaration.

The Christian theological appraisal of rights must be in terms of doctrine of creation and the human vocation to create creation according to the divine desire, most fully revealed and enacted in Christ, the creative Wisdom and Word of God. The Creator calls us to true freedom and true form: Jesus gives us the way, the truth and the life to follow rather than a fixed and static ideology or legalistic religion which can become idolatries in themselves. Human duties to others, including speaking the truth in love, would seem to be the way for Christians to approach rights. They were surely right to oppose, for example, Suttee, genital mutilation and forced marriages on this Christological basis, as they rejected slavery. The Gospel entails a universal horizon of human goods and therefore 'rights'.

The impact of Christianity will always be indirect rather than a code to be imposed. Its freedom and form are personal rather than structurally institutional. The Gospel goes deeper than the merely structural and yet transcends it so as to inform it and adjust to new challenges and developments in history. The Christian inhabits the narrative of Jesus for today, and the spread of the Gospel moves that way of being into social attitudes and then structures. 'Rights', we can now see, are one way of trying to prevent wrongs being done, but they can work for wrong: they arose from the Christian tradition, were secularized at their roots, and now are a kind of judicial management tool. For the Christian, they need to be related to the way of Jesus, and be seen as recognizing the identity of people to be that of the image and likeness of God in a form of relationship implementing love, justice and the sanctity of life. And of course a Christian view of human rights might well include the rights of the unborn child as well as the 'right to abort', even multiply, now absolutised by the UK.

The language and practice of human rights has certainly done much good around the globe since the United Nations Declaration of Human Rights 1948,[35] and we can agree with George Newlands, 'that, despite many cogent objections, human rights language and human rights culture continue to be useful instruments towards the development of a fair, just and equal society.'[36] But it is true that they are 'abstract' rights and that as time moves on and contexts change from mid-twentieth-century European Nazi carnage, they are not sufficiently linked to duties. They require a living community of good people to ensure they 'work', that

[35]The text is available at www.un.org/Overview/rights html.
[36]G. Newlands, *Christ and Human Rights*, Aldershot: Ashgate, 2006, p. 178.

the duties entailed to the poor, persecuted and vulnerable are enacted, that the money and resources are provided to heal the sick and care for the displaced. 'Rights talk' is indeed now confused over individual and communal rights, where the question of truth must be allowed onto the public forum if individuals who do not, pace Michael Ignatieff, wish to undergo female circumcision but must because of a communal custom, for example. The truly Christian view on this is that Rights can be used by God as a means of his mercy and help, but they can be turned to demonic purpose if defending the indefensible in the name of the Volk or 'community', that is if they justify a false 'form'. The Christian tradition of our duty of care to universal humanity, rooted in the history and context of Jesus, is the surest basis for what human rights seeks to defend: love your neighbour as yourself. Is approving genital mutilation in any sense 'loving' one's neighbour, we have to ask ourselves?

Secular and sacred law and authority

Western law, and Western social morality, is going through a period of deep confusion as three streams of authority collide in a kind of whirlpool or vortex. As we have just seen, the old Christian moral social tradition has given rise to and been pushed back by the modern secular tradition, which imagines that the fruit of the Christian tree just occurred without the history of Christian faith and moral struggle. So reference to religious origins and principles has been repressed, faith is to be a strictly private matter of no relevance to public policy-making. Specifically Christian ethical ideas are not given any authority in the making of law, despite the presence of bishops in the House of Lords. But the West has for so long been influenced by the Christian moral ethos that many institutions such as monogamous marriage are the product of Christianity but taken for granted as a cultural norm, as if it arose by accident or a law of nature. Christianity, to a secular government keen to woo minority faiths, is an embarrassment to be pushed firmly into the private domain, not allowed in the public forum. On the other hand minority faiths are very much welcomed into public discussion as minority groups.

In particular where secular and Islamic custom clash, the former is yielding in the interests of multiculturalism and a sense that this policy will pay dividends for social peace and order. Secularism is not demanding the privatization of Islam, as it did of Christianity. So Islamic law is gaining a public authority, and recognised identity. Muslim advisors are now integrated into government departments to shape policy where it might affect Muslims. Islam of course is not a faith that can be privatized; rather the reverse, it is a way of life and ideally needs a Muslim society and state to shape life, economic custom, marriage laws, finance, and law. That is why Turkey since Kemal Attaturk's revolution, implementing a non-religious constitution for a Muslim nation, has used the army to impose its secular governmental regime, to keep down the power of the Mullahs and allow secular – by which is meant non clerical rather than atheist – democracy to govern. Islamic law bases itself on the Qur'an, claimed to be a text dictated by Allah through the mouth of Mohammed as a blank instrument, analogous to a printer attached to a computer.

It is into this context of social morals and legal authority that the Archbishop of Canterbury in February 2008 delivered a lecture and a BBC radio interview advocating the integration of dimensions of Sharia Law into British law, or as 'supplementary' to it. This evoked a level of protest he did not anticipate, the reason being that he was understood to have argued for a fragmentation of the nation's legal system along multicultural lines. The law of the land is one of the core institutions of a nation, part of its identity, and here the Archbishop seemed to have taken knife to it suggesting that it was deficient, since it did not command the loyalty of Muslims, who allegedly would like Sharia judicial proceedings in some areas of life. The national law, the very glue binding society together, seemed threatened. Moreover the principles of British law seemed to have been found wanting and capable of improvement by Muslim law. Islam was assumed to share a parity of spiritual and moral wisdom with British law, deemed to be 'secular' by the Archbishop.

Some aspects of Sharia law were described by the Archbishop as 'out of the question' for Britain, such as forced marriages. Why there would be no question of some aspects of Sharia and not others seemed obvious to the Archbishop, but it was at this point precisely that a criterion was needed to adjudicate when there was a 'conflict of laws'. Freedom to choose whom to marry might seem like a right or expectation for all women, a universal 'human right', but this is not how Islam sees things. It might also be noted that the Archbishop's lecture and interview described the modern human rights as 'abstract' rights, that is to say not arising from a local or regional or historic community, but from an international panel of jurists intent on preventing anything like the Nazi regime from imposing its murderous laws on its citizens ever again. The Archbishop pointed to the value and sense of identity arising from particular community custom and law, especially religious law.

In doing this he was also critical of the Enlightenment and its claims to uncover universal morality and values applicable to all peoples globally: peoples are different and can have equally valid custom and law. Indeed Islamic jurists and theologians are now rejecting the human rights agenda as a Western secular imposition on Islam, which recognizes only human rights arising from Allah's will as dictated directly into the text of the Qur'an. The Archbishop's assumption or hope that aspects of Sharia, such as forcible marriage or hand lopping, would be 'out of the question', was based on those rights now deemed universal by the United Nations but rooted in a form of secularism arising from Christian civilization and its law. Yet he has adjudged such rights as 'abstract'. Below the surface of his lecture and interview, and at times breaking surface, was a real conflict of traditions between Islam and the Enlightenment intellectual, moral and legal inheritance. In fact the Enlightenment liberalism was rooted in Christian values and produced a law that did balance freedom and form, that did encourage ongoing reform, critical thinking against authoritarian clericalism and superstition, the rise of science, and the imperative to equality and fairness in society.

According to Pannenberg the 'secular' movement of Europe has its roots in taking power from religions and clerics and putting it in the hands of the laity. The Archbishop wishes to put some legal power and authority back into clerical hands, this time Islamic, creating Muslim ghetto areas requiring in time perhaps Muslim police and perhaps separate local taxation, polygamy, and the other Sharia provisions.

Not long afterwards the Chief Justice of All England, Lord Phillips of Maltravers, followed up the Archbishop's controversial remarks by endorsing them and saying that marriage law for Muslims should be dealt with under Sharia by Muslims clerics. This again evoked considerable criticism, on the principle of secular law endorsing religious courts but also on the 'chill factor' such a system would produce for women. Muslim women would be corralled into male-dominated Sharia courts by their community expectations, a total reverse of the provisions of the family courts generally where the claims of men are secondary. One very striking feature of the reaction to these speeches commending Sharia clerical courts for Muslim family law was the silence of the Western feminist lobby, a silence reinforcing the growing sense that Western feminism is culturally relative – for Western women's rights, not for women born into Muslim homes, since their rights are different and conducted by a male clerical caste. Feminism, after all, proves to be a matter of taste and not of deep moral principle – that is now the message Western feminists give their Muslim sisters who no doubt can be said to have their own, pro-patriarchal, feminism.

Contradiction in the thinking of Lord Phillips is inevitable on the basis of 'value free' secularist law, which is primarily there to manage society without any basis in moral principle. A pragmatic relativism is being encouraged in British law in order to provide for clerical law for some communities. The radical implication of the Archbishop and Chief Justice is that Britain should develop communal systems of law for different communities, that cultural relativism should be taken to a new level, the Parekh doctrine of Indian communalism that 'secularism' should apply to the 'mainstream' community only. This is the principle being suggested by the top religious and legal figures of the nation, in effect turning the law into an administrative system, a kind of ministry of justices to oversee radically different sub-systems. The lopping of limbs according to Sharia law is 'out of the question' now, but on what grounds? Halal slaughter, offending Western animal cruelty laws, is now quite normal.

'Identity' justice, complementing 'identity politics', is another way of analysing these proposals: if you are a Western woman, you access the 'mainstream' family courts; if you are a 'Muslim', or claimed by that community as such, you access the Sharia courts. If we apply the standard secularist 'liberal' test of H. L. A Hart to this situation, and ask 'what harm could be done to anyone under this legal implementation of "inclusion and diversity" policy?', the answer must itself be culturally relative: 'if you are a Muslim woman then polygamy is not damaging', if you are a non-Muslim woman then it is harmful. This secularist approach reflects the cultural relativist approach to everything. Authority is to be found in the law courts of our brave new, secular, culturally relative world, but the basis of their judgements is not connected to any shared moral ethos, not connected necessarily to 'what is right', but rather administering sets of rights for different groups of people. This is very much 'positive law', that is to say a self-defining practice without reference to any higher or deeper moral concerns or claims. It is a wonderful irony that at the same time as British law has succeeded in putting aside all Christian moral influence, it finds itself drawn to accepting a fundamentalist body of law based on religious revelation – Sharia law – for a minority group in society. In fact the Archbishop is alert to this, as he cites a Jewish writer, Ayelet Shachar, asking, 'your culture or your rights?'.[37]

Christian theology regards social law as a good for keeping order and peace, and allowing the Church space to live and preach the Gospel. Issues such as mass abortion have attracted Christian criticism, and in the past issues such as government sponsored prostitution, and indeed slavery, have been faced down through Parliamentary campaigning by Christian groups. The Authority of the law is at its highest when it reflects the values of the kingdom of God, at its lowest when it becomes brutal and oppressive as in the Nazi era. This brings us to ponder whether the deliberate move towards a deeply secular view of law, cutting away from the basic Christian moral root from which British law grew directly, will inevitably fragment British law as there is no agreed set of moral principles underlying it.

How should Christians in the UK view their contribution to the values institutionalised in social and legal structures? Ernst Troeltsch's threefold categorization of Christian types might be helpful: 'Church type', 'sect type' and 'mystical communion type' regards the church type as established churches of a nation state, the sect type as more akin to the

---

[37] http://www.archbishopofcanterbury.org/1575 see also reports of German secular courts failing to protect battered Muslim wives, judges citing verses from the Quran as cultural justification: http://www.independent.co.uk/opinion/commentators/johann-hari/johann-hari-how-multiculturalism-is-betraying-women-446806.html.

early church's fellowship of voluntary individuals with faith in Jesus who are not at all integrated into the structures of the state, and the mystical type likewise in terms of politics.[38] 'Church type' churches exercise authority in church and state, for example running church schools and hospitals, parishes open to all inhabitants, on the Christendom model. Sect type churches, deriving usually from the radical Reformation tradition, deliberately separate church from state, believing that the Church has no mandate structurally to govern society, it should be the Church and as such of course influence opinion through the Gospel and so indirectly affect public policy. The mystical groups likewise adopt the same view of church and state. One important point this tradition makes is that the state should not have power in controlling the church in any way, and yet in established churches the state often has a major say in appointing bishops, as in England the Archbishop of Canterbury is in fact appointed by the head of a secular state. Also the establishment model gives the church money from the ordinary tax payer to pay for church schools, for example – a practice unhealthy for a genuine church and unfair on the secular tax payers. The stance of the sect type church has increasingly found favour and logically leads to a secular state, which relates to different groupings in society, religious and otherwise.

This secular view of the state was adopted by the Constitution of the United States of America in its famous separation of church and state, the beginning of the end of the Christendom model, followed soon after by the French Revolution of 1789. This new era ushered in the plural state, allowing different groupings space to be free to practise their own faith, but not to break the law of the land, as polygamist Mormonism did. In fact this 'secular' theory was presupposing a basically Christian post-Enlightenment history of institutions and customs, for example monogamous marriage, equality of women, hospitals for the sick and freedom of thought, and it raises the question as to whether a state can simply declare itself 'value free' and without an historical tradition of social customs and morals. Why should polygamy be off limits in a purely open, pluralist, secular state? Christianity gives the clear answer that women and men are wholly equal as human beings, and that polygamy slides women into the class of domestic servants and providers of sexual pleasure. If we go by sheer freedom of choice of women to take this role, then is no good answer to this and many other such questions apart perhaps the legal statement that the law is the law, an answer based on

---

[38]Ernst Troeltsch, *The Social History of the Christian Churches*, 2 vols, trans Olive Wyon, London: Allen & Unwin, 1931, vol. 1, pp. 376–382 and vol. 2, pp. 688–694.

the notion that the law is a self-resourcing enterprise, not governed by any values or ethical system.[39]

The secular state seems only mandated to uphold liberty of belief and practice without any discrimination. It has to uphold individual 'rights' allocated by the United Nations, but defining rights in terms of marriage may possibly uphold polygamy as a religious right, or indeed a right chosen by women in such a domestic arrangement. Under the communist secular regimes of the twentieth century the state decreed, in the name of the people, what was allowed and what was not. In liberal democratic states today the government exercising the power of the state rests its authority on the electoral mandate of having gained a majority of votes in the last legally scheduled election for the legally appointed time of office. The people, the *'demos'*, is the source of the state's authority and Parliament can pass legislation implementing the policies voted for accordingly, subject to the international agenda of human rights now standing in authority over all state law. The EU, for its members, passes laws via national Parliaments acting as 'rubber stamps' to govern nations, so as Bobbitt points out the nation state is decreasingly self-governing, autonomous and democratic. But the *demos* is the source of state authority, and – subject to human rights international law – the *demos* through Parliament can make new arrangements for the structuring of the state. In fact human rights were devised to prevent the *demos* from being able to elect a government to oppress certain people in the nation.

Rights are granted by the state and now by the supranational United Nations, certainly according to the secularist doctrine, clearly put by

---

[39]An interesting case in France was reported in the British press concerning a clash of marital culture and law, leading to a public call for 'primitive' marital custom not to have any status in family law. An outcry over the annulment of a Muslim marriage after the wife lied about her virginity has prompted the French justice ministry to ask for an appeal against the ruling. The decision by a court in Lille has raised concerns that the country's secular values are losing ground to cultural traditions from its fast-growing immigrant communities. The case involved an engineer in his 30s, named as Mr X, and a student nurse in her 20s, Ms Y, who married in 2006. The wedding party was still celebrating when the groom came downstairs to complain that his bride could not produce the customary evidence of a blood-stained sheet. The court ruled that Ms Y misrepresented herself as 'single and chaste' and that, in this particular marriage, virginity was an 'essential quality'. The decision, which went unreported until it was revealed by a legal journal, was condemned by cross-party politicians, the media, feminists and civil rights organisations. The ruling 'is a real fatwa against the emancipation and liberty of women,' said Fadela Amara, the urban affairs minister and the daughter of immigrants from Muslim North Africa. 'We are returning to the past.' Rachida Dati, the justice minister whose parents also were born in North Africa, initially shrugged off the ruling. But the public clamour reached such a pitch that she asked the prosecutor's office this week to lodge an appeal (*Daily Telegraph*, 5 June 2006). See also Agnes Poirier 'Britain could never debate the Burka like this' for the French understanding of secularism as upholding national commonality, in http://www.timesonline.co.uk/tol/comment/columnists/guest_contributors/article6565064.ece.

the French political theorist M. Combes: 'There are no rights but the rights of the State, there can be no authority but the authority of the republic.'[40] J. N. Figgis, an Anglican political thinker, took great issue with this secularist viewpoint, and criticized Combes along lines echoing those of Edmund Burke in his criticism of the French Revolution, since it destroyed the authority of historic groupings, vital to society, which are intermediate between the state and individuals. Religious groupings, guilds, professional bodies, academic bodies, and families exemplify this kind of group that exists and has rights and authority at its own level. Such bodies are realities and should be recognized with their own rights to exist and function, society should not be reduced to the relationship of individuals to the state, according to Figgis and the proponents of the plural state.

A century on from Figgis we can see his point: Western states now behave as if they confer rights rather than simply acknowledging them as realities. Figgis is historically correct to say that our rights in fact 'are the result of age-long struggles and the expression of the English character' rather than the grant of the state. What seems to be happening in the Anglo-Saxon cultures is that the state has decided to speak for all the 'mainstream' cultural people and push away their religious and cultural heritage as significant, while at the same time endorsing 'multiculturalism' and accepting minority faith groupings in the way Figgis hoped for his own Church. A very asymmetrical plural state is developing.

Christian approaches to the authority of the state, after Christendom, have generally tried to acknowledge the importance of groups in society. Indeed the uniting of men and women in marriage covenant to have children and raise them in a good way is theologically a matter of creation – family and marriage therefore have a greater authority than does the state. The Dutch Protestant school of social theology represented by Dooyeweerd criticizes individualism but understands the state to have its own proper sphere of sovereignty. This should not impose on other spheres such as family, school and economic enterprise, which are part of God's gift in creation with a right to their own existence and authority. It is notable in the contemporary Western world that the state does seem to take itself the power to rule such spheres of life directly.

The power and authority of the state is penetrating to the very roots of society, bestowing freedoms and technological access to ensure that lesbians can be given IVF treatment, for example. It is the direct power of the state alone that has enabled such drastic change in sexual potential to happen, and the banning of traditional social and sexual ethics in this area, even for very large and respected religious minorities, makes state

---

[40]J. N. Figgis, 'The Church and the Secular Theory of the State', Church Congress Report (1905), pp. 189f, cited in David Nicholls, *The Pluralist State: The Political Ideas of J. N. Figgis and His Contemporaries*, Oxford: St Martin's Press, 1994, p. 157.

interference even more penetrating and conditioning, and all in the name of increasing freedom.

The Church does not claim to be a world government, nor a state government, but rather a moral and spiritual voice in the world calling men and women to Christ. Living 'between the times', between Christ's resurrection and the final fulfilment of history with the Judgement of Christ, the Church wrestles with living in a sinful world, and seeks by the Gospel of love and holiness to bring the hearts and minds of all people freely to become disciples. Jesus left no blueprint for world government, but rather for faith in the changes and chances of sinful history, seeking to influence rulers to do good and show kindness and justice. This corresponds with the Trinitarian shape of Christian authority and the importance of subjectively free consent to the authoritative and objective message of the Gospel of Jesus Christ as it directs us to God the Father. The Holy Spirit brings about true freedom in the hearts and minds of disciples and vocation to all kinds of tasks in creation. The science of medicine, of food production, of power generation, for example: these are clear callings for disciples to take up for the betterment of all humankind. The Gospel message of freedom for God, empowered by the Spirit and shaped by the Christ-like way of serving others, fosters the immense and useful diversity of gifts.

There is no one Christian template of government, unlike that of Sharia for Islam. Gospel speaks to changing circumstances and the Spirit enables the imaginations of disciples to seek what is good and influence social, political and economic structures as they continue to develop over the centuries. Freedom, form and historicity, the Trinitarian self-revelation to us in time, gives space for the evolution of politics and yet gives the divinely revealed and commanded focus of human relationships as ordered by love, care and justice, this focus to be woven into social patterns through free consent and mutual respect. The Christian view of political structures will no doubt look historically at the rise of liberal democracy and regard that as the best structure developed for fairness, justice and care for the weak, giving every individual a vote in the form of government.

This system emerged in Europe and the Americas on the basis of the Protestant Christian notion of the sanctity of life and the importance of each person in the eyes of God. Freedom of thought and expression is also an important Protestant principle. Pope John XXIII in his Encyclical *Pacem in Terris*[41] affirmed these democratic freedoms, rights, and the acceptance of all in society as enlightened by their being creatures of God, and subsequently Pope John Paul II's Encyclical *Centesimo Anno* endorsed liberal democracy as the way of government allowing each person the maximal freedom to participate in government:

---

[41]Rome, 1963.

The Church values the democratic system inasmuch as it ensures the participation of citizens in making political choices, guarantees to the governed the possibility both of electing and holding accountable those who govern them, and of replacing them through peaceful means when appropriate. Thus she cannot encourage the formation of narrow ruling groups which usurp the power of the State for individual interests or for ideological ends.

Authentic democracy is possible only in a State ruled by law, and on the basis of a correct conception of the human person. It requires that the necessary conditions be present for the advancement both of the individual through education and formation in true ideals, and of the 'subjectivity' of society through the creation of structures of participation and shared responsibility. Nowadays, argues the Vatican, there is a tendency to claim that agnosticism and sceptical relativism are the philosophy and the basic attitude which correspond to democratic forms of political life. Those who are convinced that they know the truth and firmly adhere to it are considered unreliable from a democratic point of view, since they do not accept that truth is determined by the majority, or that it is subject to variation according to different political trends. The encyclical observes that if there is no ultimate truth to guide and direct political activity, then ideas and convictions can easily be manipulated for reasons of power. As history demonstrates, a democracy without values easily turns into open or thinly disguised totalitarianism.[42]

The encyclical also makes a very significant point in affirming the value of Christians in democracies as those who uphold objective moral truth to guide political activity, rather than allowing it to float freely and take pathways not compatible with freedom. This very much fits in with the view of this book that Christianity authentically influences society indirectly, rather than by erecting Christian structures or institutions for the purpose, thus avoiding the temptation of religion and power: the Gospel is about freedom and the form of Christ, not any sort of oppressive form.

Does Western society need Christian influence?

State authority is necessary to prevent anarchy and chaos, and Christian theology accepts this as part of the gift of human created ability to cope with the threat of negation. Christians can accept the government while being very critical of aspects of its rule, so for example Christians under the Soviet Union were oppressed and were desperate for reform, but they nevertheless accepted the government as the government, albeit an unjust and vicious one.

---

[42]*Centesimo Anno*, Rome, 1991, para 46.

But the contemporary secular state regards itself as the sole sufficient and necessary agency of human good, and this is 'after virtue' – to return to MacIntyre's phrase, this is pure managerialism. 'When a political structure makes this claim,' says O'Donovan, 'we call it "totalitarian"'. O'Donovan makes a penetrating appraisal of the current secularist view of government. The ideology of secularist rule 'centres on the notion of the abstract will, exercising choice prior to all reason and order, from whose *fiat lux*[43] spring society, morality and rationality itself.'[44] The secular state defines everything, is as if the creative divinity setting up what is real, good and true – with no reference whatsoever to a common moral base.

The fact that Islam is the one group able to stand up to the secular state is interesting, and that religion must be credited for realizing what is happening, that the state is claiming to decide totally what is true and real and good. Unfortunately for the Christian, Islam itself politically, as in Saudi Arabia and Iran, is a totalitarian culture and produces a totalitarian state. It is not going to help reform the secularist unification of all things to itself, it is rather likely to replace one form of control with another. The way of the Gospel urges freedom and form as the life of all culture and government, not the absorption of all values into the state, whether atheist or Islamic. O'Donovan points out that the mass media tell us what is real and false, and the state is part of this apparatus.

In 1949 Karl Barth was criticized for not condemning communist regimes after 1945, since he had condemned Nazism unreservedly, notably in the famous Barmen Declaration of 1934. The context then was of the Nazis 'co-ordinating' all aspects of German society into the state, including the churches, even producing the German Christians under Reichsbischopf Ludwig Müller, placing the swastika next to the cross, *Mein Kampf* next to the Bible, and teaching racial inferiority doctrines of anti-Semitism. The Barmen Declaration rejected this on the grounds that

> Jesus Christ, as he is attested to us in Holy Scripture, is the one Word of God whom we have to hear, and whom we have to trust and obey in life and in death. We reject the false doctrine that the church could and should recognize as a source of its proclamation, beyond and besides this one Word of God, yet other events, powers, historic figures, and truths, as God's revelation.

And as regards the absolute claims of the Nazi Reich, the Declaration answered:

> Scripture tells us that by divine appointment the state, in this still unredeemed world in which also the church is situated, has the task of maintaining justice

---

[43]'Let there be light', the creative word of God bringing reality into being.
[44]Oliver O'Donovan, *The Desire of the Nations*, Cambridge: Cambridge University Press, 1996, p. 274.

and peace...The church acknowledges with gratitude and reverence toward God the benefit of this, his appointment...We reject the false doctrine that beyond its special commission the state should and could become the sole and total order of human life and so fulfil the vocation of the church as well.

This Christocentric reply to the Nazi system proved luminously clarifying of the issues at stake.

But why did Barth not issue a similar rebuttal to the communist regimes? He accepted the abuse of violence and terrible treatment of people in 'the East', but also saw the good intentions of the communists for equality and the common good entwined in their bloody methods. The 'West' is accused, likewise, of bad intentions towards its working classes, and cannot be called a Christian regime. The East is deliberately Godless, but unlike the Nazis never tried to coordinate Christian faith into its own ideology. Barth calls for 'the patience and faith of the saints' in relation to communism, rather than a Christian condemnation of the whole system. 'Not the crusade but the word of the Cross is what the Church in the West owes to the godless East, but above all to the West itself, the Word through which the Church itself must allow herself to be rebuilt completely afresh.'[45] Barth sees problems in East and West, the former suppresses freedom while trying to attain justice, the latter vice versa: Barth could see the chaos and confusion of the human condition in both, and seeds of hope in both. In Nazism he saw only real evil and threat to the Gospel itself. It has to be said that the full terror of Stalinism was not yet unveiled to the West, for example through the writings of Solzhenitsyn. Barth is surely however wise not to deify any one form of government.

More positively, the state or form of government can be a way of implementing the will of Christ. Christians in a democratic structure, even a defective one, have the chance to press for justice, care and peace in terms of policy, and for the fundamentals of family life and its bonds as following the grain of the created order, which will involve fair pay for workers and fair hours of work.

> It is not Christ's Will that there should be in this country a million or a million and a half of paupers, whose condition – whose hereditary condition – renders a happy and honourable life almost impossible. It is not His will that criminals should go on breeding criminals, and that the foul inheritance of pollution, blasphemy, and villainy should be entailed on generation after generation. In struggling against pauperism and crime...we are contending for the glory of Christ, and translating into action the prayer He has taught us to offer – "Thy Will be done on earth as it is in heaven".[46]

---

[45]Karl Barth, 'The Church Between East and West', in *World Review*, New Series, 6 August 1949, p. 35.
[46]R. W. Dale, 'Christ and Christendom', 1886, in *Essays and Addresses*, London: Hodder and Stoughton, 1899, p. 41.

These words of a great Congregational minister of a Chapel in 19th Century Birmingham get to the heart of why a Christian theology of authority must regard the state as a very important agency for the nation, an agency to be supported and reformed so as to bring the kingdom of Christ to bear on the welfare of all people. The totalizing mission of the secular state, gradually closing down 'pluralism' and not recognizing sources of moral wisdom, such as churches, other than its own decision and will to power, has to be worrying to Christians. But the state can have the power to do good, to help the poor and weak, at home and abroad. We can argue plausibly that the nation state needs a strong articulate and free Christian element in order to maximise its potential for good. The vocation of the churches is not to affirm an atheistic secularist base to government, but to seek to infuse the values of the Gospel into it, and this can only be done through freedom. The notion of a Christian revolution, to parallel the Iranian Islamic revolution, is a contradiction in terms. A Christian view might well argue for a commonality of society, and against the Parekh doctrine of competing tribes and radical differences, ignoring questions of moral right and wrong.

Capitalism

The Gospel cannot be simply an individual and private matter, of no relevance to the world of politics, economics and social welfare: there would have been no hospitals and no schools in Europe had this been the case. There needs to be radical involvement of disciples in society, but no one template for political order is mandated. Christians do not believe in rule by clergy or control of politicians by clerics with an agenda or legal system to impose. The Gospel works through the Spirit in the present situation, reforming and improving rather than tearing down, seeking change and evolution for the betterment of all humanity, not a programme forced on people but through their free consent and gladness. The kingdom of Christ is not of this world in that sense of a fixed structure. Freedom and form interlace in the historicity of human vocation, the Trinitarian pattern, and the authority of the Gospel is Jesus-like: change comes from individuals who improve the lives of others around them. Here Evangelicals can agree with Pope John Paul II in his broad acceptance of free market capitalist democracy:

> The Church has no models to present; models that are real and truly effective can only arise within the framework of different historical situations, through the efforts of all those who responsibly confront concrete problems in all their social, economic, political and cultural aspects, as these interact with one another. For such a task the Church offers her social teaching as an *indispensable*

and ideal orientation, a teaching which, as already mentioned, recognizes the positive value of the market and of enterprise, but which at the same time points out that these need to be oriented towards the common good.[47]

The encyclical is careful to say that the Christian message is very much needed in this task of government, and of business and work, to guard against the oppression that can arise from unfettered capitalist practices. In fact the Christian must say that without the shaping of the Gospel way, capitalism is bound to produce hardship and injustice – as in all the modern Western structures, Christianity is vital to ensure they do not decay and become toxic. The structures of capitalism, the banks, industries and markets, need honesty if they are to thrive and not become rotten through personal greed supplanting personal virtue.

Archbishop William Temple argued that Marx was correct in much of his economic analysis, but wrong in his rejection God and the way of implementing his programme.[48] Pope Benedict XVI has already spoken against cruelty in some contemporary capitalist practice.[49] 'Savage capitalism' is also under deep criticism from many areas of the Christian church, particularly in relation to the effects of unrestrained market capitalism in the 'Third World', which means over two thirds of the world's population whose labour is purchased at the cheapest possible price.

Daniel M. Bell, Jr. ends his book on this subject by rejecting what he takes to be the 'neoconservative' theory that the present situation of the triumph of Western-style capitalism is the permanent shape of the world order:

> Fukuyama and his neoconservative cohorts can declare that history has attained its end with the triumph of capitalism because the true end of history remains momentarily fugitive. Although the tomb is empty, the Lamb who was slain has yet to return in final victory. In the meantime, the crucified people, awaiting his return and the consummation of the judgement of grace, refuse to cease suffering.[50]

Bell argues that the capitalist system is in fact dangerous for Christianity as is mis-shapes our desire away from Jesus-like orientation towards caring for the poor and towards getting for ourselves. Bell looks back to the Medieval monastic tradition and its imperative of duty to care as an example of a 'technology' to help shape desire aright. We might in fact argue that the Marxist vision is all about just such a reshaping of desire, in secular form.

---

[47]*Centesimo Anno*, Rome, 1991.
[48]E.g. in his *Nature Man and God,* London 1935 and *Christianity and the Social Order*, 1942.
[49]Rome, 2007.
[50]Daniel M. Bell, Jr., *Liberation Theology after the End of History: The Refusal to Cease Suffering*, London and New York: Routledge, 2001, p. 195.

The global banking corporations need a moral framework and morally serious people working in it: brilliant amoral gamblers and risk takers, obsessed with their own short term personal gain and 'bonuses', led to global financial crisis in 2008 and angry criticism about this behaviour of 'unregulated' financial practice. Capitalism based on pure materialism is a cruel system indeed, but if run by people of virtue, not just by amoral 'managers', it can work. The whole issue of unfair trade relations is one that the Gospel cannot but criticize, for example. The mutual societies, arising in the nineteenth century from the Nonconformist culture, as did Trade Unions originally, show that the Christian ideal of mutual cooperation is not merely romantic and unrealistic.[51] Greed is the god to be resisted, as Jesus' temptations in the wilderness reveal. Democratic capitalist society needs to integrate kindness and goodness into its wealth creation, and eliminate cruelty and avarice. The struggle of the Gospel in creation and culture will continue against injustice and untruth until the end, according to the teaching of Jesus (Mark 13). The history of the early twentieth century shows that free market capitalism desperately needs a Christian context to moralise it, while not repressing free and creative activity in commerce, technology and science. Without some Christlike 'form' to this freedom, oppression of the poor seems inevitable. Likewise the Marxist economic systems failed to make space for freedom as it imposed rigid form.

Conclusion: synthesising freedom and form

From the angle of the nation in the UK, of whom over 70% in the 2001 census claimed to be culturally Christian, if not regular attenders of churches, the state is moving increasingly towards a repression of Christianity as significant for policy making. The contemporary driver, reinforcing liberal secularism, for this is undoubtedly now the perception that the presence of Christian ideas in public policy 'offends' other faith groups, therefore has a 'secular', or in effect empty and value free, policy core – the one value affirmed being that all values are affirmed. The state is deliberately defining the nation in diverse terms as a set of different groupings occupying a piece of land called England, with no single set of moral assumptions to be shared – although the rhetoric of pluralism continues and Islam needs to be 'managed' by the secular state.

This philosophically incoherent relativism arguably damages the future of democracy as a good mode of government, since it rejects the Christian moral ethos that has produced it. But some Christians argue that making secular relativism a condition for entering the public square of politics is bad for their faith, forcing them to leave their core beliefs

---

[51]See William Temple, *Christianity and Social Order*, Harmondsworth: Penguin 1942.

at home, for example in the question of sexual ethics and abortion. Or again it could be argued that the only way for this dualism to be avoided is for Christians to become a recognized religious minority group in society, like the Muslims, and bargain with the secular government on that basis. Roman Catholics in the UK do work in this sort of fashion, but Anglicans are stuck with the fact of establishment, and this gives the false impression of power and influence already. Just as in the first centuries of Christian existence, believers were made to worship a statue of the emperor or suffer, so now it seems that they must bow to the god of secularism or become political non-persons. Christians need to become influential minority groups if they are to be true to their real authority, Jesus Christ. And at the same time integrated into the political legislative process, or they need to engage with the brave new world of contemporary secularist culture and try to reclaim the ground.

One theological movement that raises this latter prospect is 'Radical Othodoxy', which emphasizes the swamping nature of secularism on culture and Western political order, lamenting this novel development for both nation and church life. Radical Orthodoxy, a group of theologians sharing this concern, wants to write a new form of modern culture based on Christianity and Church, to describe reality theologically. John Milbank's book *Theology and Social Theory*, perhaps the seminal book for this movement, argues against the notion of the 'secular' as a free-standing domain of human thought and culture. For Milbank, 'Once there was no "secular." ... The secular as a domain had to be instituted or *imagined*, both in its theory and in its practice.'[52] This secular reality, we are taught to think, is what really lay behind the Christendom picture of how things are, and that has now been wiped away and we know the truth: secularism now dominates our understanding of reality, and religion has to become a private hobby for those who like it. The state has now become the 'totalizing', all-controlling agency for this secularism.

The Radical Orthodoxy movement disagree that the modern state is tolerant; rather it is seen as a sovereign power that has replaced the church and its apparatus of the mass media, education, health, civil service shape us into what the state wants us to be, think, desire, and do. Religion itself becomes a sort of therapy at home for the pressures of life, but certainly not something to engage with the secular state and its current projects in the public forum, rather it provides an escape – the sigh of the oppressed and harassed, as Karl Marx put it.

Milbank would like to see the boundaries of sacred and secular to be extremely hazy, so that a social existence of many complex and interlocking powers may emerge, and forestall either a sovereign state or a hierarchical Church, so that the church is involved in politics and enterprise in the public sphere.[53] 'Tending gardens, building bridges,

---

[52]John Milbank, *Theology & Social Theory*, Oxford: Blackwell, 1990, p. 9.
[53]Ibid., p. 407–408.

sowing crops, caring for children, cannot be seen as "ecclesial" activities precisely because these activities are now enclosed within a sphere dubbed "political". They become subject to the totalizing operations of a central sovereign power, which is concerned to contain them within this sphere.'[54] Tracey Rowland's Roman Catholic analysis[55] of this problem rather ironically pins much blame onto Pope John XXIII's 'optimistic judgements' about culture. She even rejects the teaching of a full-blown ecumenical council, Vatican II, and its decree 'Gaudium et Spes' also very appreciative of God's activity in modern culture.[56] She ends her book: 'Either the Church as the Universal Sacrament of Salvation is the primary source, guardian and perfector of culture within persons, institutions and entire societies, or culture becomes an end in itself – an ersatz religion – as in the Aristocratic Liberal and Nietzschean traditions, which in turn implodes into that anti-culture known as "mass culture".'[57] No doubt her critique of modern culture is powerful, and calls for Christian influence to engage with it; but the notion of a full-scale return to Christendom looks unrealistic, and indeed open to Dostoevsky's criticism of the Grand Inquisitor cited earlier.

Judging by the 2001 Census cited, the *nation* is wanting to own a public cultural identity of a mildly Christian kind, but the state is wanting to deny this identity, while simultaneously wanting to affirm other communities identities. The majority culture is told that its one value is to affirm all values, while the minority cultures are encouraged to affirm their own values and customs and demand protection for their own 'tribe'. It may well be the case that liberal relativism has grown from liberal Christian Protestantism and its strand of charity and non-judgementalism towards others, of not seeking to impose itself or push its claims politically. Christianity perhaps uniquely has this moral ethos of stepping back in favour of others, and this has been taken up by the state in the confidence that Christianity, albeit the secularized version, will not protest at being pushed into the private sphere. Christian churches are not opposing this trend, apart perhaps from the Roman Catholic Church and its defence of its schools.

The Established Church of England has adopted precisely this quiet deferential attitude of putting up with marginalization when its whole rationale is in fact to articulate the Christian moral mores for society, so it

---

[54]Tracey Rowland, *Culture and the Thomist Tradition*, London and New York: Routledge, 2003.
[55]Passing judgement on this decree of an ecumenical council she says 'the authors of the section on culture in *Gaudium et Spes* neglected to offer an alternative account of 'religion as culture'...By depriving people of these riches through the policy of accommodating liturgical practices to the norms of 'mass culture'...the post Conciliar Church has unwittingly undermined the ability of many of its members to experience self-transcendence.'
[56]Ibid., p. 168.
[57]Ibid., p. 168.

finds itself in an impossible position, with the state now disavowing the Anglican position *de facto* and only allowing the outward constitutional trappings of 'a' national church as the social moral glue for the nation. In fact 'the nation', as Bobbitt suggests, is becoming a less and less credible reality as time goes on, as cultural fragmentation deepens, as mutually shared values diminish, as minorities that have been actively discouraged from integrating into a 'mainstream' culture expand and claim more exemptions from 'mainstream' law and custom.

The Church of England must face up to the problem of authority: whose authority does it primarily serve, that of the secular state with its agenda of soothing minority faiths, or – as Barth put it – that of Jesus Christ who alone is Lord of the Church? The Church of England is in real danger of mutating into a kind of 'ministry of religions', a neutral religious bureaucracy charged with helping all religions to get on with each other and keep a mild, nice, unobtrusive type of faith ticking over for those wanting it. This is not the role of the Church of Christ, to act as some kind of ideology support to the secular state and its, no doubt worthy, concerns to manage society in its religious dimension. The time has surely come for the Church of England to work out how it can take a path of constructive disestablishment from the structures of state power, while not detaching pastorally from the parishes up and down the land. Or else it needs to find ways of opposing the assumption of atheistic secularism as the base ideology of society and state, and to infuse Christian values into political discussion.

The question for states and churches, including the established church, is whether to seek to shore up a basically Christian moral social tradition – upholding the notion of marriage for example, and of state giving to the poorer nations of the world without religious or cultural discrimination – or whether to become privatized entirely and keep out of public policy debates. This is indeed a new moment in human history, the adoption of a wholly non-religious secular social revolution, cutting away from the Western Christian roots that supplied its moral assumptions. Can a pure relativism supply any values at all, or deny any, but only try to keep the peace between conflicted tribes on this island? Since there is no longer any common agreed set of standards, there is going to be no way of knowing what is 'reasonable' morally or intellectually – halal slaughter in the UK today, as we saw, is lawful and unlawful, depending on which group you belong to.

Another real danger for society is the secular state's abolition of 'the mainstream' as having no core moral tradition other than individual freedom and hedonism: how does secularism provide for anything else? Jonathan Sacks worries about this, since history shows that very advanced but amoral nations quickly fall prey to more primitive but more disciplined ones. He cites Russell on the fate of Renaissance Italy:

Traditional moral restraints disappeared because they were seen to be associated with superstition; the liberation from fetters made individuals energetic and creative, producing a rare florescence of genius; but the anarchy and treachery which inevitably resulted from the decay of morals made Italians collectively impotent, and they fell, like the Greeks, under the domination of nations less civilized than themselves but not so destitute of social cohesion.[58]

In other words, the withdrawal of Christianity as any sort of moral authority for the nation heralds a major experiment, one not even realized by our secular and very confident liberal elite. This ruling group appears to assume that liberal democracy is just natural for the human race and will always be there, rather than being a product of a long cultural struggle, an achievement arising from the Christian tradition over centuries. The fruit needs a tree, it does not grow from secular fresh air. It may be that postmodern secularism is detached from history, from any sense of connection with the past. As this must be deconstructed continually. Multiculturalism is also a major driver of this empty relativism at the heart of Western social policy, the idea that all cultures are equally valid and to be valued and indeed further, that 'other' cultures need privileging in the UK because they started a long way behind Christianity, which just happened to be here first and needs taking down a peg or two. The state in this way is allergic to the nation's culture and cultural history. This pathway, however well intentioned in trying to affirm people from minority races and cultures, confuses 'love' with 'truth' and makes winners and losers, the losers being the 'mainstream' and its culture which alone gave birth to liberal democracy, and as far as we know alone can sustain it.

Can our society manage without 'a' moral authority giving us a set of customs and assumptions, even to dissent from if we wish? The churches need to participate in the political, economic and social structure in order to give Christ like form to chaotic freedom of the amoralized, even animalized, will of the victims of an amoral society. If the church does not find ways of articulating the authority of Christ, the mosque is very keen to step in and fill the vacuum, with its legalistic template to control all areas of life. The renewal of the church is the condition of the salvation of liberal democracy in the West: a state whose policies are based on nothing except perhaps a keen determination to reject the moral tradition of its past, is bound for chaos then for some kind of reactive regime to restore control by force. Liberal democracy is the political fruit of centuries of Protestant Christianity; it created a nation sensitive ultimately to fairness, equality and justice for all, it broke tribalist allegiances and vendettas and fostered mutual trust.

This trust of one another is essential for democracy, a system depending on trust by losers of elections to go along with government

---

[58]Jonathan Sacks, *The Politics of Hope*, London: Jonathan Cape, 1997, p. 39.

by the winners. This mutual trust is again a massive achievement arising from the Protestant tradition and history. If it fades, then the state is faced with fissiparous resentful groups, claiming rights and resources against the others. The will of Christ, as we look back at the rise of liberal democracy, was gradually influential through the refining of democratic processes and widening of franchise, in a culture which – for all its faults – moved towards a basically Christian view of persons and their needs, and willingness to pay taxes towards the common good, in ways such as the NHS. The Church had of course been doing such social and educational work, here and around the globe, before the state took over with its massive resources. But it was not envisaged that the Christian ethos would fade and be pushed away by secularists.

The Christian tradition transcends political structures and yet influenced them indirectly as lay people reformed it towards democracy, equality and charity. This religious tradition had the power to achieve change and improvement in a way that could uphold principled pluralist government, without fostering chaos, and prevented sectarian and legalistic clerical rule. This emerges theologically and spiritually from a strong hope in the Spirit of the Triune God working at all levels in the freedom of individuals, shaped by the form of Christ to orient society to the goal of the Creator. There is no reason to doubt that a truly Christian regeneration could renew culture, before cold secularist functionalism damages society and individuals as it threatens to do, imposing form and crushing freedom, also the concern about the radical uniformity imposed by Islamic states and cultures, reflecting a radical principle of unicity of God rather than unity in diversity in the divine life of the Trinity, freedom and form. , a principle of stasis and not creative development, culturally, scientifically and morally.

The Christian revelation and the activity of the Gospel in history has surely shaped the rise of liberal democracy, of freely probing scientific enquiry, of moralizing industrial and working conditions, of health care for the sick outside our own family, clan and tribal group. As secularism grips society this achievement seems to be at risk in its many dimensions. Society as influenced by the way of Jesus will not be a domineering one, but one glad to see others and difference. 'The New Testament', says Lossky,

> speaks much of the Kingdom (*Basileia*), but scarcely ever uses the terms 'dominion' (*kuriotes*) or 'to dominate or govern' (*kurieuein*) in connection with God. This corresponds to the radical change in the condition of man after the messianic Promise, after the enthronement of Christ…The divine Kingship is revealed in an unexpected manner…in the person of the Son of God, come to earth to undergo death upon the cross.[59]

---

[59]V. Lossky, In the *Image and Likeness of God*, New York: St Vladimir's Press, 1974, p. 221.

The kingdom of Christ rules by the authority of his love and holiness, not by force covert or open. He is true authority, a personal authority and an authoritative person, whose church, 'the body of Christ' is ontologically mutual in care. The effect of the church on society will bear this imprint.

The jury of history is out as to whether freedom and form achieved up to now by our liberal democracy can be maintained without this cultural life and tradition at its core. But is the church now so divided itself as to be incapable of providing freedom of the true form of the creative Word as the dynamic for regenerating secular society? And is the church likewise able to engage with that authority called 'the market' and bring it before the feet of Christ? The Christian doctrine of creation, we recall, interprets the cosmos as a home or household, suffused with the influences and directive authority of the parents, seeking to build virtuous characters in their children and to rejoice in their diversity and freedom.

A thriving, participatory democracy seems to be the political system carrying most authority in a Christian theology, but as we have argued, it needs this tree and the soil that gave it life, and can – as all human institutions – be corrupted and abused. It needs the Christian doctrine of creation as gift to be accepted, rather than the view of the world that it is constructed by management decision, here and now. Any form for our freedom now is to be dictated to us by management, not regarded as the Christ form, promoting freedom and caring form, diversity in a common liberating unity.

Secularism has led to a loss of directive authority in the nations of the West, a common moral base for values, as commentators Jonathan Sacks, Alasdair MacIntyre, and John Milbank argue. Since all values are relatively good or bad, in fact since we have no criterion to adjudicate good from bad, it is no surprise that the public perceives a coarsening and animalization of behaviour, and the state seeks to manage the outcome with CCTV cameras and external law. Chaos and control oscillate dangerously, with diminishing moral humanizing living authority now passed on through families. Freedom is fostered without form, leaving state control to try to hold the line. The present tendency towards a cold functionalist secularist state imposing utilitarian management on the nation looks like a destructive mould on the liberal democratic tree. O'Donovan sees modernity as an increasingly macabre parody of a Christian order of society, 'as Antichrist, a parodic and corrupt development of Christian social order.'[60]

Pluralism is a concept that can apply to individualism or to 'communities' and strongly held value systems not derived from the Protestant Enlightenment, but a radically different religious tradition.

---

[60]O'Donovan, *Desire of the Nations*, op cit., p. 275; and pp 271-284 for his reasoning.

Islam is a very controlling ideology, focused on the tightest possible understanding of the unicity of God, mediated through a single text and a single divine spokesman who successfully enforced its acceptance with violent conquest, after his preaching had not been accepted at first. The purpose of Islam is to implement Islam; with no free probing questioning of itself, its text or its warrior prophet, it tends to the state and freezes the frame of developing cultural history. This world ideology is now a real option for the future of the West, an option of control to quash chaos. The Trinitarian God speaks of freedom and form, unity and diversity, and Christianity, working indirectly, has produced a political order leading to the balance of freedom with a non-oppressive form. This cannot be imposed by some clericalist vision or church control. It influences society through individual faith and virtue humanizing institutions and developing new pathways into the future. The Lordship of Christ, I suggest, is crucial to the health of the Western liberal democratic political order, law and economics. But is the church now itself too influenced by secular relativism to be able to provide a credible witness to the Lord of the Church? Perhaps the secularist elite and the Muslim Imams who speak so confidently for 'their community' will be able to hear the Gospel of freedom, love and holiness, and to see that their ideologies of totalizing unification, control and identity of nation with state does not lead to life. But is the church itself now lacking the faith and will to look to the Lordship of Christ for freedom and form? We turn now to look at the question of authority in the church itself.

Part III:

Gospel, Church and Authority:
The Divine Desire for
Church and Universe

9

The Lordship of Christ, Crucified and Risen

The secular Caesar

Western culture is facing problems of diversity, fragmentation and relativism in terms of its culture, law and authority structures, and this phenomenon was described by Nietzsche as following from the 'death of God', in whose name moral authority had held European culture together. The problems of Western society and of the church are therefore mutually intertwined. The multi-faith agenda has proved very attractive to many theologians, famously John Hick,[1] for whom God is a reality and accessed through different but equally valid religions. This mode of thinking, that a range of views is the way of regarding truth, has undoubtedly proved attractive within churches as well as outside them. 'That's my view, but I don't want to force it on others' is a well known Christian comment on why the Christian in question does not wish to commend a Christian value in public debate. It might seem arrogant, and the term 'force', or some similar term of coercion, is often used. In fact force is not in question, merely a commendation of a view for its reasonableness is more to the point, but even that is shied away from for fear of ... some strange dislike of being identified as too Christian. 'Love thy neighbour as thyself' is a Christian imperative, and even more

---

[1]John Hick and Paul F. Knitter, *The Myth of Christian Uniqueness*, New York and London: Orbis Books, 1987.

strongly 'love those who persecute you and despitefully use you' is Jesus'
own sharp focusing of his Torah inheritance. Love however is does not
suppress the truth, and this is the confusion of contemporary relativism.
It is not loving to suppress the Gospel and turn it into a purely private
'blik', or taste, possibly shared with a few friends in a closely knit club
as a language for them alone, in effect a Gnostic circle.

Or again, doctrine or theological statements can be seen as a cultural
language for the community and not statements referring to any reality
outside that culture. This is Lindbeck's view of doctrine and language
about revelation, they do not point to or describe reality outside of our
religious culture. The logic of this is that the Christian message is a
secondary matter, a matter of taste, and a private matter. This must have
some effect on the Gospel declaration of the primacy of Christ in creation
and in the church. Secularism becomes the neutral, and so somehow
reasonable, ground of moral understanding in Western culture, and this
mindset seeps into church life and thought. The secularist ideal perhaps
has become the 'real' god behind the 'nursery picture book' gods such
as Christ and the Father, which are just childish ways of talking about
something deeper. This kind of understanding was resisted in the Arian
controversy in the fourth century by the likes of Athanasius, who saw
that this kind of unknowable 'god' or principle of the cosmos cut at the
very nerve of the Gospel message that 'God was in Christ reconciling
the world to Himself.' A first principle behind the Father, Son and
Spirit makes them pagan deities alongside the Roman pantheon of gods
– and in effect the worship of the secular principle achieves just that,
the Christian faith becomes one among many religions with a quaint
iconography and stories.

Christian theology cannot accept this exaltation of secularism as the
basis for society and as the consistently repressive force on Christianity,
quietly and insistently pushing it aside and worst of all persuading
church people to make an act of obeisance to this new idol, to put the
pinch of incense into the fire in front of the statue of secular Caesar, the
new political god. In the Roman empire the emperor declared himself
divine and throughout the empire citizens had to prove their loyalty by
this brief act of worship, and Christians who refused were punished and
even killed. Secularism has grown very powerful in Western culture, and
in the USA has formally displaced 'pluralism'. Glenn and Stack chart this
change implemented by the Supreme Court:

> In contrast to this "civil liberty" regime, which permitted widely differing
> view of what religion is, as well as what its relation to government should
> be, the secular regime the Court began instituting in the 1940's attributed to
> the religion clauses [in the American Constitution] a new substantive theory
> that seems to require all Americans to understand religion as a private matter
> lacking either public encouragement or consequences …. The first blossoming

was finding unconstitutional government sponsored religious instruction in public schools as a means to combat growing juvenile delinquency.[2]

Constitutionally permitted public religious pluralism has been replaced by constitutionally mandated public secularism and this is part of the new 'civil liberties' regime in the USA. The USA is a far more constitutionally and politically 'designed' state than is the UK, which has grown and evolved for a very long time indeed, and has a monarch who is formally anointed and crowned by the Archbishop of Canterbury. But the same kind of move is clear in the British nation, secularism is pushing pluralism out, and only very politically alert and formidable religions are able to retain or gain exemptions, Islam of course being the key example. But for most Christians bowing the knee to secularism in the public forum, being forced to bracket one's real spiritual and moral beliefs and to adopt a secular ethos for this context, is damaging to the person and prevents her from engaging in moral discourse over public policy – for the 'mainline', non-minority, and now semi-officially 'secular' nation. It is hard to know how a recent majority or mainstream culture can suddenly seek to claim the minority status proving advantageous to minority faiths, given that official structures such as monarchy are historically Christian.

Unfortunately the churches themselves often are accepting the secular ideal as a basis for speaking in the public forum, and so denying the public debate a specifically Christian contribution, but also damaging themselves 'internally' by developing a dual mindset ideologically, with the secularist dimension seeping into the theological. O'Donovan describes the stance of the Church of England on public matters, such as divorce policy: 'when the church contributes to public debate on matters of concern to secular society at large, it should forget that it is the church of Jesus Christ and should address society on terms common to all participants. The attempt to be distinctively Christian belongs only to the pursuit of internal discipline among the faithful.'[3] George Lindbeck's view of doctrine seems to echo this approach,: doctrine is the 'house style' for this particular religious house, referring only to what goes on in the house, and cannot refer outside the house to the wider world. To engage with those outside this presently shrinking, perhaps 'downsizing', house doctrinal language is useless and we must pick up the common language of 'real' reality and common-sense secular assumptions. This double mind of the church in the secular and sacred realms reveals uncertainty in the Gospel of Christ as universally true and relevant for the human condition. We can note that some very acute theological judges interpret

---

[2]Gary D. Glenn and John Stack, in *The Review of Politics: Christianity and Politics*, vol. 61, 1999, p. 13.
[3]O. O'Donovan, *Resurrection and Moral Order*, Leicester: IVP, 1986, p. 20.

Lindbeck as a 'non-realist' in his doctrine of God, that is to say they interpret Lindbeck as not believing that God is a 'reality' outside of our cultural discourse.[4]

The liberal theologian gladly regards this as a development of the Spirit, part of the freedom of the Gospel, breaking down the barriers between religions by rendering secondary the technicalities of doctrine and liturgy, getting to the primary point of one God expressed in several ways according to cultural style. Christianity takes its place beside all the other faiths, affirming the very same God in its own way, and teaching a message of love as do all religious traditions – despite the fact most religions actually deny this to be the case.

The church is charged to teach not that all religions are the same, but the truth that Jesus brings the consummation of the created order into history and simultaneously the creative Wisdom itself reveals and enacts the depths of divinely desired creation. The future destiny of creation comes to it in the life act of Jesus. Jesus refocuses the divine will and authority for us from 'the legal tradition to the claim of God's future on us and on the inbreaking of this future in his own coming.'[5] The atoning death and rising of Jesus ends the legalistic system of 'the law' while maintaining its basic content of loving God and our neighbour, of holiness and love. Creation is for this, not simply a moral obstacle course, but the home where we learn to love and relish God and his will freely. It is worth noting that this is the core distinctive claim of Christianity, and it cannot be fitted into other religious worldviews. If we put Jesus into the Hindu wheel of Karma on which moral performance meets reward or punishment in the next rotation of existence, his death and resurrection breaks the whole system: his death is for the sins of humanity. Likewise the moralistic path of Islam has no place for this doctrine of costly divine reconciliation through costly grace and the atoning death and rising of Jesus, an act elected by God for us, an act of pure grace upholding holiness and grounding honest forgiveness. The church does not believe in some abstract first principle, sitting above all the religions and ideologies, but in the God of Jesus Christ, not another God. Pannenberg tells us that the 'so called theology of religions in the industrial societies of the West' merely strengthens secularists' claims that no religious claims are true or worth considering as relevant to human problems.[6]

---

[4]See Fergus Kerr, *Theology after Wittgenstein*, London: SPCK, 1997, p. 196. fn 18, suggesting that Hans Frei located Lindbeck's 'cultural linguistic' view with that of D. Z. Phillips as a 'type of theology what has no connections beyond itself, with philosophy, or anything else.'
[5]W. Pannenberg, *Systematic Theology*, vol. 3, p. 59.
[6]*Systematic Theology* vol 2, Edinburgh: T&T Clark, 1994, p. xii.

The one Word of God

The Christian Gospel uniquely claims that God is the triune Lord who is immanent and transcendent – this is how God defines himself and how God is authoritative in the world. God has declared himself in Jesus and his death, and has acted in this person, pushing us towards understanding God as triune. God has attested himself in Jesus, and draws us in to his life to be his body here in history in the action of the Spirit. The witnesses and faithful preachers who left us their legacy in the texts of the New Testament were registering the divine narrative of God into our history and culture to transform.

The creative Word arrives and speaks, 'breaks into history' but in a way that regrounds the creative order and announces who we really are and have been, most truly, bringing us to 'ourselves', to our senses from the distractedness and addiction of the world as belonging to the flesh and the devil. O'Donovan states the clear Christian position when he says that the divine Word becoming flesh

> comes to us not as a *mysterium tremendum* which simply destroys all worldly order, but as creation restored and renewed, to which God is immediately present in the person of the Son of Man. The teaching and life of Jesus must be morally authoritative if we are not to be thrown back upon the Gnostic gospel of a visitor from heaven who summons us out of the world....The moment of divine irruption is more than an irruption: it is the foundation of a renewed order.[7]

The notion that the Gospel is a cultural language game for those within the church seems impossible in the light of the core Gospel that truth itself has re-established itself in Christ and the church, for all peoples and tribes and tongues.

God reveals himself in Jesus Christ, in all that particularity – going down to the heat, dirt, blood, sweat, toil and tears of the nastiest injustice, Calvary, where God revealed our own appalling moral state and need simultaneously, where God passed judgement on that himself. The Lord of the Church, undeniably for all Christians and Churches, is Jesus Christ who gave his life for us and conquered sin and death, to be revealed as God's very Word or Son living a genuine human life. He is the authority for all Christians. To quote Milbank: 'The logic of Christianity involves the claim that the interruption of history by Christ, and his bride, the Church, is the most fundamental of events, interpreting all other events.'[8] The Church has its own way of being, introduced into history by Jesus Christ, and must seek to live and move and have its being in this way, not a way more convenient to the managers of

[7]O. O'Donovan, *Resurrection and Moral Order*, op cit., p. 143.
[8]John Milbank, *Theology and Social Theory*, Oxford: Blackwell, 1990, p. 388.

society, even those democratically elected. The Church does not invent its own way of being, it has no authority to step outside the authority of Jesus Christ and seek to amend its practice and message in ways more amenable to contemporary culture. Barth's *Barmen Declaration*, pointed to above, issued in 1934 in the context of Nazism swamping all cultural groups with its nationalism, racism and militarism, was an assertion of the ultimate Lordship of Jesus Christ and a rejection of popular cultural mores taking root in the Church. Barmen affirms Jesus Christ as attested to in Scripture to be the one Word of God', not be supplemented or replaced by other words or ideologies however popular culturally these may be.

In 1934 that ideology was Nazism, now it is consumerism, hedonism, and moral relativism for Westerners.

> We reject the false doctrine that the church could have permission to hand over the form of its message and of its order to whatever it itself might wish or to the vicissitudes of the prevailing ideological and political convictions of the day.'[9] Further Barmen rejects 'the false doctrine that with human vainglory the church could place the Word and works of the Lord in the service of self-chosen desires, purposes and plans.[10]

The church is in danger of being denatured by the power and popularity of its surrounding culture.

Barth puts clearly the Christian view of authority in the Church: it is Jesus Christ, attested in Holy Scripture, a personal authority suffusing the Body of Christ, who is authoritative and subject to no higher power. 'The Christian church is the community of brethren in which, in Word and sacrament, through the Holy Spirit, Jesus Christ acts in the present as Lord.'[11] This authority is self-attesting and self-presenting in the world. God has spoken authoritatively and finally in Christ, God appearing in time and space revealing himself as holy love in action. This drew the witness of those around him, as a wonderful work of art draws astonished admirers to stop and look and be drawn into its beauty and power. The church is the fellowship of those attracted to Jesus both then in his lifetime and now as his portrait narrated in the New Testament continues to draw people to him and his way of life. Barth himself, while famously a theologian of the Word, was struck by Grünewald's great painting of the Crucifixion, part of his triptych, in which the crucified Jesus is pointed to by John the Baptist on one side, and Mary and the disciples on the other. If the church continues to be the faithful church, it will act like such a painting or speech, it will draw people to Christ. The church should focus on being the church of Christ, rather than merging

---

[9]*The Barmen Declaration*, 1934, para 3.
[10]Ibid., para 6.
[11]Ibid., para 3.

into the secular relativist agenda and vocation of its manager, therapist and aesthete – a combination of roles often adopted by the contemporary liberal cleric.

Christ's authority

Jesus, a particular person living at a particular time in history rather than being the symbol for a general moral idea, comes from the Hebrew covenant and according to all the available sources fully embraces his faith tradition, theologically and ethically. He used the Hebrew Scriptures to correct new developments imposed by religious parties, and the prayer he gave to his disciples offers an implicit theology of God and the world in its address to 'Our Father in heaven' who is holy, just and caring for his creation. As one is drawn into this portrait of Jesus the background soon comes to be important behind the glittering focal person.

The mode of authority in the church is therefore Christ-like, seeking the free consent of the believer to the way of Jesus in the church, seeking to bring this omnipotence of love to reign in the hearts of all people gladly and freely: 'directive' authority, rather than 'coercive.' And the content of this authority makes its presence felt and known, for example the South African doctrine and practice of apartheid could not withstand this Christological test: could Jesus Christ accept the idea of some people being inferior to others? This was the way in which slavery was washed away from the Roman empire, gradually as the truth of the Gospel spread into the hearts and minds of the rulers and the common people and caused a massive cultural change.

The Gospel lays down no cultural or political structures at all, but its message influences and affects them through the centuries: the flexibility and enduring nature of the faith combines freedom and form without freezing the frame of history into a static structure. This point cannot be emphasised enough, marking out the unique character of the Gospel and its power to shape culture and institutions through the hearts of faithful people in all kinds of contexts. The way of Jesus transcends mere structure and organization, he left no plan of how his followers should organize themselves, he left no writings, he left his friends with their impression of his life shared with them, his view of the world and God, as later written down to form the New Testament. This is a personal authority eliciting personal faith – but not individualistic faith, 'we are members together of the body of Christ'. The Church is personal society and social personality, freedom and form both protected and mutually enhancing. The authority of Jesus works at the deepest and most intimate level of the human heart and mind, to produce practical free action. Christian faith in God is not fearful: perfect love casts out fear, which corrodes trust and brings about suspicion and cynicism.

Jesus entrusted the future of his work to the Spirit, the activity of God in the world, as he died utterly powerless and the victim of sheer injustice. Jesus is given all authority in earth and heaven, according to the witness of the New Testament, and the Spirit of God at work in the world continues the life of Jesus and his way: 'God has sent the Spirit of his Son into our hearts, so we cry Abba Father' (Galatians 4:6). The authority of God is the authority of Christ crucified and risen who draws us to himself by free love and response, with the Spirit. This is not the authority of the dominating deity laying down the law to the created order, to create a heteronomous religious order of submission. Nor is it a freewheeling message of autonomous individualism adrift from forming and shaping patterns given in creation. Jesus authority enacts freedom and form, bringing the human heart to loving response and worship of the Creator. The Spirit brings the life of the risen Christ to us now: freedom and form in contemporaneous 'historicity', our life act here and now, as the church is caught up in the economic Trinity, the Trinity being itself in creating the world. The authority of Jesus is of personal freedom and personal form, not a 'natural' necessitarian force or law implementing itself remorselessly in time and space, the Islamic doctrine.

This is a new kind of authority in the world. It is not that of the expert, a highly learned scholar or craftsman or artist. Nor is that of the appointed official acting for an institution. It is personal authority with the ring of truth, Jesus was authoritative not just because of his message but because his life was his message, he lived out the message he announced, not a moralist but the living embodiment of God's love and holiness in real time. The church has this authority at its heart, not an institutional authority or power, but the life of Jesus shaping our lives in the conditions we find ourselves, hence flexible and free yet formed in his likeness. Jesus was not a 'celebrity', although the people tried to make him one, nor a political or military leader who would drive out the occupying Roman legions – the New Testament emphasizes that this was not his vocation and he resisted efforts to foist it on him. On the contrary his revelation and authority was his own, not one projected on to him, he turned such projected identities back by his own identity as the suffering servant of God. His absorption of violent power, refusing to use it against others, is his decisive legacy to the church and world.

The authority of Jesus was of the 'new covenant' (Jeremiah 31) written on our hearts, not on tablets of stone as was the Mosaic law, this new and personal covenant being long hoped for by the prophets. His authority therefore is also 'eschatological', a fulfilment of the purposes of God and yet present in unfinished human history and deeply conflicted with the chaos and sin of this human condition. The authority of the Gospel is no mere impersonal moral yardstick in the heavens by which human behaviour is measured and found acceptable or wanting, a heteronomous authority imposed mechanically on us from a God who remains outside our realm of life and experience. 'Ontotheism' is now subject to heavy theological criticism by Milbank among others, but earlier by Barth and as we saw by the postmodernist thinkers.

The authority of God is not in fact an 'it' but a 'Thou', and one that is deeply involved in the human historical plight and situation. The whole point of the Christian Gospel is that God has entered our created life history, that he is not simply a Creator transcending our situation but immanent within it now by the Holy Spirit of the 'Father' and his self giving 'Son'. Holy love indwells our history as the divine act and call to us, that our sins are already judged and sin destroyed in the way of Jesus Christ, a way we are invited to join. We are taken to the doctrine of the Trinity to make sense of freedom and form: the Spirit warms our hearts with the life of the holy God, whose character is behind 'the law' now grafted personally within our characters.

This authority is personal, far more in the mode of a parent, or brother or sister, than a political or legal ruler. It is like the home, with its 'surround sound' of supportive love and virtue given to us by our parents as they give us the space, room, encouragement, and rebuke we need to grow to maturity. Their aim and their method is to bring us to create ourselves into good people, and that can only happen through our own free actions: we are different to the pet dogs in the home, we will not develop simply by being trained and ordered to obey, with no insight as to the why and wherefore of these commands, 'sticks and carrots'. God deals with us 'as friends', or sons and daughters, not 'slaves', and this is the extraordinarily new insight into God and ourselves, the covenant purpose of creation.

'Authority' will no doubt come across sometimes in purely human terms and experience as negative, a ban on what we want to do, a curb on freedom of action. Authority in human culture often has only this emphasis. God's love is always behind holy commandments to avoid some patterns of behaviour. The Latin term *'auctoritas'* is fundamentally political,[12] the authority of the state and its founding traditions, which must be kept rigidly and by threat of punishment. The Hebrew understanding of divine command comes in the context of creation and covenant, of a relationship more like that of family than state. Disciples of Christ trust that God's commandments, including prohibitions on action, are for the best and of they can be seen to be thoroughly reasonable and justified intellectually, morally and aesthetically.

The goal of divine authority is to fulfil the loving purposes of the Creator. Divine desire works to this end, with infinite patience and respect for the covenant partner created, for the freedom given to this human

---

[12]See 'What is Authority?' by Hannah Arendt in *The Portable Hannah Arendt*, London: Penguin, 2003.

colleague in working out the purposes of creation. Just as parental desire and care mediates itself through the whole, deeply subtle, context of life created for the children in the family home and wider life, so with the kingdom of God. This is revealed by Jesus Christ who is our new home, household, context of life and way of being. Christians are used to the notion of 'God as with us' in covenant relationship – Emmanuel – a constant companion on the road of life albeit at times disturbingly not 'felt' as present and in fact not felt or sensed at all, rather trusted to be there. Jesus himself clearly trusted God as his Father, despite the appalling injustices and tortures visited on him by others during his life: somehow the sufferings of Jesus were overcoming the evil and hate behind them, but of course Jesus would far rather have turned back from the path which led to Calvary, as the scene in the Garden of Gethsemane shows all too clearly and honestly. Here we see the divine desire at work in the sinful power games of human history, overturning them by entering them and absorbing their evil. And the life of Christ suffuses his church of the faithful, who indirectly influence the surrounding society.

O'Donovan teaches that the incarnation is not best understood as a general universal principle instantiated in a particular man, who in theory could have equivalents. 'What is remarkable, and what only the incarnation can tell us of, is not the representation of universal order in any one being, but the coming within universal order of that which belongs outside it, the one divine Word which gave it its origin and which pronounces its judgement.'[13] The authority of Christ then is not simply that of an example or prophet instructing us how to behave but that of the restored moral order itself personally present. O'Donovan concludes, 'God has willed that the restored creation should take form in and in relation to, one man.' This fits with Pannenberg's emphasis of the coming of the consummation of creation, in Jesus and his life action, coming to us and yet participating in our history and web of being.

The Church of Jesus Christ

The presence of God for Christians is also that of the corporate Christ, 'risen, ascended, glorified', not fixed to one place and time now but 'eschatologized' and present throughout time, his disciples being 'in' Christ, as his 'body' on earth. This again takes us to the multi-dimensional reality of God's presence and ours in God. Theologies often regard these as alternative models, but they are both true, and the household analogy remains powerful for imagining how God surrounds us in all sorts of ways, direct and indirect, objective and subjective, intensely personal

---

[13]*Resurrection and Moral Order*, op cit., p. 144.

and 'out of the corner of our eye' in the background, indeed in the very foundations of all reality. We are 'the body of Christ', mutually open to each other and gaining a new corporate identity as the church of Christ, together. Here we meet the images of the church also as 'the household of God', living stones in the temple of God, mutuality and coinherence of social personality being the difficult but yet real experience described.

This life together as church, the corporate identity as the common Jesus identity in the Spirit worshipping the Father as forgiven and glad created human beings, itself mediates divine guidance as to how we live with others, what we should do, what we should not: how our freedom should be conducted. Such churchly living together in mutuality and honesty and trust anticipates life with God, who is 'corporate personality and personal society',[14] freedom in mutual care. The more we live this life together, in the Spirit with Christ facing God the Father, the more sensitive we will become to the divine desire, the more our lives will take on the power of a witness to Jesus Christ, unknown to ourselves, and the more we find that legalism is not the way of Christian discipleship, that faith includes but transcends rules and regulations. The church then has the authority to declare the forgiveness of sins in Christ, crucified and risen, present in and with his disciples who are confident in him as the reconciler and redeemer, the one who knits together our moral wounds.

To be church people is to be formed in the likeness of Christ, with all the influences of the practices of the church, of fellow believers, of relationships and vocations fostered in that great organic flowerbed. As individuals, command meets us in the particularity of life our vocation is ours alone – as Kierkegaard spent his life and writing emphasizing. We meet with God in the peculiar circumstances of life and seek to go along with the divine will expressed to us in the most individual and personal terms, notwithstanding the common sense advice of friends and norms. No two people have the same life situations, no one else can take my moral decisions for me despite the giving and taking of strong advice. Jesus himself went ahead with his traumatic and perilous journey to Jerusalem and to the heart of religious and political power structures so hostile to him and his mission. He saw the shape of history and of the Scriptures more clearly than his disciples and his persecutors, and he was called forward by God, his Father, and he went on, in trust. This was true freedom, and also truly shaped by the authority of God, the revelation of God, foreshadowed by the Suffering Servant of Isaiah 53.

Christ-like authority in the church, as the body of Christ, shapes life action and bestows true freedom for individuals to fulfil their created potential in all sorts of ways. The wisdom of a great scientist in the cosmos is an agent of the Creator revealing some new aspect of its

---

[14]A. E. Garvie, *The Christian Doctrine of the Godhead*, London: Hodder and Stoughton, 1925, p. 478.

structure, some new wonder, and some new way of helping the human race to repair itself, feed itself, transport itself and any number of assistances, such advances are moments of revelation and disclosure of the universe's wonderful treasury. But scientific advance can of course be used as technologies of evil and mass destruction, they can never be detached from the moral context of the brilliant individual nor the community of science globally. The brilliant free mind does need the whole background context of science and humane goodness, and is in touch, knowingly or not, with the Creator's Spirit in the world. The form of true freedom is Christ's form.

Likewise in the church Bonhoeffer, the Lutheran pastor and theologian who returned to Nazi Germany from the safety of the USA, cut a pathway – against the advice of many – because he was convinced of the need to lead the 'Confessing Church' and also to support the plot to assassinate Hitler. It was a Kierkegaardian moment of decision against the moral law, and one which failed. Bonhoeffer found himself in an impossible and unique situation, caused by the sins of humanity great and small, and ultimately he took a decision against the way of Christ, but seeking to save millions from mass destruction thereby. His own death at the hands of the Nazis in fact was a passive act in the way of Christ that has had immense impact in the world, a witness to Christ and to 'true patriotism' over the claims of one's own country when it is wrong and pursuing evil pathways. The authority of Christ resonates from Bonhoeffer's martyr death rather than from his attempt on Hitler's life, although that of course reveals the clash of the kingdom of God with the sinfulness of human history and its potential for immense evil – even to killing millions upon millions of people by the most brutal possible means. With Bonhoeffer prayer and political action were combined, his vocation was unique and his freedom conditioned by this calling to be Christian disciple, leader and responsible created human being.

The ascended Christ is Lord of the universe, the cross being the wisdom of God at the very core of all reality. The authority of the crucified Christ cannot be replaced by any other authorities or powers or dominions, he has overturned all other power structures, political, economic or religious. Christ crucified and risen is the authentic authority for the human race, the restored human being who offers us all repair and healing, right relationships, true freedom shaped in holy love. Christ is the creative Word, the image of the invisible God, who knits together what has been broken by human sin and abuse of freedom. To this authority we turn in the church, and this authority we commend to the world as having the right way for society and relationships. His Lordship is loving, truthful and holy, pursuing the divine desire for his creation, inculcating true freedom for God and so true creaturely freedom as lived out in Jesus' life. No Christian practices are older or more laden with meaning than baptism and the eucharist, both take us to the death and resurrection of

Christ, to his holy self offering and total trust of God his Father, both renew our identification with Jesus and his way of holy love. That is the form of the church's life, the Jesus way. The church is the one institution, said Archbishop William Temple, that exists for the benefit of its non-members. But the present crisis of values affects both society and the church: has the church sufficient focused form to order its freedom in the Spirit? We conclude by arguing that it has, and that remaining loyal to its vocation to follow the way of Jesus is essential to itself, and so to society and state.

10

Formative Factors of Church Life

The Lordship of Christ is a fact in and for creation, but it is known in the church, in the people who have faith and live their lives in the orbit of the creative Word made flesh. In the order of being, Christ is in every rustling leaf, sustaining all life from the least to the most complex. The believer knows this, that the created order is a home or a 'surround sound' parental reality we can trust because we know the parents the richness of messages, of challenges of hope and purpose, together. The Trinitarian life is like this in its unity and diversity, reflected in the created order. Music, which absorbs us and which we can take and sing and pass on, has a rhythm, a melody, a harmony all working together in such a way that we could not conceive of pulling an aspect out of this living and enveloping and captivating reality, often therapeutic, often challenging and awakening. The great symphony multiplies diversity from a unity, Beethoven's Fifth Symphony very famously expanding from the initial four simple notes into a firework of glory and wonder. God communicates with us as God accommodating to his creatures, but not as he is not: God reveals himself, and God is love, therefore free and reaching out for free response formed by love.

In the order of knowing the church knows this, and the church knows that forgiveness and revelation, the giving of the Spirit, come through the death and rising of Christ, the absorption of the hostility of human wrong so as ultimately to kill it and draw its accumulating conditioning and imprisoning power. The church is the corporate personal society of love, expressing Christ's love to the world in its brokenness and chaos. The church is a body and so has itself, the fellowship of believers, to rely on and to help, to encourage in faith and in prayer and worship. The Spirit is at work in the church in all sorts of ways, through the deep variety of personalities and experiences, a web of fellowship and care, and one that flows into the world by way of care and invitation. How is the Lordship expressed in the world?

Preaching the word

The very first act of the new church after Pentecost was announcing to the world, as it had gathered in representatives' persons from around the known world in Jerusalem, Christ and him crucified and risen. If Christianity is an 'in-house cultural-linguistic phenomenon', how can we explain preaching to those outside the house? The authority of the preachers was only that of the content of their message, made white hot in the Spirit acting on their surrendered personalities, the message of Christ, of the Word working in the world. This was Christ's word to the listeners by way of the very undistinguished, unlearned rabble of fishermen, tax collectors and other nobodies. Preaching the Word happens by the Spirit enacting human freedom formed in the narratives about Jesus.

And we should notice that the Gospel is not preached for the church, but for the hearers of the word and for God's creative intention. This is not a project about building up a powerful world institution but about building up the body of Christ, whose centre is Christ crucified and risen: the reverse of a worldly power statement, rather a breaking of power and remaking of it in the new form of the Jesus Way. This is a message of self giving. The end product of Gospel and church is not church, a unity bound tightly inwards, but the free diversity of the message going out to the ends of the earth, with the form of Christ. This point reinforces the fact that Christianity influences and affects the world's structures indirectly, not seeking to implement a structural political edifice, which would only freeze as history moves on.

The Pentecostal phenomenon of many tongues and peoples hearing the word of preaching in their own languages is another way of putting this basic point: there is no original tongue for Christians to go back to in order to worship and pray, as in Islam with Arabic or the Medieval Church and Latin. The Gospel is freedom of worship in all languages and the Creator hears prayer and praise in every conceivable tongue, and this is of its nature, not a regrettable fact at all. Freedom not necessity, expansion not unification, diversity and not unicity: here are important and neglected hallmarks of church and Gospel, and of how the authority of Christ is mediated to us.

The people gathered in Jerusalem were there for the feast of Pentecost, and were sent out by the Spirit to Judea, Samaria and the ends of the earth: centripetalism had become centrifugalism. Christ left no relic for veneration, no shrine to visit, no footprint to adore: the tomb was empty! Nor did the disciples after the resurrection bother to mark its place, they were in the presence of Christ in the Spirit, a global reality now. 'He is not there', says the angel at the tomb. There is no equivalent of a Christian Haj, a mandatory pilgrimage to one place from around the world, this drive to unification of the diversity of disciples reverses the Gospel imperative of the presence of Christ in the Spirit, of forgiveness of sins in Christ as we worship the Father in our own languages and ways. The cultural linguistic view of doctrine flies in the face of the imperative to diversity and freedom in the Spirit, as well as its curious reluctance to accept any historical reference of biblical narratives.

The word preached is outside the house of the church is *kerygma*, the trumpet sound to the world. F. D. Maurice attracted criticism for his theology that baptism declared to the person, of whatever age, that they were a child of God, made in the divine image and restored now in Christ, but he insisted that the person needed to respond to the message given to her. He made much of the creative Word being the incarnate Word and stressed revelation, revelation of who we really are at the deepest level, but he also stressed the scope of Christ's atoning death to restore us to the people the Creator intends us to be and intended from all creation. This word must reach out to the ends of the earth, and the church must preach it in all ways it can, often in ways that restore creation in practical ways, which yet speak louder than words often. The preaching of the word now, where we are, out to those without faith and hope, the lost sheep without a shepherd, this is 'crucial', and the church badly needs to renew her efforts to communicate honestly and empathetically the word of Christ outwards in the world – to that secular world, increasingly 'off limits' to this preaching.

Attending to the preaching of the prophets and apostles: The Scriptures

Divine authority can be resisted and rejected, this is a clear corollary of the nature of the Lordship of Christ and his desire to create freely responsive disciples; no Christian can be dragooned or forcibly converted, that is a contradiction of the love of God in Christ. Jesus left no organization, highly trained and in ranks of command, no handbook for revolution or 'agenda for change' in politics and religion.[1] The Christian church emerged

---

[1]See eg Eduard Schweizer, *Church Order in the New Testament*, London: SCM 1961.

as a disorganized and tiny group of Jewish people with a lifestyle to be preached and lived out, a new way of love for neighbour and for God, a way of holiness in the world and not separated from it. Hence the divine desire at work in the church is bedded into the realities of history, politics, economics, society, religious structures, 'blood toil tears and sweat' of human chaos and sin, but is not a mechanism for control of politics or economic structures. The Gospel, in other words, works indirectly – commending itself and Christ to the world in preaching peace, healing for the sick, help for the poor, and reconciliation across bitter tribal divisions. Gospel and church must operate in the way of Jesus, who went to the cross and coerced no one. This is the same pattern we find through the history of Israel: kingship, for example, is controversial, the identity of the people with a state and state structures, did not last long and Israel and Judah in fact existed under foreign political structures after being overcome by stronger surrounding powers. Into this specific political and military situation came Jesus, not into the great Davidic kingdom of power and glory.

How does this Lordship manifest itself, implement itself, in the church and the world? Jesus as we have said left no book of rules, no 'law' beyond the Law and the Prophets which he endorsed. He left the memory of himself and the inspiration of his rising from death. He left his disciples who had known him intimately, and their impression of his life and aims. The fact that initially they got things badly wrong, according to the early church's own testimony in the first chapter of the book of Acts where 'restoring the kingdom to Israel' politically was assumed to be the goal of Jesus' messiahship, shows that they had not been given a prepared manifesto or action plan by Jesus before his death. They had celebrated final Passover meal with him, had been given an appearance of him, had been inspired by the Spirit on the day of Pentecost at a major Jewish gathering in Jerusalem, but otherwise had been left to live out the logic of his life and ministry as he left it with them, and with God. From that situation then to ours, now the church has lived out its human life in the Spirit of Christ, seeking to order its life along the way of Jesus' life in whatever conditions it finds itself.

The early disciples were immersed in Jesus' life and ministry, especially the Apostles or 'the twelve', however difficult it may be historically precisely to define these categories. They shared his Hebrew background of customs and Scripture, a whole way of thinking about history and its purpose, a whole morality stemming from the doctrine of the creation and ethics. A whole religious culture was affirmed by Jesus and interpreted for them. The story of the risen Christ teaching the disciples on the road to Emmaus in Luke's Gospel indicates that the first disciples connected Jesus with a vivid and authentic interpretation of the Scriptures, that he opened up their meaning to simple people and brought the word of the past to life now in the present. Jesus was soaked in the Old Testament and in Hebrew customary life and expressed his ministry in its traditions.

The Old Testament was therefore a major source of early Christian guidance and alignment with the desire of God, a major authority and with a focal point of interpretation, Jesus and his use of the texts. The Gospel writers envisage Jesus emerging from the Hebrew background of expectation and history, and himself revealing, and enacting, the end time purposes of God. His authority is connected with the Hebrew Scriptures and he identifies his mission in their light. His treatment of the Scriptures is theological and practical, he resists layers of tradition being added and claimed as authoritative, and looks to God the beneficent Creator as fundamental in resolving questions of religious law keeping. Should a man with a withered hand not be healed on the Sabbath, was man made for the Sabbath or Sabbath for man? Who is your neighbour? The man who needs your help as a fellow human being.

The Law and the Prophets, what we now call the Old Testament, was clearly authoritative for Jesus and had a power of self-interpretation which could resist pedantic and cruel interpretations being drawn from it since it concerned God, the Lord, full of mercy and loving kindness and abounding in steadfast love. Jesus does not seem to have looked to religious experts to interpret the Scriptures, they could make their own sense heard and cut free from traditional overlay by clerics or religious specialists. Jesus did not 'deconstruct' the text along the lines of Derrida with new and contradictory ideas being provoked by the text; rather he was 'radical' in looking to God the Creator behind the purposes expressed in the Scriptures, God who is good and caring, the character of God the Creator is that of caring Father. Few scholars would now doubt this picture of Jesus as deeply Hebraic in orientation and self-understanding, and his connection with the Hebrew Scriptures as reliable and authoritative, giving us a portrait of God as the generous Creator who is close to those who trust him.

Jesus coming into the history of Israel is a critical coming as well as a participation in that tradition, in fact that tradition always incorporated theological self-criticism even of its great figures such as David and Hezekiah. The authority of Jesus challenges every age and people and culture. Belief in this authority, as O'Donovan puts it, 'means that Christ turns these fragmentary utterances of God's voice, in warrior triumphs and legislative order, into a history which culminates in the divine manifestation and vindication of the created order.' The freedom of creation and history remain and so does the sinfulness of all history, but God's purposes were not defeated. 'Thus', he continues, 'all the time, in one sense, the story of the Old Testament was the story of that order; and in reading the Old Testament as Christians we may expect to see this story, too, emerge from its pages.'[2] Christians must read the Old

Testament in the light of Christ, as clearly the writers of the texts now forming the New Testament did very clearly.

Karl Barth must be correct, as a Christian theologian speaking of the Bible, to say that its role is to point us to God, to witness and testify to his purposes in and through all the spiritual high and sinful low points, in all the strange thickets and brambles apparently blocking the purposes of God and his servants, in all the fallibility of all those servants. Barth's simple but undeniable description of the functioning of Scripture for the church is that today's preaching depends on the narratives of Scripture, that whole messy pathway of Israel to Jesus, Mary's son, and his disciples after his dying and rising. That witness points to the revealed Word as our witness today also points, and as the Spirit brings together the freedom and form in the now, 'historicity', in spiritual materiality or material spirit, the form of Christ. The Bible is not just a curious 'in house' cultural linguistic nicety, like an ancient prayer book in a museum albeit 'our' museum, it leads us into 'the strange new world', quantitatively a minute section of history, qualitatively the section used by God to communicate his ways to us.

Jüngel rightly says that Scriptural texts do help form the identity of the church, but more than that they open up new horizons for our understanding of God. 'God's humanity introduces itself into the world as a story to be told. Jesus told about God in parables before he himself was proclaimed as the parable of God.'[3] The form of the Scriptures cohere with the theology they testify, the action of God in his empathetic coming to his creation as a creature, that has to be a story set in real time and space, in history with a context stretching back and forward. God's self-revelation is a life story, told with the rough and tumble of peasants and fishermen, with the poetry of Pslamists, with the visionary gaze of apocalyptic seers, with the regimentation of chroniclers, with the theological depth of the sage, humour and despair of faith facing destruction by the powers of evil. Jüngel is surely right: 'There is an hermeneutically persuasive reason that the eschatological event of the identification of God with the Crucified One became an integral part of the life of Jesus as it was lived and thus became a rich story which demanded explication.'[4] The incarnation of the Word means a historical narrative – not simply a concept but a life story, and one carrying back to ultimate purpose and destiny of the created world, to its eschatological end. Indeed he continues,

> In that sense no theology of the Crucified One can or may do without the narration of the life and suffering of Jesus, as a life in the act of the word which tells of God's humanity. Yes, it will not even be able to grasp the life,

---

[2]*Resurrection and Moral Order*, op cit., p. 159.
[3]E. Jüngel, *God as the Mystery of the World*, Edinburgh: T & T Clark, 1983, p. 302.
[4]Ibid.

death and resurrection of Jesus as a story which is unified in itself without going further back into the narrative context of the history of Israel.[5]

Narrative can speak of what is new and never has been, and connects it with the past. Narrative moreover is essential to communicate one's identity.

It is worth contrasting this narrative structure and content of the Bible with the Qur'an, whose structure is a long declamation by God to us via Mohammed,[6] containing largely moral instruction illustrated from stories often taken from the Bible. John Wansbrough's classic study tells us:

> The fragmentary character of Muslim scripture can nowhere be more clearly observed than in those passages traditionally described as narrative. These consist in fact not so much of narrative as of *exempla*, of the sort alluded to in the Quran itself as 'signs', and hardly qualify even for the epithet 'legend'. Exhibiting a limited number of themes, the *exempla* achieve a kind of stylistic uniformity by resort to a scarcely varied stock of rhetorical convention…Since indeed the so called narrative sections of the Quran are of essentially symbolic character adduced to illustrate the eschatological value of theodicy, it is not surprising to find such remarkable conformity.[7]

The Qur'an picks up Biblical stories and makes use of sections to illustrate moral points. Indeed 'Quranic allusion presupposes familiarity with the narrative material of Judaeo-Christian scripture, which was no so much reformulated as referred to,' and, taken together, 'suggest a strongly sectarian atmosphere, in which a corpus of familiar scripture was being pressed into the service of as yet unfamiliar doctrine.'[8] Biblical narrative is a vast sweep, incorporating all manner of literature, but a continuous story of the history of Israel, climaxing for Christians with Jesus and his impact. The Qur'an is structured as the divine voice speaking, with occasional snippets of biblical narrative 'referred to' for purposes of illustration. Again we meet the deep contrast of diversity and unity: the Bible is the story of a people in covenant with God, going through millennia of blessing and distress, a whole library of diverse texts pointing to God's purposes and saving acts. Qur'an is to a single man, Mohammed, stamped with a single personality, terminating with his fixed template, or form, for humanity, rather than part of an ongoing narrative into the open future.

That God's self-revelation and his revelation of our true identity, his calling to us and waiting for us, should be mediated by narratives in

[5]Ibid.
[6]For a brief biography, see 'Muhammad' in Hastings Encyclopaedia of Religion and Ethics Edinburgh: T & T Clark 1915 vol 8 pp 871-881.
[7]John Wansbrough, *Quranic Studies* Oxford and New York: Oxford University Press 2004 [1977], p. 18.
[8]Ibid., p. 20.

large measure, and by reflections on those narratives, is no surprise, nor that the church itself is a narrative sharing in the great story of Jesus. Narrative, we might say, bridges the order of knowing and of being, and this is the Hebrew way of describing and 'analysing' life, allowing life to bring out its meaning, joys and sorrows, questions and laments. Our lives are our stories, as the postmoderns remind us, we are not 'little mortal absolutes', thinking cased in material bodies. And God reveals his loving holy character in the world of disobedient human history, supremely at Calvary.

The authoritative portrait left by Jesus with his disciples

Jesus chose a group of ordinary people to follow him and help him, and knew they would speak of him when he died. He wrote nothing and left nothing but this impression of his life and trust in the Spirit of God for his vindication. These disciples did that, they acted for him and spoke for him, they put pieces of the jig-saw together with their Old Testament knowledge. They formed a core group to whom reference could be made. They preached the Word in the Spirit. And the logic of this Word began to work itself out, notably over the inclusion of the Gentiles. These Apostles who had walked with Jesus were unique witnesses, they alone could tell of his life and ways and teachings, his reactions to others, the whole story of his life, and all against the background of his Hebrew inheritance, Abraham, Moses, the Law and the Prophets, and all the practices and customs arising from this tradition, including the eschatological hope in God as the righteous judge of history. The Apostles saw how the ancient texts point to him, and how he authorizes them as read through his life and death and resurrection, a narrative given us by the New Testament. Texts point to God and to Christ and to the Spirit, not to themselves; they are servants to the overall truth and claim of God in Christ and the whole symphony of revelation opened up by him.

The letters of Paul were probably the earliest Christian documents, again very 'natural' free communications to young churches with the practical purpose of helping them keep the faith, and clarifying the implications of their faith. Gradually the deaths of the Apostles of Jesus led to the Gospels being written in order to maintain the apostolic witness to the whole way of Christ and its narrative history. These were written after the pastoral and missionary letters of Paul – the leading missionary for Christ as the fulfilment of the Hebrew covenant, as the messianic hope actually arrived in history – and he took for granted the integral connection of Jesus with the Law and the Prophets, some time before Irenaeus began to work out a theological logic of the Scriptures for the church. The apostolic witness of the New Testament includes criticism of the Apostles, notably Peter, they see themselves as frail and fallible, they see their sole task as pointing to Jesus and telling his story as honestly as they can. This gives the New Testament its 'ring of truth' and authority. The New Testament writings are varied in form and authorship, a diversity not organized centrally, just documents written for church use and gradually collected and accepted as authentic 'apostolic' witnesses.

It is again worth noting the diversity and freedom of the way God allows space to his people to develop patterns that accord to the form of his truth and calling. No central institute to organize the texts of the New Testament was set up; its emergence was a purely natural process of the Gospel as it spread. A diversity of voices is heard throughout all the Scriptures, Old and New Testaments alike. God rejoices in this diversity and employs human experience of all kinds as his messengers, direct and indirect, named and anonymous, great and tiny in their role, from the dizzying insights given to Isaiah to the often bitter accounts of rebuilding given in Nehemiah, from the Gospels to the letter of Philemon about a runaway slave. God conducts his purposes like a river, not a canal.[9] He uses conditions, personalities, free decisions good and bad, through which to reveal his ways and enact his will in space and time; he does not blast a straight line through the recalcitrant granite of sinful human resistance, eradicating sin by force – as if that could be done in any case. The Old and New Testaments are a whole chorus of voices of people who have experienced the grace and justice and love of God, stories of people who have gone astray, of those who have repented, of praise, of lament, of wisdom. God chooses to work through free personalities in the chaos of history.

Critical examination

For the contemporary historical scholar keen to subject the documents of the Bible to ongoing scrutiny, as has been happening now for over two hundred years, this means that the texts of the Gospels have not been processed early, have not been coordinated to iron out inconsistencies, have not been cut and squared by a human process of editing. A leading Jewish scholar of the New Testament, Geza Vermes, regards the Synoptic Gospels as very largely authentic, as fitting the known history and custom of its age like a glove. The church today can take the historicity of the New Testament about Jesus as reliable even on secular critical grounds, it is the 'metaphysical' claims of the early church that Vermes does not agree with, but these claims, about Jesus having an identity which is eschatological and divine as well as human, are not matters which secular reason can adjudicate: God cannot be placed on a dissecting board or viewed through a telescope. The factuality of the narratives of Jesus, the contexts narrated and the interest groups debating with him, the historical

---

[9]A luminous phrase of John Oman in his *Grace and Personality*, Cambridge: Cambridge University Press, 1917, p. 1.

data of the Roman authorities, customs and so forth, Vermes regards as secure and reliable; he disagrees with the Apostles and Evangelists on their interpretation of the history and narrative but that is no longer a matter of historical judgement but spiritual and moral.

Jesus allowing of healing on the Sabbath, and of his disciples eating grain in the fields on the Sabbath, are upheld on the grounds of Scriptural and theological truth, against a legalistic tradition developed by men, not God. He does not uphold his practice by denying his tradition in the name of some autonomous freedom, nor claim an exception to the normal rule; he looks to the Hebrew view of God and creation, and uses that to interpret the Sabbath laws, against a negative and harsh view. His teaching is not to abandon 'form' in the name of 'freedom' but to discern in Scripture the desire of God and find true freedom formed by the holy love of God, and applicable in a particular situation. Jesus rescues 'the woman taken in adultery' from the fate of stoning to death by the ultra religious, but tells her to go 'and sin no more', not encouraging her to create her own new prison of 'freedom', denying the pattern of marriage. Jesus' validation of Hebrew ethical form, linking to the divine desire as Creator, is basic to the debate about homosexuality in the church. Freedom has a creative form in Jesus' teaching, while legalism and mere rule keeping are not the basis of his way.

Like a great painting, the picture we have of Jesus is profoundly attractive to the reasonable enquirer, and this is part of the structure of self-attestation which emerges from the New Testament writings. Written some decades after his death by disciples who will have witnessed the spread of the Gospel remarkably and powerfully, we can assume a carefulness in setting down what was known of Jesus and his ministry, for example the Synoptics eschew adding a magical dimension to his life as is seen in the Gnostic Gospels. The main point is that Jesus stands out from the texts, and expresses the divine desire to us.

We look at this portrait, or hear this narrated life, as we do an impressionist painting, with the main object clear but with the light playing upon it, a light of faith and disclosure of depth. We are drawn into this figure, this story, and wish to follow, to become a disciple and know God through him. He maintains the Hebrew tradition of God and holiness, loving God and our neighbour, in a spirit of mercy in the name of the Creator. Perhaps this is an impressionist painting, suffused with the tints of the painter, but certainly no 'abstract' or 'expressionist' painting, the historical lines are clear and recognizable to the expert, non-Christian, historian. We might say that the core of Christian preaching is to say: 'look at this figure', or 'read this story', and respond as you will. The church's task is merely to bring people to look or listen.

Christian prayer – in Christ

Geza Vermes places Jesus teaching close to the ancient Hasidim.

> A negative, but significant feature…of Jesus' representation of God consists in the absence of any royal figure, and of a corresponding self-deprecation and abasement before a divine Lord. On the contrary, the piety practised and preached by Jesus, like that of the Hasidim of old, is characterised by simple trust and expectation. Before the tremendous majesty of a divine Judge was foreseen as following the coming Day of the Lord, Jesus and his co-workers in the establishment of the Kingdom turned for inspiration, help and strength of purpose to the heavenly Abba.[10]

This is no sentimental view. Jesus knew of the tragedies of life, the 'fall of the sparrow', unjust suffering and wrong. 'But what lies at the heart of his intuition and gives individuality and freshness to his vision is the conviction that the eternal, distant dominating and tremendous Creator is also and primarily a near and approachable God.'[11] Vermes surely captures the heart of Jesus' human spirituality, although he does not view Jesus' deepest identity as taken up by this transcendent yet approachable Father.

One particular place in the New Testament giving us a window into the mind and heart of Jesus and his orientation to God and the world is his teaching on prayer. The 'Lord's prayer', on purely historical critical criteria, almost certainly goes back to Jesus' teaching, they are his words, and so we have an insight into his theology of God and the world, an insight that is authoritative for all Christian disciples in their understanding of prayer and of God to whom Jesus prayed in filial trust. God is transcendent, 'in heaven', and immanent, 'our Father' who 'gives us our daily bread' in all the changes and chances of the world. God the Creator of the cosmos cares about us; that is the deep claim in this prayer. God is holy, his 'name' is 'hallowed', he forgives our sins and this is linked to our becoming forgiving people, fulfilling our identity as being in the image of God. Jesus urges us to pray the radical prayer that 'thy will be done, on earth as it is in heaven', and that God's kingdom come: human beings are joining in with the causes of God, their prayers being somehow important for the fulfilling of the divine will, the divine desire.

Our freedom is taken up into the will of God as if a means to facilitate divine will in human history, again emphasizing that the divine authority is far from simply being 'over against' us, a detached judge applying his rule book like a bacon slicer, but far more like a sensitive parent keen to see his children grow into themselves for what is good and Godly,

---

[10]Geza Vermes, *The Religion of Jesus the Jew*, London: Penguin, 1993, p. 180.
[11]Ibid.

into people who are supporting 'kingdom of God'. The virtue of such children growing up to support the household and form other homes cannot be compelled, issues from good characters fostered by wise parents, and so the divine parental desire is accomplished, it has to be through free personalities allowed space and forming themselves in the way God wishes us to be formed.

This rich and yet simple prayer can serve as an ethical pattern for life: can I do this act while praying this prayer, is it in the will and desire of God? We note that Jesus' prayer contains no note of threat by God to get his will enacted; this is far more the loving parent we know wants our best and is working with us for it. But the Lord's Prayer does pray in the context of a battle with evil and temptation. And for us now who prayer this prayer, we pray it with Jesus who taught us to pray, we pray in Christ to the Father. We know the ethics of Jesus, not throwing out the Hebrew way but re-rooting in the will of the inbreaking of God – our ethics is bound up with the 'Jesus of history', who is 'Christ crucified' for our sins and sinful disobedience. We are not encouraged in any soft sentimental selfindulgence, or radical change, especially damaging the created order – ecologically or personally. To pray in Christ is to orient one's life for the kingdom.

Baptismal and eucharistic praxis

A key practice of the church filled with the divine desire and authority of God in Christ is the eucharist, taking us back to the last supper of Jesus with his friends, the last Passover meal with them, the self-interpretation by Jesus as the 'suffering servant', the sacrificial lamb. The church breaks bread and pours out wine in remembrance, making present in the memorial of his passion, Christ crucified and risen, entering into the self-offering of Christ by our giving of ourselves into him. We know the kind of Lordship of Christ as church people, we know the way of Jesus is the way to human reconciliation, forgiveness and peace through self-giving and truth telling, not as just a difficult moral code to obey but a sharing in the risen life of Jesus by the Spirit. We are invited into Christ crucified and risen, in his story of human being, and so share in that new way of life and being. 'God has sent the Spirit of his Son into our hearts, so we cry Abba, Father' (Gal. 4:6).

The person of Jesus draws us to his way of being through the portrait of himself – immensely subtle and yet simple – painted by the prophets and New Testament witnesses. He offers himself to us and for us, rather than imperiously demanding submission, and we offer ourselves to God in him. His life is deeply attractive to the whole of humanity, we know he is the perfect human being, that his way offers hope to human history, that he has authority over evil through truth and love rather than through retaliation power play. We are called to enter Christ's self giving, to be broken for the world, to be scattered in the world to be his body. And this has happened for two millennia. This liturgical practice fuels pastoral care and service to the stranger, Christ's ministry in his church to the world. Here we practice love of God and of neighbour, empowered by Christ crucified.

The Jesus way is authorized authoritatively by Jesus' life, a lived and living way, which goes beyond a structure of rules and yet affects daily life in a powerful way. Freedom and form remain woven together, in a freedom and joy rather than a dour attempt to keep the rules. For example Jesus, through the narrative picture of his life left naturally to his disciples, by his love and care and challenges those with large amounts of the creation's resources to share more with the poor, and to find our self-giving in Jesus' self-offering to his Father. Here is the very core of creative purpose, here is God's desire for us human beings, here in the way of this man we see humanity and we wish to be part of him, his way, and put ourselves under his authority, as given in Matthew's Gospel: 'come to me all who labour and are heavy laden, and I will give you rest. Take my yoke upon you and learn from me, for I am gentle and lowly in heart and you will find rest for your souls, for my burden is easy and my yoke is light' (Matt. 11:28–30). This was the message of the Christian community's experience as expressed in Matthew's Gospel, that Jesus calls us to himself with the authority of caring healing love. This is taken up in our worship of God, transcending the hard moral treadmill of a worthy ethic, the way of Jesus is a liberating way, with the form of his life not just a template but a life shared in the Spirit.

That is true authority in the order of God and of God's creation, as free human beings. We are in the household, the 'surround sound' of this Jesus Christ and his Spirit orientating us to the Father. We know it as we live it, and we know it as we hear the Scriptures read; we sing hymns forged over the years, we celebrate the Lord's Supper with its sonar resonances backwards into the rock of creation, of Abraham and Moses, the sufferings of Israel in slavery, the refocusing of that in grotesque injustice and inhumane judicial murder of Jesus, the best human being there has ever been. Inhabiting this narrative of Jesus, this way of his life, means sharing in his prayer, giving alms as he taught, caring for the sick not only of our own tribe, clan and family but for whoever we see in need, even those who attack us and wish us eradicated from the face of the earth. Such assumptions have indeed penetrated Western and United Nations views of humanity from the church. Only the Western tradition donates charitably, in terms of state giving to different nations, cultures and traditions, and this derives from the Christian ethos of charity to all, the parable of the Good Samaritan institutionalized by the West after centuries of Christian influence.

In the broken bread and poured wine we are given redemption by Jesus, and our responsive self giving depends wholly on his self offering to the Father in the Spirit, again we are reaffirmed in being in the divine redemptive life, described in the dynamic Trinitarian insight of the New Testament. The life of responsive self-giving to Jesus' self-offering is true Christian praxis, and is the power house of all the Christian social and indirectly political and economic reform: leading to the welfare state, proper pay and working conditions, and full democratic government. How can we be Christ-like as a church and how should this convert wider social structures away from cruelty and towards the will of God? That is the agenda set by the Gospel and repeated in the action of the Lord's Supper, Holy Communion or Eucharist, a deeply forming act in church life and a gift to church life directly from Jesus, his past and future.

In a remarkable foreword to a book on nursing, written in fact during the last months of the writer's life, Lord Morris of Castle Morris described his time in a hospital ward. He describes compassion as rooted in the vocation and the Christian moral tradition.

> Compassion is an inconvenient concept: it cannot be measured, rationed or costed. It cannot be planned or delivered, but it will not go away. I had reason to be regularly reminded of this when I spent two periods of about five months each as a patient in an NHS hospital. Only a few days after I was admitted we were all distressed and sleepless because a young man with severe head injuries kept up a nerve-racking unearthly wailing noise for hours on end, and no form of sedation seemed to help. In the end a nurse came in, sat on his bed, put both arms around him and cuddled him for an hour. She rocked him gently, like a baby, and murmured things to him. His mind was too far away to know what was happening, but the simple human contact, the compassion, calmed him and relieved him when no drug had been effective.[12]

Here we have the anamnesis, the representation, of kindness to the stranger in desperate need spelled out in Jesus' parable of the Good Samaritan. Caring for the unpopular patient in this way was Christ-like, and while unintended as such was a kind of preaching also, the sounding note of the care of the Creator for his creature through that nurse. In the 'order of being' – even if she did not know it herself – she was living wisdom in the ward and world. As Lord Morris said, this cannot be produced by sociological or psychological training, nor by the MacDonaldized 'have a good day' commercial conditioning: but from genuine humanity as intended by God.

The other scene was of a staff nurse running the ward in the absence of the ward sister. It was a day of crises:

---

[12]Foreword to Ann Bradshaw, *The Project 2000 Nurse: The Remaking of Modern Nursing*, London: Churchill-Livingstone, 2001, p. ix.

her young nurses were flying about dealing with a series of emergencies. In the midst of this I suddenly caught sight of her walking slowly and calmly down the ward to the sluice room carrying before her a bedpan covered with a length of toilet paper. Nothing special in that, but the image stayed in my mind. A few days later I saw the hospital chaplain on his rounds, taking communion to the patients, carrying before him the paten and chalice, covered with burse and veil. The contrast between faeces and sacrament could hardly have been greater: the comparison of the two 'icons of service' could hardly have been more striking.[13]

This comparison made the observer realize that the nurse's 'status' must be 'considered far more profoundly, imaginatively and (dare I say it) poetically than it has been over the last twenty years.'[14] Surely this takes us close to the heart of Word of God communicating in the world, and divine communication effects what it says, effects the way of the deepest service, freely given, in the utterly authoritative form of Christ. The way of the cross – taken by God and made present in the eucharist, in the courageous and kind nurse, in the Spirit here and now – represents divine authority in Christ-like form, reaching into the dark and hurt places of creation to heal and reconcile.

The church surely has made a dreadful mistake in withdrawing itself from nursing training, from specifically Christian vocational work, and from offering nursing care however it can. The caring professions need the form of Christ, not simply the freedom of the 'autonomous professional'. Lord Morris' deep insight that his work is 'poetic', not functional, not to be mass produced, cut or squared, but somehow attuned with the depths of humanity and the heights of deity, true wisdom at work. It has been folly by the anti-religious secularist bureaucrats to attack the Christian tradition of altruism as a basis for care, even as one option on a menu of such bases. For the church to accept the verdict of secularist planners, that the altruistic tradition has no place in the caring professions, indicates a loss of nerve and temptation to abandon the Gospel of 'the way of the Son into the far country.'

The free and glad caring for the sick and broken is an expression of the love of God in Christ, made present in the practice of Christians and sacrificial love. The origins of the hospital are in Jesus and his church, this practical care being authoritative healing and mending of creation, a great sacrament of Christ in action – even if many of those benefiting know nothing of Jesus. Western policy-makers seem unaware of the cultural roots of hospital care for those outside one's own 'tribe'. This whole tradition of caring for individuals, irrespective of their colour, creed, or nationality, stems directly from Jesus and his acts of healing the desperate and needy. The parable of the Good Samaritan crystallizes

---

[13]Ibid., p. ix.
[14]Ibid.

this imperative to care. This Lordship has freed people from all sorts of oppressive practices, for example the ritual 'uncleanness' of women. His Lordship, working outwards into society through the microcosm of the church, has created freedoms thanks to his view of the sanctity of human life for everyone, even traditional enemies and outsiders. The form of Christ's life breaks down barriers between enemies and empowers reconciliation rather than tribal resentment and vendetta, thus fostering real freedom over enmity and strife. We see that the Christian social ethic, so powerful in this profession, is vital to maintain, and if the churches give up on it then they are surely depriving society of a crucial impetus to care. Altruism has its root in the Gospel, and politicians are worried at its increasing scarcity.[15]

The practice of Baptism also focuses on the dying and rising of Jesus stressing our new and true identity with him, as his disciple. This is who we are at the deepest level of our being. This brings the joy of security of acceptance and love by God, the verdict has been declared and shared with us in Christ. When Christians take difficult decisions ultimately their baptismal identity is the basis on which they decide and act: can we in Christ do this, or make this change? Our identity as a person of a particular race or disposition or conditioning is secondary to our identity in Christ, although that of course will be challenging if we want to 'baptise' a pattern of behaviour that is not authorized by the Apostolic way. This relates directly to the debates about human sexuality now raging in the church, and the assertion of identities based on sexual desire.

This may also be a good way to seek to practise the 'table fellowship' of Jesus with the deeply unpopular of society, those shunned and not accepted. If our identity is in Christ, if our old false identities of respectability and fashionability have been broken, then we can also seek to keep 'bad company' for God. He practised 'table fellowship' with the poor, eating with those shunned by respectable society such as prostitutes and the hated tax collectors operating for the Roman occupiers, stressing God's grace in seeking out the lost while not affirming their lifestyles, as was the case with the rich. Uniquely he broke down tribal barriers of all kinds. He observed the Sabbath mercifully, not legalistically, in tune with the mercy of the creative purpose of the Sabbath day. He taught in parables, evoking real understanding and response, rather than promulgating decrees.

He lived out what he taught, the Sermon on the Mount being a kind of summary of his way of absorbing hatred and resentment rather than retaliating, his was the way of the suffering servant. His way was a

---

[15]See eg Health Care Commission. *Investigation into Mid Staffordshire NHS Foundation Trust.* London: Commission for Healthcare Audit and Inspection 2009:12. and Johnson A. (2008) /Hansard/. House of Commons, London, 30 June 2008: c 604.

liberating way, freeing us from the prisons of our exclusive patterns of fellowship. To be baptised and share in the Holy Communion is to be shaped in the way of Jesus and his self giving for others: this imperative lies at the foundations of western civilization.

The apostolic office and pastoral ministry

Jesus called disciples who were witnesses to him, and formed the early church and its ministry as it evolved into a missionary and pastoral movement. The pastor and teacher, the local minister, perhaps in teams rather than as individual leaders, was always a figure in church life in some form. The Apostles were able to explain the significance of Jesus, in the light of Jewish scriptural tradition, to the crowds of Jewish pilgrims at Pentecost, and to lead new believers in 'the way', as the writer of Acts puts it: 'So those also who received his word were baptised, and there were added that day about three thousand souls. And they devoted themselves to the apostles' teaching and fellowship, to the breaking of bread and the prayers' (Acts 3:41).

In the letters of the New Testament we read, for example, of the Apostle Paul, as he left small groups of converts to Christ, who seems to have ensured some sort of pastoral leadership for them, and from their own group. The task of this pastoral leadership was to read the Scriptures to the congregation, to 'break bread' with them, encourage care for the sick and seek the gifts of the Spirit for vocations, to pray and baptise and keep disciples in the way of Jesus. Paul and his fellow missionaries kept in touch with the churches they had founded as a wider tangible network, and indeed the letters of Paul to new churches are the earliest texts of the New Testament, examples of Apostolic teaching and encouragement, keeping the churches close to Christ. Paul knew Peter and other eye-witnesses and friends of Jesus; while not one himself he had experienced a radical conversion after encountering the risen Christ on the road to Damascus and drew his authority from that encountering of Jesus Christ and commissioning by him to turn from persecuting the church to preaching to the Gentiles and building it up. In a typically unorganized way, Paul becomes an Apostle, one sent out to spread the word. Congregations were part of a wider network of church life rooting back to those who knew Jesus and the divine desire revealed in his ministry, death and rising. The letters of such Apostles, and narratives of how they took decisions as new challenges arose, are now part and parcel of the Apostolic guidance mandatory for all congregations and pastors and missionaries.[16]

---

[16]See Edward Schillebeeckx, *The Church with a Human Face*, London: SCM, 1984.

John McKenzie sets out the striking new kind of authority brought about by St Paul in his exercise of his Apostolic role of founding new churches and maintaining contact with them to help and build them up in Christ. From reading his letters to the young churches we see that Paul's dealings with these churches were intimate and unconstrained; his epistles were not the communication of a superior to subjects or of an administrator to subordinates so much as an unabashed disclosure of the heart to close friends … Paul belonged to his Christians and they belonged to him; and this is the way they treated each other. The relation of apostle and Christians which he established is unique; it is not like the relations of members of a family or of a civil society. Paul … brought into being an entirely new and original idea of authority.[17]

The words *diakonos* and *diakonia*, says McKenzie, characteristic designations of the mission of Jesus in the Gospels, commonly characterize the role of apostle. Paul's dedication to this role was to persons, rather than to a message or an institution. He was personally dedicated to Jesus, and inseparably to his brothers and sisters in Christ. Personal love was practically worked out in mutual love of Christ: authority is *diakonia* only if it is service given to existing persons. This apostolic authority was also what Paul inculcates in the ministers of local congregations.

As time went on the writings of the Apostles and of those who knew their testimony – those who were able to speak with people who actually knew Jesus – became important and were collected in a 'canon' which became the New Testament. The 'Conference of Jerusalem', described in Acts 15, for example, brings together Peter, Paul, John, James and other followers who clearly could interact and share their memories and impressions of Jesus. The church today is responsible to these voices and finds they come to life in the present as the Spirit links the church together across time and space. Likewise the practices of 'breaking the bread', declaring the Gospel to outsiders, baptising into the Jesus way of life, praying, caring for the sick, accepting women as people rather than chattels, being taught and encouraged by the Apostles and their witness to Jesus, the kind of activity presented in the Book of Acts, however stylized that may be, was the simple way of the early churches as they grew after Pentecost.

This lifestyle of the Gospel was kept and shaped by the cluster of these customs, teachings, traditions, and practices, and they shaped responses to changing conditions such as the expulsion of followers of 'The Way' from the Synagogue, the inclusion of Gentile believers, and later the shifting relationship with the Roman Empire and the problem of power. Authority in the church is that of Jesus, whose narrative portrait was painted by his friends, in all their weakness but all their loyalty to tell his story, a narrative that did not end at the cross but burst into history

---

[17]John L. McKenzie SJ, *Authority in the Church*, London: Geoffrey Chapman, 1966, p. 56.

through his resurrection and the Spirit's action, a narrative all Christians inhabit, always looking to his portrait as the Lord of the church. The divine desire is portrayed as this unity but through a great diversity of free voices and painters, testifying to life-changing form of life, the Jesus Way.

The ordained pastoral ministry of the church has a special task of trusteeship, which is not simply freezing the truth but maintaining it while explaining in for every age. The music of Mozart needs to be played by an orchestra, and the orchestra with its conductor will give performances all slightly different, but still of the same piece of music. The whole text of Scripture, its whole message read in the light of Christ's climax, shapes the performance of the church today. No church or leadership is free to break this form of life, the apostolic way of Jesus. The Anglican bishops at the 1998 Lambeth Conference gave their judgement on the issue of gay sex, 'rejecting homosexual practice as incompatible with Scripture' and not being able to advise blessing of same sex unions or ordination of people engaging in homosexual sex. That was clearly right as far as Scripture is concerned, and Scripture is the key apostolic authority. But this decision was accompanied by a resolution to care for those who see their identity as homosexual and who do not accept the New Testament ethic. This is definite and also pastorally caring. It seems apt for the Jesus way. It seems the best way forward for society and young people with plastic natures feeling their way into adult life. It is very much in tune with Jesus' appeal to creation and form for our freedom, while avoiding legalistic judgementalism, and fits with Foucault's work on the social construction of identities.

Expecting the Spirit

The history of the church is certainly more like a natural river than an engineered canal, and this again shows that God gives freedom to his disciples including freedom to commit grave mistakes. This for example has happened in relation to state power, but we also have a flexibility in recovering from mistakes and reordering itself by returning to this Jesus lifestyle. This way of life left by Jesus in such an apparently unorganized, but definite, way is the way of the church, all its practices and teachings have their roots in the historical Jesus, with all the richness of meaning in his person and work. According to Max Weber's famous typological description of the church, it moved from an initial era of charisma to a later mode of establishment and bureaucracy, from being a movement inspired by the Spirit, with travelling charismatic prophets spreading the word and teaching small communities, to a Roman 'diocesan' civic organization with a hierarchy of rulers and the lay people doing what they were told by their leaders, and now, finally, it has fixed into a regional pattern. This typology has some value as a description of how the waves of church history develop, and as a warning to churches against becoming a quasi-state, either ruling the state structures or becoming a vassal of the state. The development of 'mono episcopacy' in church leadership, itself capable of being seen in its early form as a charismatic role and pastoral role, as the centuries went on developed into a role of immense wealth and power, so that the 'prince bishop' was a common figure in medieval Europe.[18]

Hannah Arendt suggested that when the Roman empire was invaded by barbarians, the church gave it a new lease of life and a new identity, with a new founding moment in Jesus replacing Romulus and Remus, a founding historic criterion of loyalty and value. Arendt said this changed the church drastically from a movement looking to the risen Christ now, to an establishment religion looking back to a founding historic figure: form without the freedom of the Spirit now, we might say. Church and Empire, Pope and Emperor, coordinated themselves, giving the church immense power, and under Hildebrand, Pope Gregory VII, the church asserted its autonomy and power over the state. The church held the keys of the kingdom and could withhold grace and forgiveness of sins even to emperors. Arendt's reading of the medieval doctrine of hell was that its roots were in Plato, who saw that the polis needed a sanction beyond the grave to compel citizens to do what they did not want to do, the threat of death not being sufficient. The church wielded this power effectively, rooted out heretics and even waged war in the name of Christ – but this was surely an abrogation of the authority of Christ. The use of violence was not part of the authority of Jesus. His authority was a sort of counter authority, and yet not some nihilistic movement against all authority, 'render to Caesar the things that are Caesar's'.

The presence of the Spirit has been of the essence of the church, and all the practices listed above are also connected with the Spirit – prayer especially being a work of both the people praying and of the Spirit, but also mundane acts of caring, difficult acts of witness in the secular world, the church constantly trusts in the Holy Spirit. And this is in complete harmony with the origin of church practice and lifestyle in practices of the historical Jesus, since Jesus himself trusted the Spirit throughout his ministry and saw himself as serving the Father in the Spirit. Freedom, form and historicity combine, mutually condition and act, when the church is most truly the body of Christ, the kingdom of God, the will of the Father being done on earth as in heaven. The Spirit is the Spirit of God shown in the life of the Jesus of history, the Spirit ungraspable by us but not a crazy and destructive spirit against all order

---

[18]See Eduardo Hoornaert, *The Memory of the Christian People*, London: Burns & Oates, 1989, for a critical appraisal of such developments.

and form. The form and order of the Spirit of freedom is freedom from
sin and death not for it, freedom revealed humanly in Jesus, freedom for
love and care, not for brutal power and indifference. This ties in with
Jesus and his theology of God the good and caring Creator, found in the
Hebrew tradition, a mutually confirming pattern.

The Spirit, as we survey church history, does not allow the calcification
or deadening of a false form of being to petrify the church, as we see
from the many reform movements down the centuries. The monastic
movement was one such impetus towards holiness against worldly and
purely formalistic Christendom, fleeing the world to the common life of
prayer together in varying forms. Francis of Assisi recovered the Jesus
way of life in his simple wandering and preaching, gathering a group
of friends and becoming friars, not with a set monastery but peripatetic
and charismatic in kind, a movement of the Spirit and of creation, and
a challenge by implication to the immensely wealthy and powerful
medieval church establishment. It was to the credit of the latter that the
Franciscans were accepted as an order within the church. Wesley's revival
movement met only rejection unfortunately by the established Church of
England after he began preaching to the poor in 1740, another movement
of the Spirit bringing the New Testament Gospel to the people and
causing spiritual revival. The freedom of the Spirit was bringing new
life to the ancient forms of church life, bringing the letter to life in the
present, resulting in the form of Jesus' life making itself present in all
manner of ways.

The freedom of the Spirit in history is coloured with the personal
form of Jesus way of being. Something authentically Christ-like is often
the mark of a genuine movement of the Spirit: the caring for the sick and
destitute by Mother Theresa of Calcutta seems to have been a movement
of the Spirit, within the forms of the church and certainly strengthened
by the Eucharistic sacrament to a great degree. The 'German Christians'
movement which Barth so opposed clearly convinced many contemporary
German church members, but Barth showed its fundamental conflict with
Christ and his way, and of course historically it revealed its disastrous
moral bankruptcy and political motivation. The Christological test is
always powerful in pondering the work of the Spirit.

Some important movements in Christian history have pointedly
appealed to divine creation, including Francis of Assisi who was so
close to creation and the Creator through the created works; his gospel
message was preached in the way of Jesus but with this distinctive
stress. The 1930s 'German Christians' appealed to orders of creation to
validate their claim to national progress and vitality and superiority, but
with a totally different note of aggression and power. Today's ecological
movement has clear affinities with the Christian doctrine of creation,
with Francis, and Jesus' deep assumption of the beneficent Father of the
universe, but it is conceivable that some directions it can take break with

the Christian way. The near worship of some animals gets close to a pagan deification of created beings and 'the planet' is almost given an absolute value. A Christian view must ultimately trust in God and not human plans for the future, having done all that is reasonable to be a responsible carer and steward of the universe.

Freedom in the Spirit, for the Christian, involves the diversity of gifts and abilities, of vocations, a great garden of flowers and possibilities. 'But', as O'Donovan says,

> Christianity has never been prepared to leave the matter there, at the level of vocation or gift, which would amount to no more than an ethic of differentiated self fulfilment.' The freedom of the Spirit is not to be reduced to that of the autonomous self, or spiritual supermarket consumerism, since 'over against the varieties of gifts, varieties of ministries, varieties of expressions, there is the unity of God, Father Son and Spirit, whose work underlies all these differences and there is the unity of the confession "Jesus is Lord" which marks the authentic presence of the Spirit (1 Cor. 12:3–6).[19]

Ultimately God's self revelation in Christ of love as the core form of life interweaves with the freedom and diversity of the same Spirit to bring about the fullness of life. The church is in danger of yielding to the temptation to replace this Christological form with that of the secular, and to accept relativism as the truth of freedom, rather than reappropriating the Trinitarian pattern in her own life and as her contribution to social ethics in theory and more importantly individual practice. Freedom and calling alone are not sufficient for a Christian view of moral decision, the form of Jesus and his historical personal way of life will always accompany the freedom of the Spirit. This pattern of divine desire for us is another clear dimension of directive authority for the church in its debates and disagreements.

Worship

The practice of corporate worship is a very obvious church practice, so much so that it escapes notice, but it lies at the heart of Christianity and the divine desire. To repeat a key verse of St Paul, capturing how we are caught up in the life act of God by the holy love of Christ, 'God has sent the Spirit of His Son into our hearts so we cry Abba, Father' (Gal. 4:6). The chief purpose of human life is to freely worship God in love, joy and peace. The commitment of the faithful to gather together on the Lord's Day, the day of the rising of Jesus for our justification, is paramount and also a sign to the surrounding population of our responsive love to God.

---

[19]*Resurrection and Moral Order*, op. cit., p. 222.

The divine desire is surely worked out in this, and the gathering speaks of the love of God for all, and all are welcome to join the assembly.

It is our duty and our joy to gather to worship, notwithstanding the deep imperfections of our worship, the music, the often poor sermons and half-hearted singing: yet this is taken up by God as an 'eschatological' event, a piece of heaven come ahead of time. The Eastern Orthodox tradition makes much of this and regards the Eucharistic celebration gathered around the bishop as literally the coming to earth of heaven, the inbreaking of the kingdom of God in the human liturgical theatre.[20] Christian worship claims to worship God 'really', not be an obedient act to a command which is morally meritorious, but 'worship in the Spirit', caught up by God with Christ to the very presence of the Father. This dimension of freedom in the Spirit, of end time glory and praise, whatever the situation now in history, is unique in world religions, and a quite different understanding to that of Islam whose deity transcends being 'glad' at the praises of his people but requires a pattern of life including times of prayer each day: again we see form as the distinguishing factor, requiring submission.[21] Daily prayer for the Christian disciple is not a matter of strict form, but of speaking to God 'as Father' from the heart, bringing the concerns of daily life, as well as praise, thanksgiving and confession of sin.

This eschatological worship of the Father in the Spirit promotes diversity of tongues, of styles, of new hymns and free prayer from the heart, it is not restricted to any historic form or formula. The logic of worship together before God in the Spirit breaks down barriers, notably of men and women needing to sit separately or in particular vesture. Any Christian socialism should be rooted in this common worship, unfolding the implications of our unity in diversity, of our mutual caring in the body of Christ, and joy in serving each other. And in terms of guidance, directive authority and the implications of worship, the created order is perfected in offering worship, the healed creation glad in its own God given pattern and form. The eucharist being the most distinctive act of Christian worship, the pattern and form is revealed as Christ crucified and risen, marking our worship and our way of life, conformed to the mind of Christ in holiness and glad trust for everything.

---

[20]See John Zizioulas, *Being as Communion*, New York: Crestwood, 1985.
[21]See 'Prayer (Muhammedan)', in Hastings Encyclopaedia of Religion and Ethics Edinburgh: T&T Clark, 1918, vol 10, pp. 196–9. Muslim law prescribes in great detail how a Muslim must perform his ritual prayer.

11

Patterns of Authority in the Church: Control and Freedom

Bishops in the church

The church has been guided through its phases of life, and in many different contexts, by attending to the 'Prophets and Apostles', that is the witness of Scripture, and seeking the guidance of the Spirit in the church today, form and freedom in a wonderful harmony. Christian tradition has also been engaging in this struggle of self-clarification as difficulties have arisen, and some key markers have been laid down, or guide posts set up, which the church has accepted as authoritative interpretations of the faith that have stood the test of time – critically the Nicene Creed of 381, which established the Trinitarian identity of the Son as what the Apostolic Gospel entailed. Such creedal formulae are stated in the language and concepts of their day and so need explaining for each new generation and culture, but the burden of Nicaea is clear and the truth it strives to convey fits with the lived experience of the church down the centuries. The teaching of the church has an orientation from the past, like a great ocean liner leaving its path marked in the water behind it, and it has a lighthouse as its destination. The spirituality, praxis and sacramental shaping of the church, cohere together in this rich interweaving patterning of divine directive authority. Scripture remains the core of this authority, and questions of its interpretation for each contemporary age are guided by this patterning of church formative factors. And *diakonia*, the new form of authority of Jesus and the apostles, is at the heart of the episcopal role of oversight over the beloved brothers and sisters in the Lord.

Bishops developed early in the history of the church as key trustees of the faith, pastoral and sacramental leaders of their local flock, people trusted to hand on the message of the Gospel, to lead worship, to foster fellowship, *koinonia*, in Christ, and to encourage charity and good works by the faithful. The bishop was therefore linked to the Apostles by handing on and living out their message. The bishops were trusted with 'oversight', *episcope*, and their presbyters were helpers in this task. Bishops would meet together in councils and synods to discuss important matters, to consult each other, and the Council of Nicaea in 325 was the first major 'ecumenical' or world wide church council with the churches represented through their bishops. How has this tradition of authority and oversight developed in current denominations?

Eastern Orthodox churches

The Eastern churches emphasize the role of the bishop as the leader of the diocese or local church, standing in the living tradition of the Apostles and so the trustee of the faith, the figure who can be relied on the teach the faith in the Spirit. The bishop is in living continuity with the past, with St Paul, St Peter and the saints who are 'contemporary' now with us in the church. The Bishops in Synod convened by the Ecumenical Patriarch are the ruling body of the Eastern churches. They do not accept the primacy of the Pope, agreeing with the Anglican Communion on this:

> within this communion a position of seniority has come to be ascribed to the ancient See of Canterbury. But this seniority is understood as a ministry of service and support to the other Anglican Churches, not as a form of domination over them; and, like the Ecumenical Patriarch, the Archbishop of Canterbury makes no claim to a primacy of universal jurisdiction.[1]

The Anglicans and Orthodox have a similar structure of bishops and synods of bishops, although the Anglicans include more lay participation in their synodical structures. But the basic unit of the church is the diocese led by the bishop, and there is no doubt that the Orthodox structure does equate to the situation found in church life in the early centuries, with bishops as the leaders of dioceses in mutual consultation and fellowship. This is an ancient pattern, far older than that of Rome.

Eastern Orthodoxy is an Episcopal tradition, but the local church is regarded as the diocese, and the bishop the local minister over this unit,

---

[1] *Anglican-Orthodox Dialogue: The Dublin Agreed Statement*, London: SCM Press, 1984, p. 18.

a far larger one than a single congregation which worships together in a town or area – rather it could well include tens of thousands of Christians who rarely see their bishop. The clergy are regarded as delegates of the bishop as they lead congregations of the diocese. The bishop is the key figure for teaching and practice, and he is a trustee of the Apostolic faith, maintaining the truth and handing it on to the next generation. The Ecumenical Patriarch is the leader of the Orthodox bishops, first among equals and not with a jurisdiction to interfere in other dioceses, as has the Pope. The Orthodox seem able to maintain their historic tradition and traditions of faith and ethics, deeply rooted in the patristic theologians and early creeds and councils: they have not needed a super bishop to be given power over the other bishops worldwide – a move they see as political power play rather than catholic and apostolic spiritual authority.

But the problem of authority which plagues the Orthodox is that of territory and jurisdiction: thus the USA has many Orthodox churches with national identities – Russian, Greek, Serbian, Georgian, Ukrainian and so forth – all jostling together and apparently wholly unwilling to set up an 'autocephalous', self-standing, American Orthodox church and let that be the national church. The church of Estonia is not recognized by Russia as an autocephalous church but is claimed as being under Russian jurisdiction; likewise now there is an argument over whether the Orthodox church of Georgia in Eastern Europe should be autocephalous or be under the control of the Moscow Patriarchate, a growing power wanting more control and a possible rival to the Ecumenical Patriarch based in Constantinople. Moscow is perhaps showing that the temptations of Rome, a Curia and a need to control, are at the door of the Orthodox churches. The Orthodox have this particular problem of authority – one of jurisdiction, not one of doctrine and ethical diversity – and the Anglican Communion is envious of this ethical consensus, which is its particular problem.

Roman Catholic church

Roman Catholicism has opted for its papal structure, the pope being the global leader of all individual Roman Catholics, with power over all bishops around the globe, and a teaching authority that must be obeyed. This decision was taken in 1870 at the First Vatican Council, amidst great heart searching by many bishops who accepted the notion of papal infallibility in certain circumstances, and direct global papal jurisdiction over all churches, with extreme reluctance. After all, this structure renders Roman bishops little more than papal curates and even synods of bishops are relatively unimportant: this is a long way from the episcopal structure of the early centuries of the church, and could even be seen as a sort surrender to modern managerial practice of the 'CEO', the chief executive officer, dictating policy and installing his underlings as bishops in dioceses at his choice, not considering the desires of the local churches whose pastors the bishops are to be.

This resolves the sort of jurisdictional problems of authority felt by the Orthodox, but it has deep problems in terms of ethical leadership in the West. For example the famous ban on artificial contraception declared by Pope Paul VI in 1968 in his Encyclical *Humanae Vitae* has not been 'received' by the lay people who ignore the authoritative teaching. 'Reception' by the church as a whole is a theological and also real factor in assessing the authenticity of an authoritative pronouncement, and therefore this teaching must as time goes on find itself in a limbo as it falls into disuse; the alternative would be for the pontiff to excommunicate those who cannot comply and so lose vast swathes of lay people to the church. This problem of a very powerful centralized authority structure is, for example, the reverse of the Baptists' structure of very local congregations under the direct command of no higher figure or body, but in covenant with other churches and so mutually seeking guidance in such matters. Rome is a church which has developed its distinctive forming factor, the Petrine ministry, overshadowing other forms and offering in exchange on point of authority which will tell you, without grey areas, what is 'the truth' and how Christian life is to be lived.

The place of the 'laity' as church, as well as the place of bishops, is a major theological weakness in the system of the Roman Catholic Church. The laity have no active role in saying anything 'in the Spirit', they must passively listen to their clerics, and the clerics are instructed directly from Rome, making local Christian initiative to relate to specific contexts at the guiding of the Spirit redundant and not possible. J. H. Newman wrote in 1870 that he feared the great divide between the *ecclesia docens* and the *ecclesia discens*, the teaching church and the learning church, the clerics and the laity, would lead to indifference in the educated faithful and superstition in the poor.[2] John McKenzie makes the same point of this system when he says that 'the members must accept authority as paternal in the sense that the members are children incapable of adult responsibility…When adults can be trusted on to obey without question, they are not being trusted at all. Over valuation of authority is under valuation of those who are subject to authority.'[3]

The Second Vatican Council of 1962–5 was something of a movement away from the very defensive mode of 1870, speaking of the church as 'the people of God' for example. But the Pontificates of John Paul II and now Benedict XVI have done much to re-establish the centralist

---

[2]J. H. Newman, *On Consulting the Faithful*, New York: Sheed and Ward, 1961, p. 106.
[3]John L. McKenzie SJ, *Authority in the Church*, London: Geoffrey Chapman, 1966, p. 173.

pattern and have disappointed many. *Humanae Vitae* had given an early disappointment to the laity in 1968. The local church has become used to having bishops imposed from outside its locality, for example the Brazilian Catholic Church, and the laity are not included in consultative decision making. The notion of papal infallibility has been strengthened. The feel of the age is that Christianity is under threat, as in 1870, and now is the time for defensive retrenchment and consolidation, not for experiment.

Questions of authority are not usually raised unless the church has some distressing problem to address, which is causing disagreement. The really major disagreements in church history often revolve around questions of power, for example the West and the East split when the Bishop of Rome claimed jurisdiction over the bishops of the East, and the Reformation in the West when Rome excommunicated large groups of Christians who were urging reform of the church triggered by selling 'indulgences' in order to fund large building schemes in Rome. In terms of this problem of political authority, unity and diversity, freedom and form, Hannah Arendt[4] points interestingly to Plato's *Republic* which, in order that order be kept and wise government implemented, was ruled by the 'philosopher king' and a group of 'guardians' – a structure uncannily like that of the Roman Catholic system – the *demos* or people being untrustworthy and vulgar. The European Community takes a similar view of the need to keep authority to those 'who really know', the experts in government. The role of the laity is to 'pray, pay and obey', for the Roman church, the lay people say 'Amen' to the Lordship of Christ mediated through the clergy, bishops and papacy. Today's authority structure in the Roman Catholic Church is very centralized again, very much about direct control rather than fellowship of councils of bishops, let alone laity, and focused on the person of the Pope – this version of the cult of celebrity does indeed ring bells with contemporary culture.

The Anglican Communion

The Church of England rejected the control of Rome over its church and its state at the time of Henry VIII and Elizabeth I, but retained the structure of bishops and the historic line of bishops – 'the historic episcopate' – as an important link with the early church and the wider church catholic. The Church of England and its historic formularies base themselves doctrinally on the Scriptures, the first four ecumenical councils and the historic formularies expressing the faith for the people.

---

[4]Hannah Arendt, 'What is Authority?' in *The Portable Hannah Arendt*, ed., P. Baehr, London: Penguin, 2000.

The Church of England quickly enabled worship to take place in the vernacular, language understood by the people, and had translations of the Scriptures read in church services a great deal. Scripture, Tradition and Reason became a well known threefold cord typifying Anglican theology. As Gary Bennett's last *Crockford's Preface* showed, Anglicanism was a conservative, thoughtful Christian family, without any felt need to write everything down in a code. Apostolic doctrine and ethics were simply assumed as being of the warp and weft of a church.

The Anglican Communion spread around the world with British trade and grew into a global communion. Anglican polity is most simply found in the 'Lambeth Quadrilateral' of 1884, which says that the four essentials of the church are the Scriptures, the decision of the ecumenical creeds and councils of the first five centuries, the dominical sacraments of Baptism and the Eucharist, and the historic episcopate 'locally adapted'. This is a statement which describes the forming factors of the church. The Scriptures include the teaching of the Apostles about Jesus, including his whole Hebrew inheritance; the ecumenical creeds and councils give broadly the Trinitarian and Christological traditions about Jesus and God common to all Christian churches, including teaching about the Spirit; the sacraments are clearly a forming factor of ethical and spiritual life and accepted by almost all Christian churches; and the historic episcopate means not only Episcopal form of oversight of congregations but with a connection going back to the earliest pastoral care and mission of the church as it developed into monoepiscopacy. The Apostolic leadership of the church, another forming factor, is affirmed.

The Church of England is now an Anglican oddity with its structure of establishment dating back to the middle ages, monarch and church being interwoven, and this tradition means that politicians technically appoint Anglican bishops, hardly an apostolic practice – although one that has occurred throughout most of the history of Christendom. The Anglicans' system worked well until the present strife over sexual ethics. Liberal Anglican leaders claim there never was any core ethical teaching on this subject, when in fact it was of course assumed under the Scriptures, tradition, sacramental ethical imperative, and whole role of trusteeship and guardianship of the way of Jesus committed to bishops and church teachers.

The Church of England has various strands to its authority structures – the archbishops of Canterbury and York, the bishops of dioceses, the synods and General Synod which has the final say – including lay people, men and women. This involvement of laity shows the Anglican commitment to the whole church in the Spirit having contributions to make to church policy making and action, and this marks it out from Rome and Orthodoxy. In addressing problems such as birth control the Anglican church has taken the voice of its members seriously, and does so in regard to the current issue of homosexuality.

The Anglican Communion has run into trouble, as set out at the start of this book, now that some elements of its global communion do not accept the traditionally assumed interpretation of Scripture, on sexual ethics in particular, and have felt free to cut loose from the apostolic form of life requiring celibacy for those not married. This assertion of freedom by some 'liberal' Anglican provinces has led to a crisis of authority and to the development, still in process, of a covenant for all the global Anglican churches, but the liberal members do not wish their autonomy to be disturbed by an authoritative covenant. It had been assumed that the Anglican family abided by the tradition, the tradition kept by the East and by Rome, on sexual ethics.

The American Anglicans could never really have imagined homosexuality being practised and commended by a bishop as having ever been acceptable in the history of the Christian church. The peace of the family was in fact recklessly broken by the American cousins firstly acting unilaterally by consecrating women bishops, then a divorced man announcing himself as engaging in same-sex activity. There was a tacit knowledge that their action was an innovation of a radical kind, with no support in most Anglican provinces and none at all in the Eastern bishops nor Rome – so such consecration had no realistic intention of being 'catholic' or accepted in the Anglican family nor by the wider groupings of Christian bishops. And the Bishops of the whole communion had voted overwhelmingly in 1998 against this move. It therefore could hardly have been a 'consecration' carrying any 'authority' at all. It was rather a piece of theatre to grab public attention for the gay cause, using the Anglican Communion for the purpose.

But this crisis in Anglicanism has led many to look for some more 'centralized' body, or instruments of authority, to impose more churchly discipline or 'form' on the freedoms claimed by some provinces to autonomy – and yet to ongoing membership of the global family. The problem of endless diversity, as we saw at the beginning of this book, had been seen by the likes of Gary Bennett before the 1988 Lambeth Conference, and in 1998 the Virginia Report was presented, discussed and endorsed – a report suggesting deeper 'instruments of unity'. For example, the primates of the Communion meeting with an authoritative voice can evolve into such an instrument to offset the centripetal tendency of the Communion, without leading to an Anglican papacy. This again follows the kind of structure of the Eastern Orthodox. But such developments, at the time of writing, are merely in discussion following the Windsor Covenant and the responses to that document, in the firestorm of the crisis caused by the American and Canadian members of the Communion.

ARCIC Agreed Statements on Authority

The idea of the Anglican 'covenant' is one idea being pursued, but with much disagreement from the innovating provinces. The ecumenical developments are also significant, notably those of the Anglican Roman Catholic International Commission [ARCIC], and some of their agreed statements are worth considering in terms of the issue of authority.

The claim of Rome is that the bishop of Rome succeeds directly to the role of Peter in the early church, that is a charismatic leader and teacher who leads the Apostles, and was specially commissioned by Jesus. This concept was raised by the bishops of Rome when it began to wield power several centuries after Jesus' death as a justification for its claims to jurisdiction and influence, the link between Rome and Peter being that Rome was probably where Peter met a martyr death. The first ARCIC report on authority[5] agrees that the Roman primacy was a gradual development that occurred as the need of the church of for a figure to adjudicate on questions of doctrine and practice arose, a development of the Spirit's guidance.

The claim is essentially that there is Petrine 'forming factor' of the church's life, a ministry echoing that of Peter in Acts. ARCIC I agrees that there is no evidence of Jesus setting up any sort of successor to Peter. Peter was in fact a unique foundation 'rock' figure, a foundation preacher and leader on whose work others were to build, but could not 'succeed' as his contact with Jesus was unique to himself. There is no doubt that the early church used councils and synods to discuss debated questions, as we see in Acts 15 and Galatians 2, where leading figures including Peter, John, James and Paul reportedly spoke with authority. ARCIC I spells out a structure whereby the church is in spiritual fellowship, *koinonia*, with Christ in the Spirit, and has pastoral leadership locally to focus and foster this *koinonia*. This local level then needs regional level leadership, the bishops, who themselves meet in councils. Archbishops form a still higher layer of leadership to focus unitive *koinonia*. These councils of leading bishops finally need a coping stone at the top of the pyramid, a primacy with and over the conciliar leadership. This is the pope, the bishop of Rome, and he is the sole candidate for any ecumenical global primatial role. ARCIC I agreed that this role could be important in crises where an outside senior leader might step in with authority to sort things out – although this conflicts with the Anglican Orthodox Agreed Statement in Dublin, 1984, we note. ARCIC I was not happy with the notion of papal infallibility, regarding that notion as applicable only to God, but did open up the issue of emergency global jurisdiction for a primacy, but with a reformed version.

---

[5]Anglican Roman Catholic International Commission, *The Final Report*, London: SPCK, 1982.

The Second ARCIC document on the issue of papal primacy, *The Gift of Authority*,[6] controversially sees the Anglicans agreeing to the ministry of the Pope as it now is, with no call for reform, and also surprisingly accepting that a special charism of interpretation of Scripture has been given to the Roman Primacy, a gift of authority for the church to resolve such disagreements and tensions. ARCIC II does not seem entirely consistent with the reasoning of ARCIC I and its view that the ministry of primacy slowly evolved to meet occasional needs.

In fact ARCIC II appears to relapse to the sharply divided clerical church which teaches – and the lay church which listens and says 'Amen' to – precisely what so many acute Roman Catholic theologians found lamentable in their system. ARCIC I had built up its theology of the church on the spiritual *koinonia* of the whole church, in Christ in the Spirit, and only then began to speak of the ordained ministry as a focus of unity. This biblical and apostolic basis seems to have been forgotten in ARCIC II. The theological argumentation for this is complex, using the analogy of Eucharistic practice and a heavy identification of the teaching ministry with that of Christ, and the lay people as the hearers of his words whose role is to say 'Amen' to the Word. In terms of the forming factors of the church it is unfortunate that Peter, on which this typology rests, was far from infallible in the New Testament and indeed rather a maverick leadership figure, who needed the guidance of Paul to sort out his position over the Gentile mission. Interestingly the International Commission for Anglican Orthodox Theological Dialogue sent some telling questions to ARCIC asking for clarification of this doctrine, but received no reply, including the issue of the laity as passive recipients.[7]

The Gift of Authority to many Anglicans is worrying, and could lead the Communion from apparent chaos to deadening control in a way that would not help patient theological ethical reasoning and pastoral development. This document has oscillated towards 'form' at the almost total sacrifice of 'freedom' in the Spirit for the whole church, including her bishops. Despite the febrile state of the Anglican Communion over sexual ethics and need for some sort of structures of authority globally, the Church of England has its national General Synod as its own final authority over such matters. Anglican polity very deliberately includes laity in its decision making, having a 'house of laity' in its General Synod with full voting rights for all decisions, and lay people are invited to the Lambeth Conferences to participate, although not to vote formally. This participation of lay people is distinctive to the Anglican way. The

---

[6]ARCIC II, *The Gift of Authority*, London: SPCK/CTS, 1999.
[7]Since then the Orthodox and Roman Catholics have produced the *Ravenna Agreement*, which takes seriously the need for primacy, more as did ARCIC I, without going to the extreme of ARCIC II and *The Gift of Authority*, and stressing the regional authority of the local bishop.

authority of the church entails the whole church, not only its leadership, and this requires expression in synods at all levels. Members of the church have a role, their gifts and abilities are needed in helping the church forward in all sorts of situations, including for example people in the professions whose minds are wonderful resources for pondering difficult questions related to the faith, one thinks of the many natural scientists who are also Anglican believers.

This makes it very difficult for Anglicans to agree that ARCIC II'S 'Gift of Authority' can be the solution to its difficult disagreements over sexual ethics, however troubling and unsettling. The matter cannot be resolved by the diktat of a hierarch whose word is absolute and with whom there can be no discussion. The Anglican way regards reason as an important divine gift to all humans and that it should not be paralysed in the members of the church. It is important to allow questions to be put to doctrine and dogma to help the church keep pace with contemporary learning, not as a separate secular strand of content with different roots to the Apostolic Scriptures or the ecumenical tradition. The gift of created reason was not regarded as a dangerous human capability, and helped Anglicanism maintain links with science, the arts, and music, and to cope with radical new developments such as Darwin's *Origin of Species* far better than Rome.[8]

McKenzie sets out the damaging results of rendering the laity very passive and obedient to the hierarchy in its understanding of what the church is and how it conducts its mission.

> False identification of authority with the Church makes authority exclusively responsible for the mission of the Church. In such a false identification the individual member is absolved from any personal responsibility except for his own personal welfare. His own welfare is then reposed exclusively in his obedience to authority. There is no warrant for this way to salvation anywhere in the New Testament.[9]

McKenzie shows alarmingly that this passive and irresponsible view of unquestioning dumb obedience has had disastrous effects in twentieth-century history, as with Adolph Eichman, who on trial for his concentration camp crimes of mass murder claimed that he was only obeying orders and so was not culpable. This is a social sickness, and not to be espoused by the church of Christ as a way of building up the faith in clergy or

---

[8]While the Vatican could only pronounce anathemas on such scientific work, with the 1865 anti-modernist decrees and successive similar pronouncements, the Anglican Church quickly produced responses keen to engage with the implication of the theory of evolution, for example in *Essays and Reviews* (1860) and *Lux Mundi* (1889). Anglican theologians and lay thinkers were free to ponder the new situation. Rome permitted such freedom only in the 1930s. Control can stifle freedom.

[9]McKenzie, op cit., p. 113–4.

laity. The option to choose unquestioning obedience to the Curia has parallels with the option to choose the mosque: a culture of deep control and possibly deadening form, quenching the life in the Spirit. Needless to say, this is not to discourage ecumenical work continuing, Christians need to reunite formally for mutual strength and encouragement, healing the tears in the body of Christ.

This is the core theological and spiritual reason why Anglicans would find it less than Apostolic to jump into the current version of the Papal system as a quick and easy solution to their disagreements over sexual ethics. To opt for a system of pure control in order to avoid apparent chaos would be to sacrifice both Christian freedom and proper Christian form in seeking to deal patiently with pressing issues using Scripture, Tradition, and careful modern cultural analysis. In fact, the Church of England has already the resources to show that the Apostolic way of sexual life is the healthiest and should be upheld, as at present. But objections and problems need to be attended to, in Christ-like fashion. The Anglican formative factors for the church, Scripture, early church traditional conciliar teaching, the dominical sacraments and the historic episcopate, are surely clear enough to resolve the issue of sexual ethics now causing it such distress. The apostolic forms are there but need to be applied rather than set to one side in favour of secular forms. I am suggesting that the Anglican Communion in fact is doing the right thing in maintaining a patient theological discussion, gathering the Communion together in the light of this new radical innovation which does not seek peace but a sword, and staking out the nature of itself as a worldwide, catholic and evangelical Christian body. It is being forced to clarify itself, to make explicit what was always implicit, to return to the roots of the faith, its Christological form and freedom in the Spirit. It needs not to panic and opt for a Curia to deal with makers of chaos, but keep faith in its bishops as leaders rooted and grounded in Scripture and Nicene orthodoxy. And the extraordinary thing is the utter neglect of the strand of 'reason' in all this, notably by the radical revisionists: where do we see any analysis of Western culture, notably Foucault and scholars such as Jeffrey Weekes[10] (as noted in a previous chapter) – nowhere. All we hear from TEC and its fellow travellers is of experience of sexual desire for the same sex and the claim that this therefore necessitates major reversals of the Apostolic way of life.

Looking to some of the Anglican doctrines and practices, let us take the 'historic episcopate' forming factor and apply this to the consecration of the bishop of New Hampshire 'as a gay bishop'. This consecration took place after the Anglican Communion told the American Anglican church of its strong disapproval, and yet the consecration went ahead. There is a very strong case that the consecration was not valid since it

---

[10]See above ch 5.

was known that it was not going to be accepted by the college of bishops of the Anglican church, let alone by the Orthodox and Roman Catholic bishops, hence it could not be regarded as consecration into the 'historic episcopate' as recognized any way now. It was not 'catholic' in that it could not command global assent. This simple and obvious point merely needs to be registered by the Anglicans, it has already the forms and instruments of apostolic desire, shaping and authority.

It should be added that the Anglican church views itself as *part of* the church worldwide, hence its bishops constitute part of the *global* college of bishops,[11] and that means taking into account the Orthodox and Roman bishops: Anglican bishops on their own cannot possibly conceive of themselves as an independent 'college of bishops' of the church catholic and apostolic. The American Episcopalian bishops continue to insist on their right to autonomy in governing themselves, and yet be members of the Anglican Communion with this wider body denying their practice: it is in effect advocating a congregationalist form of episcopacy, detached from the apostolic forms and failing to apply their clear implications, and consecrating people 'bishops' in the sure knowledge that they will not be accepted in the wider church catholic even within the Anglican family. It is also significant that TEC does not accord the same freedom to its minority conservative members and bishops that it expects from the majority Anglican Communion, seeking to coerce their minorities to accept their own radical innovations, to abuse their authority at home while seeking generosity in the Anglican Communion. This is not equitable in secular terms, let alone in the church of Jesus Christ.

Again, let us take the sacraments as a core Anglican practice, and the clear truth that baptism confers our true identity, we are in Christ and transformed in that new state, since to be baptised is be baptised into Christ crucified. St Paul begins Romans 6 with this basic Apostolic truth: he rejects the 'antinomianism' suggested at the end of chapter 5 because we are baptised into the death of the Lord; our old habits and ways of amorality are judged in baptismal identification with the judgement on sin at Calvary. The notion of a 'gay identity' would be washed away in the waters of baptism, as would 'a slave identity' – we are now in Christ, not our old allegiances and loyalties and self-understandings. Our natural theologies of our inner selves are included in this baptismal transformation and claim of Christ, the incarnate Wisdom of all creation. This discussion, of course, which has simply not been had by TEC nor the Windsor Fathers as yet, needs contemporary analysis of the identities sold to us by our cultural supermarket, identities we can trade and renew and change often, as Bauman has shown.[12]

[11]Church of England General Synod, *Bishops in Communion: Collegiality in the Service of the Koinonia of the Church*, London: Church House Publishing, 2000.
[12]See discussions above in previous chapters 4 and 5.

Scripture is clearly foundational for all church life, and revisionists have made no kind of case against its whole ethical drift, not just some proof texts, towards marriage as the one way of sexual congress, and no other. Idolatrous self-obsession and wilful distortion is St Paul's view of sexual activity among same-sex individuals. Secular gays are happy to accept this description, the self is ultimate and the will is to be enacted, absolute freedom reigns, but for the Christian the form of Christ is imperative and not to be hidden from. Pannenberg discusses this interestingly, showing marriage to be so strongly affirmed in the New Testament as to be an analogy for Christ and his church. 'Today', says Pannenberg, 'a lasting marriage has become almost a witness of Christian life in our modern secularized society that has emerged out of Christianity.' He continues 'It is obvious, at any rate, that in the norm of monogamous marriage we have a cultural impact of Christianity, not something that by nature we can take for granted in the course of human socialization.'[13] And the church has to bear in mind that it is itself an agency in society for human socialization: to endorse gay sex in the created order as a way of life to be taken up, an option to be considered as a pattern of life, is a drastic responsibility, and one not authorized at all by the Gospel in creation.

Conclusion: Christlike Authority for Church and Society

The Anglican Communion really knows its way ahead; it has many resources and guideposts to point it in the right direction, and the authority of Christ comes through many ways and practices, connecting the church to the divine desire for creation. The form for our many freedoms is that of Christ, he is the authorization for our living and relating, and we find that liberating from the imprisoning practices of our culture: autonomous individualism, narcissistic hedonism, moral relativism, and scientific reductionism, as Oden so neatly lists them. Our supermarket consumer world needs the form of Christ. Our liberal democracy and capitalist free market system need the continual indirect influence of the Gospel through Christian people and influence on structures if they are to survive and not decay.

There is no crisis about what the authority of Christ is, only about determination to implement it and fully accept the ways his Lordship is mediated to us, in the church and into the world – how to ensure that the cross is at the very centre of the moral cosmos, making peace and reconciliation. Preaching to the lost, the bewildered, those consumed by consuming and betrayed, not just engaging in a cultural linguistic in-

---

[13]W. Pannenberg, *Systematic Theology*, vol. 3, p. 364.

house game, this is the real challenge of the Lordship of Christ and the divine desire in the great household of creation and its human guardians. The church is no private hobby, no mere personal taste, but the very core of creation, the creative impetus of the triune God to enable creation to complete itself, to acknowledge creation as gift to be accepted and to be the base of human culture. The church today is certainly in an increasingly harsh climate, but shows signs of not realizing how deep the suffocating poison gas of secularism is penetrating, to the detriment of humanity as a whole.

It may be time for the 'liberal' Christian to question whether secular pluralism is able to take on the fruits of Christianity in society. In the caring professions, altruism and care was imagined to be in the bloodstream of British young women, rather than the effect of a century of the caring tradition from Christianity woven into the profession's soul. A whole new ideology rooted more in neo-Marxist secularism displaced that Christian tradition, which was deliberately knocked out of nursing training.[14] The Christian person in the professions now commonly says that her faith is nothing to do with her work, and indeed it would wrong to 'impose' her view on others – which actually means 'wrong to present to others as truth relevant to policy discussion'. She has been silenced – and colluded in regarding her silence as a virtue, a charitable attitude of kindness and love. Here is a very dangerous situation for Christians and for society: it is now a virtue to keep the Gospel and its values out of public life altogether. We are inhabiting, to use O'Donovan's words, 'a parodic and corrupt development of Christian social order.'[15] This ties in with the Roman Catholic worry about the way secularist democracy, and a secularist judiciary, is evolving into a utilitarian management system, albeit with the therapist and aesthete on hand to supply solace and distraction.[16]

The very reasoned scholarly German theologian can have the final word on this:

> The ideological character of modern secularism rests on certain supposedly self-evident assumptions about human nature that regard the religious theme in life as in any case secondary. Christianity must set itself in a new and basically critical relation to this ideologically characterized secularism. Christians and churches fall victim to an illusion if they view the secularism of modern society simply as a continuation of the limited autonomy and worldliness of the secular vis-à-vis the spiritual in the context of a culture that as a whole is under Christian influence.[17]

---

[14]*Desire of the Nations* op cit., p. 275.
[15]See Ann Bradshaw, *The Project 2000 Nurse*, op cit.
[16]See, for example, Michael Novak, 'Democracy Unsafe, Compared to What?' in *The Review of Politics: Christianity and Politics, Winter 2000*, 31–35.
[17]Pannenberg, op cit., p. 53.

On the other hand he warns against a 'clericalist reaction' to modern secularism, but calls for Christians and churches to advocate our rational autonomy – in the face of irrational emotivism and hedonism – in pointing to our own finitude and the divine mystery that constitutes our finite existence. The church, by its existence, is a sign of the kingdom of God and relativizes the orders of this world, which can be 'powers and principalities' needed to be conquered by the cross.

In the church the formative factors surely speak of how our freedom in Christ is formed, and it is not a freedom that is chaotic but one to be exercised in responsibility to our identity in creation and in Christ crucified and risen. Other identities given us by the secular world are to be brought to Christ, rather than baptised on their own terms. There can be little doubt that the Anglican Bishops of the 1998 Lambeth Conference were right in their judgement on this newly created homosexual identity as imprisoning rather than liberating, whatever the secularist managers of culture may propose. The Church has quite sufficient formative resources to work this out and to remain calm in the fact of febrile emotivism, again a mark of contemporary society. It is of course vital to say that Christ's pastoral care through his church for people who desire the label 'gay' remains absolute.

Christian influence on society and state is by freedom and form, working through the hearts and minds of people in the form of Christ, under his authority, a unique form of authority in the world. This is what transformed the West from the Roman Empire into a gradually Christian civilization, and a system of government involving all people. We are not conservatives, nor anarchists, says Newbigin. 'We are rather patient revolutionaries who know that the whole creation, with all its given structures, is groaning in the travail of a new birth, and that we share this groaning and travail, this struggling and wrestling, but do so in hope because we have already received, in the Spirit, the first-fruit of the new world (Rom 8:19–25).'[18] The authority of Christ, the desire of God, will not be heard if Christians gladly consent to 'go into the closet' at the behest of the secular Caesar and deprive society and state of the wisdom of the true form for freedom.

The future of the Church of England, established or disestablished, is critical for the future of the culture of England. As indicated above the temptation to secure a position with a very secular state regime, a role as the de facto 'ministry of religions and culture', looks very real, and that is a future that would mean this ancient institution decides against being a church of Jesus Christ and merely a civil service department. If the Church of England wishes to continue to be a catholic and apostolic church of Christ, then it cannot duck its task of preaching and teaching

---

[18]Lesslie Newbigin, *Gospel in a Pluralist Society*, London: SPCK, 1989, p. 209.

the Gospel of the God of Jesus – and not another god. This will entail the intellectual task of engaging the nation, notably its youth, with the rationality of faith in Christ as well as its radical challenge to western consumerism, hedonism, relativism and reductionism.

The suggestion of this book is that liberal democracy in fact needs a thriving Christianity in order to maintain that unique blend of individual freedom and diversity together with form needed for an ordered, caring, humane society. In this I suggest the Christian faith is unique over against other faiths, since the cross of Christ has alone shown the moral power to break down tribalism, to foster self criticism and reformation, and to accept the riches of traditions it has encountered in its history: 'it has transcended these traditions', says Pannenberg, 'but it has also preserved them in modified form'[19]

I am suggesting that secularism is leading to an absolutist frame of values which allows of no grey areas of free disagreement and will turn out to be a brain washing control mechanism ultimately. Islam tends to unification and stasis in its focus on moral warning. The God of Jesus, the Trinitarian life of freedom, form and historicity, fosters difference and common life together, unity and diversity, freedom to think, probe the potentiality of the created order, and debate, with the Christ like form of caring, truth and peace. The Christian view is of a purposive history in covenant with God. The final revelation is the person of Jesus, God's self demonstration of divine love and power. This is a very different vision to that of a strict legalism preventing experiment in the arts and sciences and closing the open future off. Communistic secularism proved to be a version of such suffocating legalism, not merely Islamic states.

People are free to reject this Gospel way of life with Jesus as its revealed form and the Trinitarian God of diversity in unity, freedom and form, in favour of a secularist hedonistic freedom without form or a controlling form which squeezes out freedom of thought and diversity, the way Islamic nation states have developed. For the Christian of course this is a very important but second order issue: our true citizenship is in heaven, as St Paul teaches the church. The church's only real power should be that of proclaiming Jesus as the Lord. But the indirect Christian influence on social and political structures has been decisive for the rise of democracy, science, the arts, and the whole culture of caring for the sick and poor. Indeed it is arguable that the core trust needed for liberal democracy to function presupposes this basic Christian ethos working against tribalist mentalities. Both church and society therefore need to become aware of what is at stake in this current crisis of values and authority. If the suggestion of this book can at least start some debate

---

[19]W. Pannenberg, *What Is Man?* Philadelphia: Fortress Press, 1970, p. 135. Greek philosophical insights, the poetry, painting, music, art, novels, history and all manner of cultural riches are included in Pannenberg's point.

about the foundational significance of the Christian way on British culture, and awaken church leaders to the fact that the Gospel makes universal truth claims and is not patient of being told that it is culture relative, only for a particular set of persons, I will be grateful.

Index

Humanae Vitae (1968) 218
Huntington, Samuel 154
Hymns 101, 106–110, 204, 214

Incarnation 58, 80, 94, 98, 99, 108, 132, 188, 197
Ignatieff, Michael 153, 156
Immortale Dei (1885) 149
Individualism 26, 45, 49, 56, 81, 103, 131, 162, 175, 186, 227
Irenaeus, of Lyons 97
Islam xi, 5, 13, 14, 16, 18, 37, 39, 41–44, 57, 77, 95, 133, 136, 138, 148,151, 154–158, 163, 167, 169, 174–176, 181, 182, 186, 193, 214, 230

Jardine, Lisa 41
Jesus of Nazareth x11, 9, 44, 80–82, 85–105, 107–131, 133, 135–165, 169, 170–174, 180–191, 193–200, 202–230
John Paul II 163, 167, 218
Julios, Christina 37
Justinian 144, 146

Kant, Immanuel 8, 9, 21, 65, 78, 116, 120, 121
Kerr, Fergus 182
Klein, Rudolph 93

Lambeth Conferences xii, 30, 31, 32, 33, 34, 210, 221, 223, 229
Lambeth Quadrilateral 33, 220
Law 7, 9, 14, 15, 25, 26–28, 33–39, 44–59, 66, 73, 91, 95, 102, 107, 118, 120–129, 132, 133, 134, 139, 141, 143–148, 149–152, 156–159, 161–162, 164, 172, 175, 176, 179, 182, 186, 187, 190, 194, 195, 199, 201, 214
Leo XIII 140, 147
Lewis, C.S 50, 116, 130
Liberalism xiii, 5, 8, 12, 13, 16, 17, 18–39, 40–44, 51, 56, 62, 65, 67, 79, 88–91, 103, 133, 134, 140–142, 146, 148, 151, 154, 158, 161,163, 169, 171, 173–176, 182, 185, 220, 221, 227–230
Lloyd George, David 142
Locke, John 41, 114, 148

MacIntyre, Alasdair 10, 46, 48, 51, 52, 53, 57, 70, 88, 138, 139, 165, 175

McKenzie, John.L 218, 224
MacPherson Report 13, 37
Magisterium xii
Malik, Kenan 42, 43, 44
Managerialism 42, 45, 46–61, 138–139, 148, 151, 165, 169, 183, 185, 218, 229
Mann, Thomas 48
Marcuse, Herbert 139
Mattheson, George 107
Marriage 17, 21, 25–27, 42, 52, 77,123, 124, 127, 149, 150, 153–158, 160–162, 172, 201, 227
Marx, Karl / Marxism 10–16, 18–20, 23–25, 47, 55, 57, 59, 67, 88, 126, 168–170, 228
Maurice, F.D. 194
Methodism 142
Milgram's Experiment 119
Miller, Arthur 55
Mohammed 39, 133, 136, 157, 198
Moltmann, Jurgen 87
Multiculturalism 13, 14, 16, 36, 39, 43, 44, 98, 156, 159, 162, 173

Narrative 29, 49, 59, 64, 79, 86, 87, 91, 92–112, 122, 123, 125, 155, 183, 193, 194, 197, 198, 199–200, 204, 208, 209, 210
Newbigin, Leslie 142, 229
Newlands, George 155
Newman, John Henry 121, 133, 218
Newton, John 106, 107
Nicholls, David 162
Nietzsche, Friedrich 4–11, 16, 21, 44, 48, 49, 52, 53, 56, 57, 62, 70, 87, 89, 121, 122, 136, 171, 179
Nightingale, Florence 20, 22, 23, 140
Nisbet, James 52, 117
Nursing 12, 20, 22–24, 53, 68, 141, 205, 206, 228

Oden, Thomas 227
O'Donovan, Oliver 5, 27, 30, 165, 175, 181, 183, 188, 196, 213, 228
O'Donovan J.L 152
Oman, John 92, 131
Orthodox Church 29, 109, 216
Orwell, George 12, 88,

ND - #0087 - 090625 - C0 - 229/152/13 - PB - 9781842276433 - Gloss Lamination